ONIONS

ONIONS

ONIONS

Other Books by Linda & Fred Griffith

The New American Farm Cookbook
The Best of the Midwest

ONIONS
ONIONS
ONIONS

Linda & Fred Griffith

ILLUSTRATED BY MICHAEL HALBERT

CHAPTERS™

CHAPTERS PUBLISHING LTD., SHELBURNE, VERMONT 05482

Published by
Chapters Publishing Ltd.
2031 Shelburne Road
Shelburne, Vermont 05482

Library of Congress Cataloging-in-Publication Data

Griffith, Linda.
Onions, onions, onions: delicious recipes for the world's favorite secret ingredient /
by Linda and Fred Griffith; illustrated by Michael Halbert.
p.   cm.
Includes bibliographical references and index.
ISBN 1-881527-54-9: $14.95
1. Cookery (Onions) 2. Onions. I. Griffith, Fred. II. Title.
TX7803.05G75   1994
641.6'525—dc20   94-25793

Trade distribution by
Firefly Books Ltd.
250 Sparks Avenue
Willowdale, Ontario
Canada M2H 2S4

Printed and bound in Canada by
Best Book Manufacturers, Inc.
Louiseville, Quebec

Designed by Susan McClellan
10 9 8 7 6 5 4

To the Cooks Who Made Us

Mary Fried Weller, Linda's beloved grandmother, whose passion for cooking,
always without recipes, is Linda's inheritance.

Gertrude Weller LeVine, Mary's daughter and Linda's mother,
whose respect for recipes ensured the preservation of many family treasures.

The late Fred J. Griffith, the creator of Macfarland Lunch
of Charleston, West Virginia, where his son, Fred, learned to sling hash
and use a chef's knife without fear.

And to Fred's mother, Leona Griffith, who, when the kids had grown,
took her place at the range and continued a tradition of simple, honest home cooking.

Contents

Thanks

THIS HAS BEEN AN EXTRAORDINARY YEAR reading, thinking, talking and writing about onions, not to mention dicing, slicing, mincing, blanching, pickling, boiling, sautéing, frying and braising onions. It has also been a year-long orgy of eating onions.

We have baffled the folks from UPS who have brought us boxes and boxes of Vidalias and Walla Wallas. We've marveled at the careful packaging of enormous shallots from Robison Ranch in Washington. And we've had the pleasure of opening a gigantic box of pristine leeks, lovingly labeled and wrapped by Kingsfield Garden's Rick Abernethy and Erika Koenigsaecker, who never forget to send some heavenly gray shallots as well.

At Richwood, West Virginia, we ate our fill at the Feast of the Ramson, and we thank Billy Gay, noted ramp eater, for showing us around. We were warmed by the hospitality of the families Bland and Dasher in the region of Vidalia, Georgia, where we were ably guided by Chris Barker and Robin Raiford.

Later in the year, we were helped by a host of folks around Celeryville, Ohio: Dr. Richard Hassell of the Muck Crops Branch, O.A.R.D.C.; Bruce Buurma and his family's Buurma Farms; and the storage-onion master Charles Hanline, president, Stambaugh & Co., who also introduced us to sweet onions of Arizona and New Mexico and kept us sup-

plied with superb yellow onions and delicious fresh-from-the-garden corn and potatoes.

We've enjoyed the aid of Henry Koja in Maui, Hawaii, and Craig Christensen and Marguerite Daltoso in Walla Walla, Washington. We thank Cleveland's wonderful Jenny Crimm, anchorwoman extraordinaire, for making certain we tasted a hand-delivered Maui fresh from the source.

MORE THANKS TO SOME PEOPLE whose livelihoods are intertwined with alliums: Archie Dessert, who ran the Dessert Seed Company in El Centro, California, the site of so many important onion studies; Dr. Darrell Bolz at the University of Idaho; Dr. Bill Dean of Washington State University; Dr. Leonard M. Pike of Texas A & M; Dr. Michael J. Wargovich of M.D. Anderson Cancer Center; Larry Smith; Nancy Teksten and Wayne Mininger of the National Onion Association; Kimberley Rector and John Peterson of Angelic Organics in Caladonia, Illinois, for introducing us to "The Allium Man"; John Swenson, The Allium Man himself for giving so generously of his time and knowledge; and Tom Vortmann of the Ann Thacker Group, Sacramento, for his assistance with Texas 1015Ys.

Once again, we thank our friend Donald Patz for his intriguing wine recommendations. Besides making Patz and Hall Chardonnay, Donald is sales director for another of our country's best wine labels, Girard Winery. He has a splendid ability to make stimulating wine and food pairings, a talent we have often enjoyed when dining with him and his lovely wife, Heather, at their Napa Valley table.

As in the past, we are grateful to Linda's cousin, Susan Cavitch, for our scented geraniums and lemon verbena, for her help in recipe testing and for her willingness to create recipes upon request. Thanks to her sister, Betsy Cohen, for sharing her delicious recipe for leg of lamb.

We appreciate the continued help of friends Sanford Herskovitz, a.k.a. Mr. Brisket, his partner and wife, Frances, and his mother, splendid cook and baker, Margaret Wine.

Thanks to herbalists Patti and Michael Artino of Art Forms Nursery in Chagrin Falls, Ohio, for keeping Clevelanders supplied with fresh herbs in winter. They and Pat Bourdo of Woodland Herbs in Northport, Michigan, are the reasons our herb garden is so varied. We are also indebted to Silver Creek Farm's Mollie and Ted Bartlett and Ohio Maiden's Patrick McCafferty. And of course to our Seattle fish guru, Jon Rowley. And to The Grapevine's Bob Fishman.

WE ALSO THANK our many chef and foodwriter friends. In Cleveland: Zack Bruell of Z; Stouffer's Lucien Vendome; Piperade's Ali and Marcie Barker; Joe Santosuosso and Paul Anthony of Johnny's; Baricelli's Paul Minnillo; and Shuhei's Hiroshi Tsuji. In Chicago: Jean Joho of Everest; Topolobampo and Frontera Grill's Rick and Deann Bayless; in Ellsworth, Michigan, Harlan "Pete" Peterson; in Madison, Wisconsin, L'Étoile's Odessa Piper; in Reading, Pennsylvania, Jack and Heidi Czarnecki of Joe's Restaurant; in Providence, Johanne Killeen and George Germon of Al Forno; in Williamsburg, Marcel Desaulniers of the Trellis; Jimmy Schmidt, chef-owner of Detroit's Rattlesnake Club and Très Vite; John Cunin of The Cypress Club in San Francisco; Emeril Lagasse, of Emeril's and Nola in New Orleans. In New Prague, Minnesota, John and Kathleen Schumacher of Schumacher's New Prague Hotel; Cincinnati's Paul Sturkey and Jimmy Gherardi of Pigall's Cafe and J's; and caterer Dede Wilson of Harvest Moon in Northampton, Massachusetts.

> No one we met in the onion world seemed to know where the expression *"He knows his onions"* comes from.

We have also greatly benefited from the help of the following writers: Lynne Rossetto Kasper, Carol Field, Jean Anderson, Paula Wolfert, Craig Claiborne, Jane and Michael Stern, Marcella and Victor Hazan, Lydie Marshall, W. Park Kerr, Michael McLaughlin, Hedy Würz, Nathalie Dupree and Jacques Pépin.

Thanks, also, to Susan Sack, Linda's tireless cooking-class assistant, and to the students, who have not complained about a year of onion recipes.

Arielle Kozloff, Curator of Egyptian Art at the Cleveland Museum of Art, provided us with a wealth of information. We also thank Ann Burckhardt of the *Minneapolis Star Tribune*, David Brose of the Royal Ontario Museum, Erika Lieben of the Swiss National Tourist Office in New York, and the transplanted Texans, Julie and Buster Arnim.

The people in the reference department at the Cleveland Public Library were wonderful, securing materials from distant libraries, letting us copy text from noncirculating books and teaching us how to address the remarkable databases available at their computer stations. They helped us verge on computer literacy in our onion quest, and they were always patient on the telephone. Also, we appreciate the help of the staff of the Allen Medical Library for shaking up their database with inquiries about alliums. And thanks to Cleveland's produce maven, Maury Faren, for his constant encouragement.

Every cookbook needs tasters. We're grateful to ours: David and Deborah Klausner; Sandy and Peter Earl; Evan and Brenda Turner; Anne Sethness, Peter Sethness, and Jack Smith; Diann and John Yambar; George and Mary-Ellen Hammer; John Carey; Russell Trusso; Sanford and Frances Herskovitz; and last, but far from least, Gert LeVine, Linda's mother and our number-one fan. All were willing to tell us when we had cooked a clinker.

To OUR GROWING FAMILY, our thanks for your patience: grandchildren Madison and Forrest; and children Andrew Myers and Janean Lyons; Wally Griffith and Diane Bacha; Rob and Tracy Myers; Gwen and Barry Drucker; Barbara Griffith and Rob Bialic. And to the felines Rosebud, Omar, Pooh Bear, Ginger and Sugar Charlie; and to the great giant Bacchus and the gentle poodle Dali, who enjoyed the Zucchini and Sweet Onion Bread above all.

Our love and appreciation to Lisa and Lou Ekus and publicist Merrilyn Siciak. Thanks to our friend and overseer Barry Estabrook; Cristen Brooks, who faithfully made corrections; Susan McClellan, the designer of this book; and illustrator Mike Halbert for fine work. And to Judith Weber, our tireless agent, Mardee Haidin Regan, our meticulous copy editor, and Rux Martin, the best editor any writer could hope to encounter.

Introduction

Never have so many tears been shed over a book that was this much fun. Yes, we cried. We doubt there was a day in the year of this research that there was not weeping in our kitchen. (Well, actually, on some of the days when we were dealing with the big sweets, we didn't cry that much.)

When we started to work on this book, we were drawn first to the onions that have received so much good press—the sweet onions everyone has heard about: Vidalias, Walla Wallas, Mauis, Texas 1015Ys. We confess to having given these sweets a great deal of time, space and attention.

The sweets are heavenly and sexy; people everywhere know their names and profess their love for them. But it's the anonymous and hellish hots that are still the backbone of most of the world's cuisines and integral to the most beloved dishes. Mark Twain once remarked that he would prefer "heaven for climate; hell for society," and something of the same could be said for onions. Sweet onions have none of the character flaws that might keep them outside of the pearly gates, but the hots are more interesting.

The mighty onion may rarely be the star of the show, but in our book it gets the prize for being the best player in a supporting role. When we invite someone to dinner, we first ask if they are allergic to cats and dogs. Then we ask if there is any food they don't eat. We groan silently if the answer is, "I don't eat onions." How can that be? It seems that almost any dish we make will have at least a dusting of chives, a base of leeks or onions, if not a litany of chopped sweet onion. Whether standing on their own stuffed with a wonderful filling, appearing in a salad or as part of a basic flavoring in a sauté, onions are essential to virtually every cuisine.

> The French sometimes say, *"Occupe toi de tes oignons"* (Mind your business).

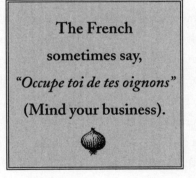

The first step in our research for this book was getting in touch with our own culinary legacies, in which onions were always the main ingredient. Linda's beloved Grandma Weller chopped onions by the score every morning as she prepared a three-course noontime meal for the large family group that would gather at her table. The meal would begin with soup, with onions forming the base. Next might come a stewed chicken or a fine roast, inevitably generously accompanied by onions. But Linda's finest memories are of the Friday mornings when her grandmother combined chicken fat with coarsely chopped onions in a large sauté pan and cooked the onions slowly until they were crisp and nearly blackened. Then Linda would have to bargain to determine how much of the onions would be her snack and how much had to be saved for the chopped liver.

Fred, who as a boy, worked in his father's restaurant in Charleston, West Virginia, remembers that there were always 50-pound, red-mesh bags of onions in the kitchen. Onions went into virtually everything. The chef put them into the mashed potatoes and cooked them with the beans. Half of the meat loaf was onion. No gravy was ever made in that kitchen that did not carry the flavor of onions. The famous lunch chili lacked cumin—in those days, who knew what it was?—but it always had more than enough onions and was so thick that it could stand up to a spoon. Grandfather Clarence Griffith, who ran the night shift, did not measure his onion slices with a micrometer. He made sure there were enough on the burger to get your attention. In our own kitchen today, we can make the same claim.

From our food notes from years of travel and cooking, we set down on paper every oniony triumph

that we could remember. Then we started testing and using, over the months, hundreds of pounds of every conceivable allium—as the far-flung members of the onion family are called.

We traveled to places where onions are grown and to watch them being planted, harvested, bagged and shipped. We talked with onion farmers, onion scientists, onion processors, onion cooks. We cut and tasted a thousand alliums, raw and cooked. We reviewed scores of scientific documents and books. Everyone was generous with ideas and recipes.

We have scoured the forests of West Virginia for the fabled ramps in late April. We have seen long green onions piled six feet high in Beijing markets or arranged in beautiful circles in the markets around Oaxaca, Mexico. We've grown weary of arm from slowly stirring pounds of thinly sliced onions for a Northern Indian dish, and we've eaten them raw and crisp. We've celebrated the arrival of Vidalias in springtime and searched the farmstands for plump, white leeks in the fall.

Although many people do not realize it, onions are a seasonal crop. Specific varieties must be selected according to latitude, altitude and temperature. Making the right decisions about which to grow is difficult, demanding work that requires enormous knowledge and experience.

Most onion growers are small operators, farming a hundred acres or less. Many make a living on just a few acres, specializing in small quantities of rare varieties that they then market creatively. But some of the onion farmers we got to know own huge operations, producing millions of dollars of onions. Because there are not enough local people to do the work on such farms, they hire migrant workers. A thousand-acre onion farm may need as many as 500 workers at peak season. Much of what we take to our tables would not be there without their work.

The soil is rich and sustaining; it is fulfilling and regenerative. We all are alive because of it. The sadness is that few of us ever think about it, or the people out there, who, ignored by the broader society, keep doing what they do. More than onions, that is what this book is about.

Ancient Onions

WOULD THAT ONIONS WERE LIKE CORN. You can trace the history of agriculture in the western hemisphere and learn a lot about the course of other human activity through the fossil record of corn. Because the woody structure of the cobs allowed them to survive in desert regions, archaeologists can track the almost accidental development of agriculture by the people who first gathered corn's ancestors and took the tiny ears to their lodges.

We cannot read the history of onions in the same way. Even the toughest onions were too small and too fragile to leave much of a record. The Egyptians often put the foods they loved into their tombs. The earliest entombed onions found by archaeologists date from the fairly recent New Kingdom, about 3,500 years ago. But we must presume that our predecessors discovered and started eating wild alliums very early. Those ancient ancestors were certainly foragers and gatherers before they became farmers.

"What's out there that we can eat?" they might have asked. "This green thing. Give it a try. Except that it made me cry, it's delicious." And as humans found they could grow the things they wanted in appropriate quantities near where they lived, they roamed less and settled down.

Many food historians place the earliest onion cultivation at the edges of the Mediterranean as long ago as 5,000 years. Others believe that the onion originated in central Asia. The National Onion Association says onions were first grown in Iran and Pakistan. But with several hundred onion cousins growing wild across the temperate parts of the world, it is likely that they have been eaten for tens of thousands of years and probably cultivated simultaneously in a number of different places.

It is hard to pin down exact dates, but there is evidence that the Sumerians were growing onions as early as 2500 B.C. Waverley Root, in his great dictionary, *Food*, cites one Sumerian text dated to about 2400 B.C. that tells of someone plowing over the city governor's onion patch. No word on what happened to the careless plowman. While the onion was clearly loved at the tables of the great and the near great, the Code of Hammurabi stipulates that "the needy shall have a monthly ration of bread and onions." (There ought to have been some beer there, too, since many texts indicate that those three commodities were basic staples consumed by the poor of many ancient Mediterranean communities.) Root says there is also evidence that one small sect of Egyptians refused to eat onions for religious reasons, but some scholars believe that in Egypt, onions were actually an object of worship.

Arielle Kozloff ought to know if anyone does. She is the curator of ancient Egyptian art at the Cleveland Museum of Art and internationally known for her work on the life and art of Amenhotep III, who reigned from 1391 to 1353 B.C. Her studies of Egyptian art and history have led to a better understanding of what daily life was like, not only in the precincts of the royals but in the villages and farms. The early Egyptian name for the onion, she told us, most likely was *hdw*, a word written with the hieroglyph of the ceremonial mace carried by people of authority, a staff with a head that resembled an onion.

From her files, Kozloff produced photographs of painted sarcophagi in which piles of spring onions

> A Turkish legend has it that when Satan was cast out of heaven, garlic sprouted where he placed his left foot, and onion where he placed his right.

are pictured as a major part of the tribute left for the dead, suggesting that the deceased probably liked onions. Onions also were found to have been used in mummification, one or two being placed in the thorax or pelvis, or in the ear or near the eyes, perhaps because they were believed to improve breathing. Paintings of onions appear on the inner walls of the pyramids of Unas (c. 2423 B.C.) and Pepi II (c. 2200 B.C.), in tombs of both the Old Kingdom and the New Kingdom. During the First Kingdom, onions were worn as garlands for certain festivals. Throughout Egyptian history, onions seem to have had a dual quality, sometimes greatly revered and relished, eaten at the tables of kings and buried with their bodies, and at other times avoided or forbidden because of their pungency.

The Roman writer Juvenal, an equal-opportunity satirist, after spending some time among the Egyptians, poked fun at their infatuation with onions:

How Egypt, mad with superstition grown,
Makes gods of monsters but too well is known.
'Tis mortal sin an Onion to devour,
Each clove of garlic hath a sacred power

Religious nation sure, and best abodes,
When every garden is o'errun with gods!

THE ISRAELITES PARTOOK of Egyptian onions before Moses led them into Canaan. In the book of Numbers, in the story of the hardships of the odyssey, the Israelites speak fondly of the foods they had enjoyed: "We remember the fish which we did eat in Egypt freely; the cucumbers, and the melons, and the leeks, and the onions, and the garlick." Three of the six things mentioned were alliums.

Centuries later, Pliny the Elder, Rome's keen-eyed observer, wrote of Pompeii's onions and cabbages before he was overcome and killed by the volcano's heat and fumes. Excavators of the doomed city would later find gardens where, just as Pliny had said, onions had grown. The bulbs had left behind telltale cavities in the ground.

Pliny wrote of foods, but he didn't give quantities or cooking techniques. That chore fell to Apicius, a Pliny contemporary. He compiled a 10-volume cookbook that guided cooks for a thousand years. And, yes, he knew his onions. Actually, he knew his *bulbos*, the Latin word that signified all of the bulbs that were used in Roman kitchens and by Roman apothecaries—despite a common belief during the Roman period that onions were unholy. As translated by John Edwards in the remarkable *Roman Cookery of Apicius*, the recipes read so well that you want to try them.

Onions also seem to have had a place in the history of India, not so much in the kitchen as in the infirmary. Texts from as early as the sixth century B.C. celebrate the onion as medicine—a diuretic, a physic, good for the heart, the eyes and the joints. Some believed that because of its strong odor, the onion was not fit for the table, not meant to be eaten except by the afflicted.

The ancient English also venerated the onion and believed it had magical powers, according to Richard Folkard, the nineteenth-century English writer. "In olden times," he wrote in *Plant Lore, Legends and Lyrics*, "country lasses used to resort to a method of divination with an onion named after St. Thomas. This they peeled and wrapped in a clean kerchief, then placing it under their heads, they repeated the following lines:

Good St. Thomas, do me right,
And let my true-love come to-night,
That I may see him in the face,
And him in my fond arms embrace."

From ancient times, onions have marched through history, a staple and universal foodstuff. They remained that way until the dawn of science, awaiting the magic of contemporary botanists, who would make the humble onion, *Allium cepa*, blossom into a bewildering array of shapes and forms.

Onions and the Scientists

WHEN THE SCIENTIFIC ERA STARTED, the onions that were cooked in the soup of the eighteenth-century university professor were similar to the onions that were grown at Pompeii. And those onions were very much like the onions of ancient Egypt. Early botanists, who started the unending chore of finding, examining, describing and cataloging every living plant, were observers, not experimenters. Their work set the stage for a scientific explosion in plant cultivation.

Still, disagreements abound about how to classify some plants. Even today, there are scientists who will insist that the onion you had on your hamburger or sliced in your salad belongs in the amaryllis family instead of among the lilies. To further complicate matters, a recently emerging school of thought holds that the alliums are complex enough and different enough from both the lily and the amaryllis to be elevated to the rank of family and called Alliaceae.

Here is how most contemporary botanists place the garden-variety onion into the world of plants:

Division Spermatophyta
(from a word with Greek roots meaning a seed-bearing plant)

Subdivision Angiospermae
(from the Greek, referring to plants that grow their seeds in a closed vessel)

Class Monocotyledoneae
(also from the Greek, meaning plants having only one leaf growing from a seed at germination)

Order Liliales

Family Liliaceae
(from the Latin word for lily)

Genus *Allium*
(from the Latin word for garlic)

Species *cepa*
(from the Latin word for onion)

Group Common Onion

Cultivar—the specific variety
(Spartan Banner, for example)

You want big?
Call V. Throup in Silsden, England.
One of his onions made the *Guinness Book of World Records* —10 LBS. 14 OZ.

THERE IS ALSO DISAGREEMENT over the number of onion species that exist. *The New York Botanical Encyclopedia of Horticulture* says that there are about 450 species in the *Allium* genus, all in the northern hemisphere. Food historian Waverley Root wrote that there are 325 species of alliums, including about 70 that are native to North America. Onion scientist Henry Jones believed that the vast, unwieldy genus has at least 500 species, including 80 in North America. One researcher counted 1,100 specific names but figured 600 were synonyms.

But there is agreement on the best way to check out a suspected member of the *Allium* genus: you crush its tissue. If you cry, it is one. Or, better put, if you get an alliaceous, or onionlike, odor, it is an allium; they all have it. Those that don't, aren't. Another universal allium characteristic: the foliage is basal—all of the leaves are attached to an underground center or stem. Of the 325, 450 or 500 species, only a few have made it into cultivation, either as food or as a flower. The rest are out there in the fields, prairies and mountains.

Every allium that we take to our tables can be found under one of these species:

• *Allium ampeloprasum* includes the leek, both wild and cultivated; the rare kurrat, a small leek; and the great-headed garlic, known now as elephant garlic. (Some argue that the domestic leek should be called *A. porrum*.)

• *A. ascalonicum*, the shallot. (Onion scientist Henry Jones disagrees and includes the shallot in *A. cepa*.)

• *A. cepa* includes three groups, differentiated by the way they reproduce. The Common Onion group includes most of the onions eaten in the world. They generally produce seeds. Rarely seen and of little commercial value, the onions of the Aggregatum Group send out shoots along the ground, while the onions in Proliferum Group propagate by means of bulbils, or tiny bulbs that grow in the flowers on top, like the Egyptian, or walking, onion.

• *A. chinense*, called Rakkyo, is widely grown in Japan, China and Southeast Asia. It is frequently pickled to preserve it for winter use. It can sometimes be found in Asian markets in this country.

• *A. fistulosum*, the Japanese bunching onion, more commonly called a scallion.

• *A. sativum*, the garlic found in our gardens and markets.

• *A. schoenoprasum*: chives.

• *A. tuberosum*: Chinese, or garlic, chives.

HERE ARE A FEW OF THE BETTER-KNOWN wild species that have from time to time been gathered and eaten:

A. canadense, a wild North American onion (*Gray's Manual of Botany* says wild garlic), sometimes confused with the tree or top onion.

A. cernuum, a wild nodding onion.

A. drummondi, another wild onion.

A. mutabile, a wild spring onion.

A. oleraceum, another wild garlic.

A. reticulatum, a native onion.

A. stellatum, the prairie onion.

A. textile, another wild prairie onion.

A. tricoccum, the wild leek or ramp.

A. ursinum, the European bear leek or wild garlic, gypsy onion.

A. vineale, field garlic.

ONCE THE BOTANISTS HAD DECIDED where to place the onion in the scheme of things, the plant breeders took over. By the turn of the century, scientists had already started shaping the species to meet the needs of the farmer and the consumer. But the seed catalog of 1900 was thin. It offered red, yellow and white colors, oblate, globe and spindle shapes, and a few different flavors and different dates of maturity. Progress in developing new onion varieties came slowly, and the work was hard and uncertain.

But the accidental discovery of a male-sterile onion by Henry Jones in 1925 changed everything. Now hybrids could be efficiently produced by crossing the sterile line of onions with other lines having desirable characteristics. Eventually male-sterile lines were distributed to university cooperative breeding projects all across the nation. That gave local researchers an opportunity to develop new varieties in response to specific growing conditions in their area.

For example, researchers in Wisconsin found traces of the chemical phenol in the dry covering of colored onions. In concentrated form, phenol is a powerful poison. Diluted, it is carbolic acid. The researchers discovered that carbolic acid helped protect onions from smudge, a naturally occurring moldlike condition that could ruin a whole crop. They were able to breed for darker onions with a greater concentration of phenol, providing the onions with more resistance to smudge.

Black mold, downy mildew, pink root, purple blotch, neck rot and yellow dwarf are other mortal enemies of the onion, capable of dramatically reducing a farm's yield. And over the years, onion breeders have been able to strengthen the plant's resistance to such diseases. Today, farmers can buy special varieties that are immune to most of these diseases.

Other scientists studied the little-understood role of day-length in onion development. Onions start growing a bulb when the day achieves a particular length. Farmers in the north, where summer days are long, want an onion that will not start to form a bulb until the longest day. If the bulbing begins too soon, while the plant is small, the bulb will be small as well. Southern farmers, on the other hand, want onions that will be triggered by their shorter summer days. If they use common northern varieties, the days may never be long enough to make the bulbs develop properly, and the result will be green onions without bulbs. Using the new breeding techniques, agricultural scientists created varieties to meet these special needs. Researchers also discovered ways to control bolting, the unwanted production of flowers and seeds instead of a bulb.

By 1945, chemists had analyzed the elusive sulfur compounds that cause us to weep when we cut an onion (see page 186). Breeders, on hearing the news, figured that if they could create a larger, juicier onion, they might be able to dilute that onion power and come up with something sweeter and not so hot. Our most popular sweet onions grew out of that research.

Now onion varieties have been developed for every climate and latitude. There are large onions and small, perishable sweets and long-lasting hot storage onions. We have varieties that resist diseases and insect pests and enough different cultivars across the country that there is rarely a month when you cannot find a recently harvested onion in your supermarket.

Classifying Onions

SCIENTISTS MAY ARGUE over where to place the onion in the plant kingdom, but the people in the onion industry are interested in more practical classifications. Here are some of the ways they do it:

◆ **Fresh or storage:** The National Onion Association says it's this simple: there are two types of onions. The fresh onions are spring and summer onions, high in water and sugar content and coveted for their sweet, mild flavor. They don't store well and ought to be used as soon after harvesting as possible. Mauis, Vidalias and Walla Wallas are examples. Storage onions are available through the fall and winter. They are stronger in taste, usually smaller, have the traditional onion heat and keep well.

◆ **Sweet or strong:** Some onion growers and marketers use these words in describing onions, putting the emphasis on how much of those potent sulfur compounds that make you cry are contained in the flesh. Fresh onions tend to be sweet, and storage onions tend to be strong.

◆ **Color:** The National Onion Association says there are three colors: yellow, white and red. Other onion scientists say that there are also brown onions. Fresh and storage onions come in any of these colors, which is significant to growers because colored onions have compounds in their scales, or dry coverings, that inhibit smudge and neck rot, two important onion diseases. Onion processors prefer to work with white onions to ensure that their product looks absolutely pristine.

◆ **Size:** Owing to the thousands of special-purpose varieties that have been developed over the years, mature onions come in an enormous array of marketable sizes. You can find a mature *Allium cepa* as tiny as a grape or as big as a cabbage, from ⅛-ounce pearls to 6-pound giants.

❧ **Shape:** Botanist Henry Jones used nine distinct terms to describe onions of various shapes: globe, flattened globe, high-globe, spindle, Spanish, flat, thick-flat, Granex and top. A globe is round; a flattened globe onion has a slightly flattened top and bottom; and a high globe onion has a somewhat elongated middle. A spindle onion, sometimes called a torpedo, is long and tapers at both ends. A Spanish onion is perfectly round. A flat onion, on the other hand, may be twice as wide as it is thick. A thick-flat onion is similar but not quite so dramatic. A Granex has a wide, flat top and round bottom. A top onion is a similar shape, except that the bottom is much more elongated, like a toy top.

❧ **Long-day or short-day:** For the grower, this may be the most important category. Most onion varieties are developed for specific day-lengths and temperatures, with a combination of the two triggering the bulbing of the onion. Some experts draw a line roughly from North Carolina to San Francisco to divide northern long-day and southern short-day onion planting zones.

❧ **Place of origin:** Although not particularly discussed among onion professionals, in the popular media there is a lot of talk about Vidalia, Maui and Walla Walla. These names are used for marketing purposes, to take advantage of carefully developed promotion strategies. Such promotions are usually reserved for sweet onions. (You will also often hear of Bermuda or Spanish onions, both of which are large yellow storage onions. Neither comes from the place in its name.) Most onions grown in North America are anonymous storage onions.

❧ **When harvested:** Archie Dessert, who has worked with onions for 50 years, first at the Dessert Seed Company in El Centro, California, and later at nearby West-Gro Farms, and has helped develop hundreds of cultivars, notes that it is important to have a continuous flow of newly harvested onions to the market. "You have very early onions, early onions, medium-early onions, midseason onions, late onions and very late onions," he told us—an onion for virtually every month of the year.

❧ **Whether a bulb forms:** Sometimes a bulb doesn't form when it's supposed to. That can mean the grower has made a mistake, that the weather hasn't been right or that something else went wrong. Some varieties, however, are deliberately used in the "wrong" place, so they won't form a bulb. A scientifically selected cultivar in one latitude might produce a bulb, but when it is used in another, it will behave like a scallion.

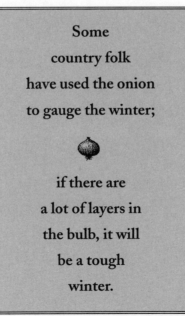

Cultivar: In horticultural work, the term ultivar is used instead of variety when dealing with a food plant. Onions never come to market under these variety names, but the specific cultivar is of crucial importance to the farmer when ordering seed.

Where Onions Grow

MOST OF THE ONIONS EATEN in North America are storage onions. They are grown in quantity in several states, with the heaviest concentration in western Idaho and eastern Oregon, where as much as a quarter of our entire fall and winter crop of storage onions is produced. Colorado is big onion country, too. Washington, New York, Michigan, Wisconsin, Nevada, Utah, Nebraska and Ohio also contribute to the harvest of storage alliums.

But California is the number-one onion state by far. At least 25 percent of America's onions are grown there, including sweet onions, storage onions and special onions for processing. (Half of the state's production goes to the companies that dehydrate onions, can them, freeze-dry them or put them in mixes.)

If you ask supermarket customers where sweet onions come from, many are likely to say Georgia, thanks to the powerful Vidalia publicity juggernaut. But actually, that state, home of Vidalia sweet onions, is good for only about 5 percent of the nation's total onion acreage.

California is ahead of Georgia in sweet onion production, much of it in the Imperial Valley, where many of the sweet varieties were developed. New Mexico, Washington and Arizona also produce substantial quantities of sweets, and Texas grows nearly twice as many sweets as Georgia, mostly the big 1015Ys.

Unfortunately, the onions that do most of the nation's onion work—that flavor most of the stocks, soups and stews—are bereft of the glamour that attends the sweets. No one at an airport, seeing you toting a bag of dry storage onions, is likely to cry out, "Take me home with you and make me a hamburger," something they may do if they see you with some fresh Mauis.

But without storage onions in the house, expect a bland dinner.

Some country folk have used the onion to gauge the winter;

if there are a lot of layers in the bulb, it will be a tough winter.

What's in an Onion

DURING WORLD WAR II, the government sponsored a study of vegetable efficiency. The goal was to learn which of the 31 most popular vegetables had the most nutrients in relation to the cost of producing them. The work was carried out on the farms and in the laboratories of the California Agricultural Experiment Station system. John H. MacGillivray, a well-respected agronomist of the time, designed the project and supervised its execution. The results were published by the station in 1943.

The planners of the study assigned values to the different nutrients and worked out an average for the nutritional content of each of the 31 vegetables. They then calculated the nutrients per pound, per acre and per man-hour of labor.

The authorities never ordered a halt to the production of an inefficient vegetable. But if they had, the onion surely would have survived. In nutrients per pound, the onion was bunched in the middle.

Nutrient Composition   One Medium Onion

The National Onion Association in Greeley, Colorado, wants you to know exactly what you get when you partake of a medium-sized (5-ounce) onion.

Serving Size	150 grams (5 oz)	Serving Size	150 grams (5 oz)
Calories	60	Riboflavin B$_2$ (mg)	*
Protein (gm)	12	Niacin	*
Carbohydrate (gm)	14	Vitamin B$_6$ (mcg)	120.1
Fat	0	Folic Acid (mcg)	24
Cholesterol	0	Calcium (mg)	38
Sodium (mg)	10	Iron (mg)	*
Potassium (mg)	200	Phosphorus (mg)	40.3
Vitamin A	*	Magnesium (mg)	16
Vitamin C (mg)	11.9	Copper (mg)	.03
Vitamin B$_1$ (mg)	.06	Dietary Fiber (gm)	2.8

* Less than 2 percent of United States Recommended Daily Allowance (US RDA).

But in nutrients per man-hour invested in their production, the onion ranked sixth, and in nutrients per acre, third. A very efficient vegetable indeed.

Oddly, a vegetable that is not widely eaten was the most efficient by far—mustard greens. Also ahead of the onion were broccoli, white potatoes, sweet potatoes and cabbage. Sweet spring onions were efficient, too, in ninth place overall, behind winter squash and spinach.

Trailing the onion in efficiency were the radish (the least efficient vegetable), watermelons, cucumbers, cantaloupes, asparagus, Brussels sprouts, turnips, carrots, beets, tomatoes, cauliflower, lettuce, beans and peas.

THEN AS NOW, you get your money's worth when you buy an onion. Eat an onion and you will get no fat, no cholesterol, few calories, a surprising jolt of vitamin C and enough fiber to do your gizzard some good. Taste aside, it is a food well worth eating.

Although an onion makes a nice contribution to your daily vitamin C needs, it is not in the league with oranges. A medium-sized Valencia orange (2⅝-inch) has 58 milligrams of vitamin C, compared to the onion's 11.9. On the other hand, the onion has 2.8 grams of fiber, while the orange has only 0.6.

The onion is a good fiber performer, with about twice as much as a ½-cup serving of cooked kidney beans, and only half of the calories.

An Allium a Day

Eat leeks in March and ramsins in May,
and all the year after the physicians may play.
—Old English proverb

THROUGHOUT HISTORY and in all cultures that incorporated them in their cuisine, onions have been recognized for their healing powers. As anyone who grew up in rural America and had grandparents born in the 1800s can tell you, onions were a common folk remedy for various illnesses well into the early part of this century, valued as a medicine as much as a food. Grandmother Edith Dean Griffith, who worked as a country doctor's assistant in rural West Virginia in the 1900s, never allowed the doctors to dissuade her from the notion that a poultice containing onions is what you put on a kid with the croup, a cough or a fever. The stronger the onion, the more likely it was, in her view, to cure what ailed you. Her faith in the healing power of onions put her in good company.

In her book, *An Ancient Egyptian Herbal*, Lise Manniche writes that in Egypt the onion was an important curative. In pharaonic medicine, onion juice was prescribed for coughs, colds and stomach ailments. It was rubbed on cuts and acne and used to treat the ears. To stop a woman from menstruating, onions and wine were made into a paste and placed in her vagina. To cure night blindness, one Egyptian text recommends "leek and fresh urine. Fill his eyes frequently with it, so that he will get to see well." Kohl, a cosmetic powder of antimony, was ground together with dried leeks and mixed with honey to treat warts on the private parts. An onion poultice was used to try to grow hair.

If the medicine failed, and the patient died, the Egyptians would resort to onions again, tucking them into the body cavities of the dead, thinking that in a future life the onions might stimulate the deceased to breathe. Even today, some Egyptians still use a freshly cut onion to induce breathing in newborn babies.

IN ANOTHER SCHOLARLY BOOK, *Food: The Gift of Osiris*, the authors report that Pliny the Elder cataloged the Roman beliefs on the efficacy of the onion: "a cure of feebleness of vision . . . used to induce sleep . . . chewed with bread heals sores in the mouth . . . with vinegar, honey, and wine [used against] dog bites . . . toothache . . . boiled onions given to eat to those affected by dysentery or lumbago, . . . eaten daily on an empty stomach [they] preserve a good state of health, loosen the bowels by putting the air in motion, disperse haemorrhoids when used as a suppository . . ."

While onions may not grow hair or cure blind-

"De soltz vahcksen a zoy vi a tzibele mit dem kop in der erd un mit di fes in der hoykh!"

You should grow like an onion with your head in the dirt and your feet in the air!

—*Yiddish curse*

ness, mounting scientific evidence suggests that their therapeutic powers are real. In Texas, Dr. Leonard Pike, the Texas A&M horticulturist who developed the Texas Sweet onion, is working with Dr. Michael Wargovich, a cancer researcher at the M.D. Anderson Cancer Center in Houston, to isolate natural substances that inhibit or prevent cancer. Wargovich is particularly interested in compounds in onions that seem to reduce the risk of cancers of the gastrointestinal tract, such as colon cancer. His task is to isolate, analyze and document the compounds, while Pike's assignment is to develop an onion variety rich in the cancer-fighting compound.

"All that folk medicine, all that business about the power of onions, has a basis in fact," said Dr. Pike. "Now, we are starting to understand it."

The two scientists believe that the sulfides in garlic and onions may work against cancer by stimulating the production of enzymes that neutralize or detoxify certain molecules or atoms in the body called "free radicals." Created as a by-product of the metabolic process, these free radicals have lost an electron and are therefore unstable. If they are not neutralized by natural enzymes, they can latch onto genes and change them, thus opening the way for cancer. The greater the concentration of these enzymes, the less the chance of the disease.

"For those who have had cancer," said Wargovich, "we are doing trials with high doses of the garlic and onion compounds in pills, to see if we can prevent a recurrence. For the general population, we will go the 'designer food' route, with cultivars that are fortified with the cancer-preventing agents."

Other researchers in the past decade have been studying the effect of alliums on reducing cholesterol levels, lowering blood pressure and preventing the formation of potentially lethal clots. Chemists at East Texas State University have found a substance known as Prostaglandin A in ordinary onions. It has the ability to reduce blood pressure and has already been extracted and used successfully in animal trials.

Investigators at the George Washington University School of Medicine have found that onions and garlic contain a compound that can block the formation of thromboxane, a natural substance in the blood that causes it to clot. The clotting agents keep us from bleeding to death when we are cut or hurt. But sometimes blood will clot spontaneously in the blood vessels, causing blockage to the brain, heart or other parts of the body. This onion compound behaves like the chemical anticlotting agents frequently given to heart-attack victims to stabilize them.

From her research post at Tufts University, Dr. Isabella Lipinska has published a number of papers that report that some onion compounds have in-creased the amount of good cholesterol in heart patients. She also has found that these compounds tend to inhibit clotting.

OTHER EVIDENCE OF THE THERAPEUTIC EFFECT of alliums surfaced in an Indian study published in 1991 in the *Indian Journal of Experimental Biology*. Researchers fed a group of rabbits a cholesterol-rich diet and then gave them a substantial supplement of garlic. The dangerously high levels of blood cholesterol in the rabbits dropped dramatically.

A number of other studies have confirmed the ancient belief that alliums have bacteria-killing properties when applied directly to wounds. According to the *Indian Medical Journal* in January 1991 (A. K. Chowdhury, Z. U. Ahmed, et al.), allium extracts "showed significant in vitro antibacterial activity" against a variety of drug-resistant strains, including the infamous *Escherichia coli*, which causes severe gastrointestinal illness. Using a population of infected rabbits, the investigators found that those treated with onion extracts survived, while those that were untreated died. Finally, during cold and sore-throat season, you may do well to note the words of one Russian scientist, who says chewing raw onions for five minutes sterilizes the mouth and throat.

Whether any of this ultimately will get the onion reclassified as a drug remains to be seen, but one thing is sure: There is no downside to eating your onions.

Tasting the Alliums: A Glossary

WHEN YOU GO TO THE MARKET, all you really need to know is which onions will do what you want. Do you want them sweet or hot? Are you going to eat them on a hamburger or in a stew? Will they be sliced raw into a salad or caramelized for a pasta sauce? Will they be creamed as a side dish for dinner or diced and packed into a meat loaf?

While it pains us to confess this, when cooking, one can usually substitute one variety of onion for another with little discernible change in taste.

But that's not to say there are not differences, because there are. However, unless you possess a remarkably educated palate, the change in flavor is not dramatic when you substitute a sweet onion for a hot one in a stew. Small boiling onions work just as well as pearl onions in a cooked dish.

Other substitutions may pose a problem. For example, many people do not enjoy a thick slice of a raw, hot storage onion on their burger. But if you don't happen to have a sweet onion in the refrigerator, a thinner slice of a Spanish onion will do, or even a slice of a red onion.

For your salad, if you don't have a red onion, use a yellow or a white. The only difference is that it won't be as colorful. And you could substitute the bulbs of scallions, or better still, a plump-bulbed green "creaming" onion, if those are what you happen to have in the house.

BECAUSE ONIONS ARE SEASONAL, certain types may not always be available. Storage onions can be found anytime, as can red and Spanish onions. On the other hand, sweet onions are usually in markets only from April through the summer (although there is now a fall release of Vidalias that have been stored in a low-oxygen environment). Torpedo, or bottle, red onions are common on the West Coast during the summer and fall, but you will be hard-pressed to find them elsewhere, unless you have access to a specialty farm.

Medium-sized and small onions tend to be sold by the bag; large and jumbo onions are usually offered individually, by the pound.

HEAT INDEX

❧

Sweet & Mild

❧ ❧

Moderately Hot

❧ ❧ ❧

Hot

❧ ❧ ❧ ❧

Hot & Sharp

YELLOW
STORAGE
ONIONS

White (Storage) Onions

THESE ONIONS ARE HOT, but with a slightly sharper, cleaner flavor than yellows. They also tend to have a slightly shorter shelf life because they lack the pigment that affords them protection against mold and because they have proportionally more water than the yellows. They are most commonly used in Mexican cuisine. It is not unusual to find white onions weighing as much as 1¼ pounds. The first taste of them is sweet, but then the sulfur flavors kick in. Larger white onions are usually sold individually by the pound, or when smaller, in blue net bags.

Yellow Storage Onions

THE MOST COMMON COOKING ONIONS, yellow storage onions are sold in red net bags. They are hot and usually will make you cry. They range in size from very small to medium-large, but their heat does not vary with the size. They are a dry onion, with a heavy brown wrapper, little crispness and a faint sulfur taste that lingers on the tongue. Their heat disappears with cooking. This onion is the workhorse of cookery—good in any heated dish, or any other dish in which subtlety is not an issue.

WHITE
STORAGE
ONION

Spanish Onions

SPANISH ONIONS ARE A LARGE YELLOW storage onion, as round as a globe. They usually have a slightly higher water content, and so generally are less hot, sweeter, somewhat crisper and more perishable than the storage onion. They have some heat—just enough to let you know that they mean business. Although some people refer to these onions as Bermudas, they are misinformed, according to Nancy Teksten of the National Onion Association. The death of that venerable line occurred in 1985. We use Spanish onions as a substitute for specialty sweet onions out of season. They are sold individually.

RED ONIONS

SPANISH ONION

Red Onions

RED ONIONS ARE SIMILAR to Spanish onions in their characteristics: Their flavor is sharp, sweet and pungent; their texture is a bit coarser, with a very thick wrapper. Uncooked, red onions make a handsome addition to salads of all types. However, when cooked, these onions lose some of their color, sometimes taking on a greenish hue. They are usually sold individually.

Boiling Onions

BOILING ONIONS ARE VERY SMALL yellow or white storage onions, usually about two inches in diameter. They will be hot to the taste before cooking and are best when left whole and boiled or simmered in a stew. They are usually sold in bulk.

BOILING ONIONS

Pearl Onions

PEARL ONIONS ARE BETWEEN 1 inch and 1¼ inches in diameter with a thin, white wrapper. They are crisp, with a surprising sweetness, and only after chewing does a little sharpness kick in. Pearls are very good when marinated or pickled. You can easily substitute small storage onions for them in any dish that is cooked. Pearl onions are most commonly white, but occasionally, pink pearls are available in the marketplace. They are sold by the pint.

PEARL ONIONS

Green, or Creaming, Onions

to

GREEN, OR CREAMING, ONIONS are fresh onions with a large white bulb still attached to their long green quill, or stem. Sometimes these are scallions that have been allowed more time in the ground.

Most often they are fresh young bulb onions, picked before maturity. They have a clean, crisp flavor, and although somewhat hotter than the thin scallion, they are good both raw and cooked. Green onions make an excellent substitute for red and/or sweet onions in salads. They are sold by the bunch.

Specialty Sweet Onions

SPECIALTY SWEET ONIONS are very high in water content, low in heat and high in sweetness. They are extremely crisp and fairly perishable. These are the onions that most often are sold under a regional name (Maui, Vidalia, Walla Walla) and have a limited season. Most sweets weigh ½ to ¾ pound when they come to the market. Usually yellow, most are shaped like globes or slightly flattened globes. The smaller ones are often slightly hotter than the large ones. These onions are excellent raw, delicate when cooked, and they caramelize nicely. Try them for your next onion rings. They are usually sold individually.

The sweet onions include:
The **Texas Sweet**, sometimes called the 1015Y, so named because it is

SPECIALTY SWEET ONION

29

traditionally planted on October 15, is crisp, probably 85 percent water. It explodes when you bite it, releasing loads of sugar. It has little sulfur, yet enough onion character that you know what it is you are munching. The 1015Y is available from March to June.

The **Maui** tastes almost like it has been soaked in sugar syrup. Crisp and full of water, Mauis seem almost thirst-quenching. A little heat sets in as you chew, not much, but enough to linger for awhile. Although hard to find, Mauis are available year-round.

The **Arizona** impresses first with its sweetness. It is not quite as full of water as the Maui, not quite as crisp, nor quite as hot. Its overall sweetness gives it a lovely refreshing finish. It is available May through June.

The **Vidalia** (Vy-DALE-yuh) is very sweet and crisp. A hint of heat tends to linger just a moment after chewing. When we tested one that had been in foil in the refrigerator for six weeks, we were struck by the fact that the sweetness and fine texture were unchanged—only the heat had diminished with time.

Baby Vidalias come to the market in December, and mature onions are available from April through June. Some are stored in a low-oxygen environment for release in late fall.

Walla Walla Sweets come in July. They are astonishingly sweet, with barely enough sulfur to confirm that they are onions. They are as delicate as a chilled jícama, and as refreshing; you can eat them out of hand, like an apple. They are available in July and August.

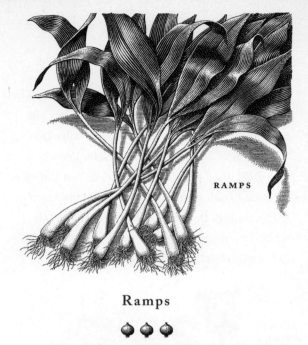

RAMPS

Ramps

WILD MOUNTAIN LEEKS that can be found throughout the forests of the eastern United States, ramps are picked by foragers and can sometimes be purchased off the back of a pickup at mountain ramp festivals. They resemble scallions but have wide, flat leaves and a much more pungent flavor. They are available in April.

Leeks

LEEKS HAVE A TOUGH GREEN TOP that is discarded. You don't often hear of people munching raw leeks—and for good reason. In flavor, the garden-

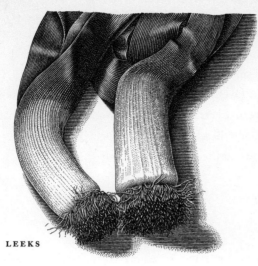

LEEKS

Scallions

SCALLIONS have a white bulb that is mild in flavor and enjoyable both cooked and raw. When chopped, the greens make a handsome garnish. Scallions are a common ingredient in Chinese cuisine; the bulb is cooked to add flavor, the raw greens tops are chopped and sprinkled on at the end as a garnish (the scallion top burns very quickly when cooked in a stir-fry). They are sold by the bunch.

variety leek is like an offbeat onion, very hot, coarse and chewy. The heat persists, and as you chew, the leek releases a bitterness and a more complex flavor than almost any onion, mellow and astringent at the same time. When cooked, leeks develop a warm, oniony flavor. When chopped and sautéed, they become almost buttery in texture. A yellow storage onion can be substituted for chopped leeks, but the flavor will not be the same. Leeks are usually sold individually.

One day, we tasted five varieties of leeks grown at Kingsfield Gardens in Wisconsin. They ranged in flavor from heavy, rich and slightly bitter to light and fresh, with a tinge of sweetness. Then, we braised some of each of the varieties and found that, while there were differences after cooking, they were subtle indeed. Leek varieties can be used interchangeably.

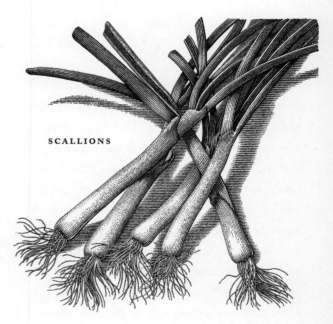

SCALLIONS

CHIVES   GARLIC CHIVES

cious, delicate onion taste. When gently pulled apart into individual petals, the deep pink flowers make a delicious garnish to most cold dishes.

Chives are now frequently sold by the ounce in supermarkets and can be grown in small pots on the windowsill and clipped as needed. They are easily grown in the home herb garden.

Garlic Chives

GARLIC CHIVES have gray-green, broad, flat stalks. They are rarely seen in the market but are easily grown at home. Their flavor is heartier than that of the common chive.

Chives

CHIVES ARE THE GENTLEST of all alliums. Their tender green stems have a delicate onion flavor that is vastly diminished by cooking. Therefore, chives are best added raw at the last minute and are usually used snipped into small bits. Their cylindrical leaves are similar to those of the scallion or green onion but much finer–rarely more than an eighth of an inch in diameter. It is easier to use kitchen scissirs to cut them than a knife. Chives are far more tender than scallions and sweeter, too. While they are clearly oniony, they have not even a hint of heat. It is possible to substitute minced scallion greens for chives as a garnish, but the scallion top is significantly less pleasing in flavor and texture. Chive flowers have a deli-

Garlic

AVAILABLE YEAR-ROUND, garlic is best when fresh. While there are many varieties, the most common are pink-headed garlic, so named for the color of its exterior, and white-headed garlic. Each head consists of many cloves. While there are minute differences among varieties, all fresh garlic should have a pungent, sharp flavor, a tinge

GARLIC

of sweetness and a lingering aroma. If the head is sprouting, the garlic will be bitter. The flavor is released when the clove is cut, and mashing it is said to make the taste even stronger. Because of its pungency, it is generally, but not always, cooked. A small amount goes a long way, especially when raw. Garlic is usually sold by the pound.

ELEPHANT GARLIC

Elephant Garlic

A VERY LARGE FORM OF GARLIC, elephant garlic is said by some to be an ancestor of today's leek. While each clove is very large, the flavor is actually milder than that of ordinary garlic.

Shallots

SHALLOTS, which are like tender, delicate onions in taste and aroma, come in a variety of sizes. They make a superb base for sauces and a splendid addition to omelets. Cooked whole, they hold their shape and caramelize beautifully, making them an excellent addition to anything braised or roasted. Like the leek, the shallot is not for eating raw: A raw shallot tastes nothing like a cooked one. It is hot enough that you wouldn't often try it. Shallots are usually more expensive than the other alliums and are sold by the pound.

The thin-skinned red shallot is the one most commonly available in this country, while the thick-skinned gray shallot is popular in France and rare in the U.S. Although the gray shallot does have a sharper flavor when tasted raw, both varieties mellow out quite nicely in cooking. Because of its thick skin, however, the gray shallot holds its shape better than the red one.

The World of Onions

FLAVOR, IN ITALIAN DISHES," writes Marcella Hazan, "builds up from the bottom. It is not a cover, it is a base." And inevitably, as she sees it, at the bottom of the base is the onion.

Few in the world write more knowledgeably about food than Hazan, and as a student of Italian cooking, she has no peer. She holds doctorates in both the biological and physical sciences, and she thinks about cooking, food and flavor from both a structural and architectural point of view. Her *Essentials of Classic Italian Cooking* begins with an essay on fundamentals and what she sees as the key to understanding and mastering Italian taste.

Whatever the dish, she continues, "a foundation of flavor supports, lifts, points up the principal ingredients." To understand this, she asks the reader to learn three techniques, *battuto, soffritto* and *insapoire.*

Battuto is the beginning, in the Hazan world view, of any consequential dish, especially of the first courses, the pasta sauces, the soups, the risottos. The *battuto* consists of the all-important chopped onion as well as parsley, lard or olive oil, plus garlic, carrots, celery or bacon and anything else that might enhance the dish. A *soffritto* is the *battuto* sautéed until the onions become translucent and the garlic takes on a little color. Take care in making it, she warns. Let nothing scorch; make sure every component has

yielded its best. *Insapoire* is the technique by which the flavors of this onion base engulf the other major ingredients as the *soffritto* is tossed over vigorous heat. By shortcutting the process, the cook will execute a dish that is pallid in taste.

THE FRENCH, TOO, know their onions, which in one way or an other, touch virtually everything cooked in their kitchens. Bases, sauces, essences, reductions, stocks, broths, bouillons, consommés, aspics, gelatins, mirepoix—the critical building blocks of French cooking—all have at their heart the flavor of the onion. A culinary student is likely to struggle for the first two years of schooling with the principles of taste, learning the sophisticated techniques that will produce these vital elements, but all will be for nothing until he or she understands what to do with the onion.

Onions play a similarly fundamental role in the cooking of Transylvania. "If the Transylvanian onion were lifted out from the pyramid of our dietary culture," notes food writer Tibor Balint, "the structure would collapse." In Paul Kovi's *Book of Transylvanian Cuisine,* his friend Balint catalogs the important essential flavors—marjoram, thyme, savory, dill, tarragon, caraway, and above all, onions. Kovi, who is also the co-owner of New York's Four Seasons restaurant, puts onion in virtually every savory dish in the book.

In the traditional Hungarian kitchen, too, onions get preferential treatment. Susan Derecskey, in *The Hungarian Cookbook*, declares that "the slow 'stewing' of chopped onions in hot fat until they turn soft is a fundamental technique . . . Use enough fat, keep the heat very low, and never allow the onions to brown."

And in most of the cuisines of India, onions loom large. Julie Sahni writes that they are the most important ingredient used in the dishes of the North, more important than garlic or gingerroot, the other two essentials. "Onions are added to virtually every dish," she writes in *Classic Indian Cooking*. They show up in an astonishing array of forms, from crisply fried garnishes to smooth and creamy sauces.

IN ADDITION TO ACTING as the foundation of flavors, onions can conceal many a culinary sin. The Australian writer Oscar Mendelsohn in his *Salute to Onions* in 1965 suggests that virtually every major

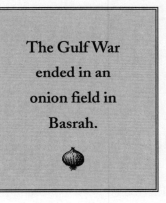

The Gulf War ended in an onion field in Basrah.

national dish from the British Isles owes its continued existence to the ability of onions to cover up what's in it. The Scots, he alleges, use onions to make the ingredients of a haggis less recognizable.

After all, he says, a sheep's stomach filled with oatmeal, lungs, heart and liver is going to need all of the onions it can get. We are not among those who would malign the cooks of the British Isles. But it is often said that cockaleekie soup, made from a decrepit chicken, is edible only because of the leeks.

Though the ordinary onion is rarely encountered in Chinese cuisine, alliums like scallions and garlic will do whatever work the dish demands, from adding grace to the most ethereal preparation to putting a solid base under the earthiest. Scallions are used in hundreds of preparations, tops and all, chopped into almost any imaginable stir-fry, snipped and coiffed into fanciful garnishes, formed into brushes to spread the Peking duck with hoisin sauce, or paired with ginger and given a yin-yang assignment.

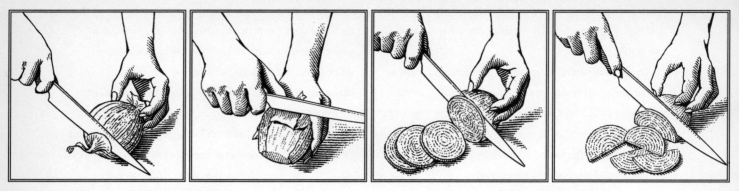

PEELING AN ONION   SLICING AN ONION

Cutting Techniques

BE SURE TO USE VERY SHARP, high-carbon stainless-steel knives in handling onions. Pure carbon steel will tend to discolor the onions. Do not chop onions in a food processor because they tend to pulverize and turn to mush; we have found the processor useful for grating and slicing, though.

Bulb Onions

To slice an onion: Make a small slice across the neck end of the onion; peel the skin off down toward the root. If it is not necessary to keep the onion whole, be sure to divide the onion lengthwise in half, directly through the center of the root. Place each half, flat side down, on a board and begin to slice crosswise from the neck end to the root end. Leaving the root intact will facilitate handling, keeping the onion together while you cut it.

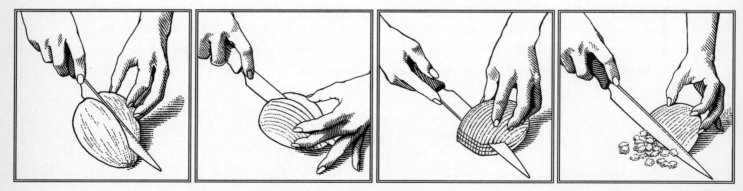

DICING AN ONION

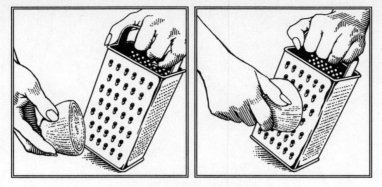

GRATING AN ONION BY HAND

To dice or chop an onion: Make a small slice across the neck end of the onion only; peel the skin off down toward the root. Cut the onion lengthwise in half, directly through the center of the root. Place each half, cut side down, on a board and make even, parallel, lengthwise cuts, cutting to but not through the root end (the farther apart these cuts are, the larger the dice will be). Make even, parallel, crosswise cuts perpendicular to those cuts. These cuts will help determine the size of the dice. Then, carefully cut across the onion from the neck end to the root end; again, the closer together, the smaller the dice.

To grate a whole onion in a food processor: Make a small slice across the neck end of the onion, then slice across the root as well and remove the skin. Cut the onion in half. Place it in a food processor fitted with a grating blade. Insert the pusher into the feed tube in order to pressure the onion to stay in place while it is being processed.

To grate a whole onion by hand: Make a small slice across the neck end of the onion, then peel the skin off down toward the root. Keeping the root intact while you grate the onion will make things easier.

Pearl Onions

To peel pearl onions: Plunge the onions into a pot of boiling water and blanch for 1 to 2 minutes. Drain and chill in ice water. Using a sharp knife, cut off the root end and stem end and peel off the remaining skin.

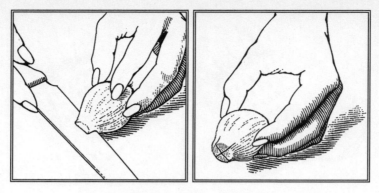

PREPARING AN ONION FOR BOILING

Boiling Onions

Any small storage onion, between 1 and 1½ inches in diameter, is good for boiling. To make peeling easier and to keep the onion intact, blanch the onions in boiling water for 30 seconds, then drop them into very cold water. Trim off just a bit of the top of the onion with a sharp knife and the skin will slip off easily. To prepare the onions for further boiling, make an X in the root end to facilitate even cooking.

Dicing Shallots

The red shallot, which is the most commonly available, has a skin similar to that of the yellow storage onion. The skin on a gray shallot is like rough cardboard. It is tough to cut and requires a very sharp knife.

Peel the red shallot without cutting off the root end. Then slice the shallot lengthwise in half and proceed as with an onion. To peel the gray shallot, cut off both the top end and the root end and remove skin before slicing.

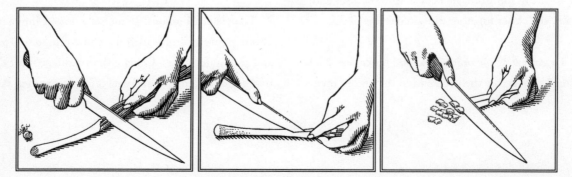

SLICING AND DICING A SCALLION

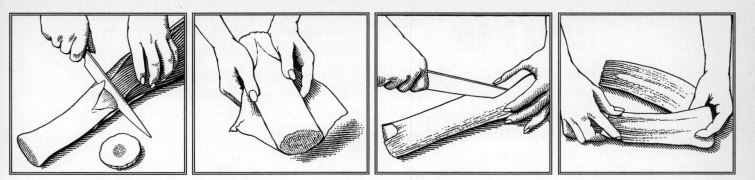

PREPARING A LEEK

Scallions and Green Onions

To dice a scallion: Trim off the tough greens and the root ends. Slit each scallion lengthwise in half, then cut crosswise as finely as needed.

Leeks

Leeks are usually sandy, so thorough cleaning is essential. Cooks unfamiliar with leeks should be warned that the sand lurks within the layers, particularly where the white bulb joins the green shaft.

To clean a leek: Carefully slice off and discard the roots. Cut off and discard the tough green top at the point where the white bulb turns light green in color. Split the leek lengthwise in half and rinse under cold running water to remove any sand, but try to keep the leek from falling apart. If you are using very thin leeks and trying to keep them whole, slit them down one side without cutting through the base. Hold the leek under running water while gently fanning the leaves so the water can rinse away all of the grit.

Chives

Fresh chives will be less bruised if you snip them with sharp scissors instead of mincing them with a knife.

For Best Results

◆ Use the freshest organically grown produce whenever possible. If you need help finding organic growers in your region, check with the agricultural extension service or with chefs at fine restaurants who are apt to know local growers.

◆ When available, use fresh herbs: They impart full flavor without the harshness that often characterizes dried.

◆ We use kosher salt in our recipes, preferring its flavor to that of ordinary table salt, which may, of course, be substituted.

◆ For extra-virgin olive oil, we like to use those labeled "fall harvest, cold-pressed," indicating that they have been made from the first pressing of green olives rather than from ripe olives. They have a particularly fresh, slightly herbaceous flavor.

◆ In recipes where chicken or beef stock is called for, the flavor will be heightened if you use a rich stock. We make our stocks by adding extra bones at the beginning. Then, before we freeze the stock, we further intensify it by reducing it by one-third.

◆ Two high-quality, modestly priced table wines are R. H. Phillips Night Harvest Sauvignon Blanc and Night Harvest Cuvée Rouge (a Rhône-style wine), made in Yolo Valley, California.

◆ We like to use kosher-style processed poultry, which is dipped in cold water rather than hot before plucking; we find that it tastes fresher than ordinary poultry and stays more moist during cooking.

◆ The best-quality Parmesan cheese is genuine Parmigiano-Reggiano, from the region of Emilia-Romagna, Italy.

About the Recipes

◆ We refer to onion sizes as Jumbo, Large, Medium and Small.

Jumbo: Over 1 pound
Large: ¾ to 1 pound
Medium: About ½ to ¾ pound
Small: Below ½ pound

Cooking with onions does not require the kind of precision required for measuring flour and spices. It's usually just fine to have a little more or a little less. For baking, boiling and braising, cooking times may need to be adjusted slightly for variations in size.

◆ We call them *scallions* when they have little or no bulb. We call them *green onions* when they have a large, fresh white bulb with no dried skin on it and a long green quill attached.

Hors d'Oeuvres & Appetizers

White Beans with Red Onions, Tuna & Fresh Basil . . . 43

Red Onions, Walnuts, Cheese & Sage . . . 44

Zack's Roasted Onion Tapenade . . . 45

Shellfish Fritters with Roasted Shallot Mayonnaise . . . 46

Crab & Shallot Wontons with Green Chile Sauce . . . 48

Fresh Oysters with Chive & Corn Vinaigrette . . . 50

Roasted Red Peppers & Sweet Onions with Garlic & Anchovies . . . 51

Egg, Olive & Scallion Pâté . . . 55

Parma Pierogi's Potato & Onion Pierogi with Onion-Butter Sauce . . . 56

Pork & Scallion Pot Stickers with Chili-Scallion Dipping Sauce . . . 58

Shrimp & Scallion Spring Rolls with Plum Sauce . . . 60

Chinese Barbecued Spareribs with Scallions & Shallots . . . 62

Fried Scallion-Shrimp Balls . . . 65

Chicken Liver Pâté with Applejack, Scallions & Chives . . . 66

Soft Cheese with Shallots . . . 67

Pickled Lox & Onions . . . 68

Chive Crêpes with Smoked Salmon, Red Onions & Chèvre . . . 70

Deep-Fried Chive Crêpes with Chèvre, Scallions & Prosciutto . . . 73

Maui Salmon Mousse . . . 76

Helofa Hot Sauce Chicken Wings . . . 77

White Beans with Red Onions, Tuna & Fresh Basil

THIS SIMPLE AND RUSTIC DISH has its roots in a wonderful lunch served to us by Italian food and wine maven Faith Heller Willinger in the kitchen of her handsome apartment in Florence. While one can make this with canned beans, we prefer to cook them ourselves. In fact, we try to keep a supply of cooked Great Northern beans in the freezer, especially in summer.

MAKES ABOUT 4½ CUPS; SERVES 10

3   cups cooked Great Northern beans
1   medium-sized red onion, halved lengthwise and thinly sliced crosswise
1   6½-ounce can water-packed tuna, drained
3   tablespoons red-wine vinegar
7   large, unblemished basil leaves
½   cup extra-virgin olive oil
1   teaspoon kosher salt
1   teaspoon freshly ground black pepper
    Lettuce leaves and chopped fresh flat-leaf parsley for serving

In a large bowl, combine beans, onion and tuna. Toss with vinegar and set aside. Stack basil leaves, one on top of the other, and roll into a tight tube. Using a sharp knife, cut into fine strips. Add basil strips to bean mixture. Gently stir in olive oil. Add salt and pepper, mix and taste. You may wish to add more vinegar or other seasonings.

Cover and chill for at least 2 hours. Line a serving bowl with lettuce leaves; fill with bean mixture. Sprinkle with parsley.

Wine: Zamo and Palazzo Chardonnay (Italy: Friuli)

Red Onions, Walnuts, Cheese & Sage

THIS UNUSUAL COMBINATION has its roots in Tuscany, where many dishes served before the main meal include red onions. The onions, walnuts, sage and garlic are first gently warmed in olive oil—just to release their flavors—and then poured over the shaved cheese and cooled. We use a vegetable peeler to shave thin slices about 1 inch long and ¾ inch wide from a chunk of room-temperature Parmesan cheese.

We serve this dish all summer long, when the sage comes right from our garden and the red onions are at their sweetest.

SERVES 4

½ cup shaved Parmesan cheese (about 3 ounces)

⅓ cup extra-virgin olive oil

½ cup coarsely chopped red onion

1 cup coarsely chopped walnut meats

2 tablespoons chopped fresh sage

2 garlic cloves, slivered

Freshly ground black pepper

Place cheese in a medium-sized mixing bowl and set aside.

Over low heat, heat olive oil in a small saucepan. Add onion, walnuts, sage and garlic. Toss for 2 minutes. Pour warm mixture over cheese. Gently toss until mixture cools. Add pepper to taste. Serve at room temperature.

Wine: Isole e Olena Chianti Classico (Italy: Tuscany)

44

Zack's Roasted Onion Tapenade

APENADE, a thick, lusty Provençal spread, features ground black Mediterranean olives and olive oil and is usually served in a crock, accompanied by fresh, toothsome bread. At Zack Bruell's acclaimed Cleveland restaurant, Z Contemporary Cuisine, a crock of tapenade awaits diners at every table. This version, with its caramelized roasted onion, has proved to be irresistible, especially when spread on Focaccia with Rosemary & Onions (page 184). Zack likes his tapenade with lots of oil; we prefer it with less—it's up to you. Be sure to save some tapenade for the Butterflied Chicken with Roasted Onion Tapenade (page 310).

MAKES 2½ CUPS; SERVES 8 TO 10

1   large Spanish onion, unpeeled
     About ½ cup extra-virgin olive oil
1   packed cup pitted kalamata olives
2-4   tablespoons oil-packed or water-softened sun-dried tomatoes, drained
3   plump garlic cloves, peeled

Preheat oven to 375 degrees F. Rub onion with 1 tablespoon olive oil, wrap in foil and bake until very tender, about 2 hours. Remove onion from foil and let cool to room temperature.

Peel onion and place in the bowl of a food processor fitted with the metal blade. Add olives, 2 tablespoons sun-dried tomatoes and garlic; pulse until pureed. Taste and add more tomatoes, if desired. With the motor running, gradually add ¼ cup olive oil. If desired, add more. Scrape tapenade into a clean container, cover and store in the refrigerator. Bring to room temperature before serving. Stir in more oil, if you wish.

Shellfish Fritters with Roasted Shallot Mayonnaise

THIS LIGHT FRITTER BATTER contains morsels of seafood, and the accompanying mayonnaise takes on richness from the roasted shallots. When the fritters are made small, they are a great appetizer for a group. But you could also serve them as a dinner for six. Save any extra mayonnaise for a cold chicken and tomato sandwich.

Note: The egg yolks used in this mayonnaise are uncooked. If you are concerned about the danger of using them, substitute 1¾ cups commercial mayonnaise blended with the shallots, chives and 2 tablespoons fresh lemon juice.

MAKES 3 TO 4 DOZEN SMALL FRITTERS;

2 CUPS MAYONNAISE

Mayonnaise

½	pound shallots (6-8 plump), unpeeled
¼	cup olive oil
2	large egg yolks
2	tablespoons Dijon mustard
½	teaspoon dry mustard
⅛	teaspoon cayenne
¾	cup vegetable oil
¼	cup fresh lemon juice
	Kosher salt and freshly ground white pepper
1	tablespoon minced fresh chives

Fritters

⅓	pound sea scallops, chopped
¼	pound minced clams
¼	pound fresh crabmeat, picked into pieces
¼	pound peeled and deveined raw shrimp, chopped
½	cup finely diced red onion
¼	cup minced shallots
½	cup buttermilk
1	large egg
2	tablespoons minced fresh parsley
2	tablespoons minced fresh cilantro
1	small dried red chile pepper, crumbled
½	cup yellow cornmeal
¼	cup unbleached flour
2	teaspoons dry mustard
1½	teaspoons baking powder
½	teaspoon baking soda
1	teaspoon kosher salt
½	teaspoon freshly ground white pepper
2-3	cups vegetable oil for frying
	Lemon slices and fresh parsley and cilantro for garnish

To make mayonnaise: Preheat oven to 300 degrees F. Combine shallots and olive oil in a small ovenproof dish. Cover and place in the oven. Roast until shallots are tender and slightly caramelized, about 1 hour. Uncover the dish and set aside to cool. Peel shallots and set aside; reserve cooled olive oil.

In the bowl of a food processor fitted with the metal blade, combine egg yolks, Dijon mustard, dry mustard and cayenne; pulse several times. With the motor running, very gradually add reserved olive oil and vegetable oil and process until mixture is thick. Pulse in lemon juice, salt, pepper and roasted shallots. Process for 6 seconds. Fold in chives. Cover and chill until needed.

To make fritters: In a large mixing bowl, combine all fritter ingredients and blend well. Cover with plastic wrap and chill for at least 1 hour.

Pour oil into a wok or deep-fat fryer to a depth of 1½ to 2½ inches and heat to about 330 degrees F, or until hot enough to quickly brown a cube of bread. Drop fritter batter by rounded teaspoonfuls into hot oil and fry, 6 to 8 at a time, until golden on one side. Turn and fry on the other side, 1 to 2 minutes total. If oil is too hot, fritters will burn. Remove from oil with a slotted spoon and drain well. Fry remaining fritters in the same manner. Do not crowd them or they will become too oily.

Serve fritters hot, with mayonnaise and garnished with lemon slices and herbs.

Wine: Spottswoode Winery Sauvignon Blanc (California: Napa Valley)

Crab & Shallot Wontons with Green Chile Sauce

WE LIKE THE FLAVOR of shallots in this dish, but it is certainly possible to substitute white onion or even scallions for them. These wontons are always popular as a nibble before dinner, but we also serve them as part of a special Chinese dinner.

MAKES ABOUT 24 WONTONS; SERVES 6 TO 8

Wontons

3	tablespoons unsalted butter
⅓	cup minced shallots
1	plump garlic clove, minced
¾	pound crabmeat, picked into pieces
¼	cup chopped fresh cilantro
	Kosher salt and freshly ground black pepper
	Pinch cayenne
	Cornstarch for dusting baking sheet
24	wonton wrappers (gyoza skins)

Green Chile Sauce

6	plump scallions, trimmed to include 1 inch of green
1	jalapeño pepper, halved and seeded
1	plump garlic clove
¼	cup loosely packed fresh chives
¼	cup loosely packed fresh parsley
¼	cup loosely packed fresh cilantro
8	fresh mint leaves
¼	cup soy sauce
3	tablespoons rice wine
2	tablespoons Oriental sesame oil
	Freshly ground white pepper
½	cup vegetable oil

To make wontons: Melt butter in a medium skillet over high heat. Add shallots and garlic and stir until their color begins to change, about 2 minutes. Add crabmeat and cook until hot, about 1 minute. Remove from heat and cool to room temperature, 10 to 15 minutes. Add cilantro, salt and pepper to taste and cayenne.

Cover a baking sheet with wax paper and dust lightly with cornstarch. Arrange 6 wonton wrappers on a flat surface. Distribute a rounded teaspoonful of filling in the center of each. Using your fingers, moisten edges of wontons with water, fold over to form a triangle and press edges to seal. Bring the 2 opposite points together and gently twist to seal. Place on the prepared baking sheet. Repeat until all wontons are filled. Cover lightly with plastic and refrigerate for at least 1 hour.

Meanwhile, make green chile sauce: Combine

scallions, jalapeño, garlic, chives, parsley, cilantro and mint in the bowl of a food processor fitted with the metal blade. Chop as finely as possible. Add soy sauce, rice wine and sesame oil and puree. Pour sauce into a small bowl and let stand at room temperature.

Pour oil into a large skillet to a depth of ⅛ inch and heat until hot. Fry wontons, without crowding, until golden on each side, about 4 minutes total. Drain on paper towels and keep warm. Repeat until all are cooked, adding more oil if needed. Serve with green chile dipping sauce.

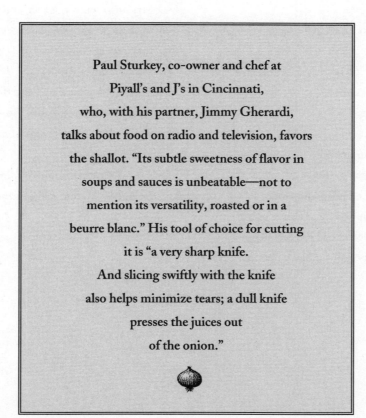

Paul Sturkey, co-owner and chef at
Piyall's and J's in Cincinnati,
who, with his partner, Jimmy Gherardi,
talks about food on radio and television, favors
the shallot. "Its subtle sweetness of flavor in
soups and sauces is unbeatable—not to
mention its versatility, roasted or in a
beurre blanc." His tool of choice for cutting
it is "a very sharp knife.
And slicing swiftly with the knife
also helps minimize tears; a dull knife
presses the juices out
of the onion."

Fresh Oysters with Chive & Corn Vinaigrette

FRESH, RAW OYSTERS are topped with a zingy salsa of corn, bell pepper, chives and jalapeño, seasoned with a little cider vinegar and sugar. This salsa is also very good with raw clams, grilled mackerel or bluefish.

SERVES 4

Salsa

1   ear fresh sweet corn
½   cup cider vinegar
¼   cup sugar
1   teaspoon ground cumin
¼   teaspoon minced garlic
½   teaspoon minced jalapeño pepper
1   tablespoon snipped fresh chives
1   tablespoon finely diced red bell pepper
    Salt and freshly ground black pepper

24   fresh, well-chilled oysters, scrubbed

To make salsa: Cut kernels from corn cob and place them in a nonaluminum small saucepan. Add vinegar, sugar, cumin, garlic and jalapeño. Bring to a boil; remove from heat, cover and let cool to room temperature, about 1 hour. Add chives, bell pepper and salt and pepper to taste.

Carefully shuck oysters and discard top shells. Divide oysters among 4 plates. Pass vinaigrette or serve in a small bowl in the center of each serving plate.

Wine: Domaine Billaud-Simon Chablis "Les Clos" (France: Burgundy)

Roasted Red Peppers & Sweet Onions

WITH GARLIC & ANCHOVIES

THIS IS ONE OF OUR FAVORITE summer appetizers. The roasted peppers are soft and silky, with just a tinge of smoky flavor, and the grilled sweet onions caramelize slightly from the fire. The flavor of the dish improves as the days pass. It keeps for at least a week in the refrigerator, but let it stand at room temperature for a few hours before serving.

SERVES 6 TO 10

4-5	large red bell peppers
1-2	large Walla Wallas or other sweet onions
3	tablespoons vegetable oil
1	2-ounce tin flat anchovy fillets, drained
½	cup extra-virgin olive oil
2	plump garlic cloves, thinly sliced
3	fresh basil leaves, torn in half
1	teaspoon freshly ground black pepper

Preheat the broiler.

Place bell peppers on a baking sheet and broil, turning often, until blackened and blistered on all sides. Transfer peppers to a paper bag and keep tightly closed until cooled.

Meanwhile, cut onion into ¼-inch-thick slices. Brush both sides with vegetable oil, and broil, turning several times, until tender. Cut slices in half and place in a large bowl.

When peppers have cooled, peel and discard skin, rinsing under running water to remove any stubborn bits of skin. Slice in half, discard seeds and trim thick ridges. Cut each half into ½-inch-wide strips and combine with onions.

Cut each anchovy fillet lengthwise in half; add to peppers and onions. Add extra-virgin olive oil, garlic, basil and black pepper and mix well. Add more olive oil, if peppers and onions are not well covered. Allow to stand for at least 6 hours before serving.

Wine: Marcel Deiss Pinot Blanc
(France: Alsace)

What's a Scallion?

WHAT IS A SCALLION? There is no single answer that is generally agreed upon by all botanists, scientists, farmers or produce specialists. The confusion goes back to ancient times. Theophrastus, the Greek philosopher, writing in the third century B.C., became the first person to catalog plants methodically. In one of his works, he describes a small onion from Ascalon, the town in Judea where Herod was born.

Three hundred years later in Italy, Pliny the Elder, the Craig Claiborne of his era, wrote that the slender onions grown in Roman gardens were the same ones that Theophrastus had described—the onion of Ascalon. But Pliny's description made those onions sound more like today's shallot than a scallion or green onion.

Noah Webster compounded the confusion. He must have read Pliny; the scallion, says his unabridged dictionary, is "the onion of Ascalon, the shallot, *A. ascalonicum*. Also the leek or any green onion with a long, thick stem and an almost bulbless root."

Neither food historian Waverley Root nor gardening writer Shepherd Ogden agrees with Webster's definition. They think the scallion is *A. fistulosum*, the Japanese bunching onion, a variety that never grows a bulb. Many modern botanists agree. But Root hedges; he goes on to say that maybe the scallion is any young onion before it bulbs.

Bruce Buurma, who grows millions of scallions on his Ohio farm, says Root is right; the scallion is simply an immature onion, pulled before it bulbs. In his view, it can be any cultivar of *A. cepa*.

In the book *Hybrid Onions*, written by onion scientist Henry Jones, we are told that "almost any of the white varieties [of common onions] are used for green or bunching onions. These include the short-day types like Crystal Wax and Eclipse; the long-day types such as White Sweet Spanish, White Portugal and Southport White Globe." They are harvested before maturity.

Most commercial producers will buy the seed of the onion they like best and plant 20 to 30 pounds of it per acre. This dense planting, using 6 to 8 times more seed than in an ordinary onion patch, crowds the onions and slows growth. When the onions are big enough, just before they start growing bulbs,

(continued on page 54)

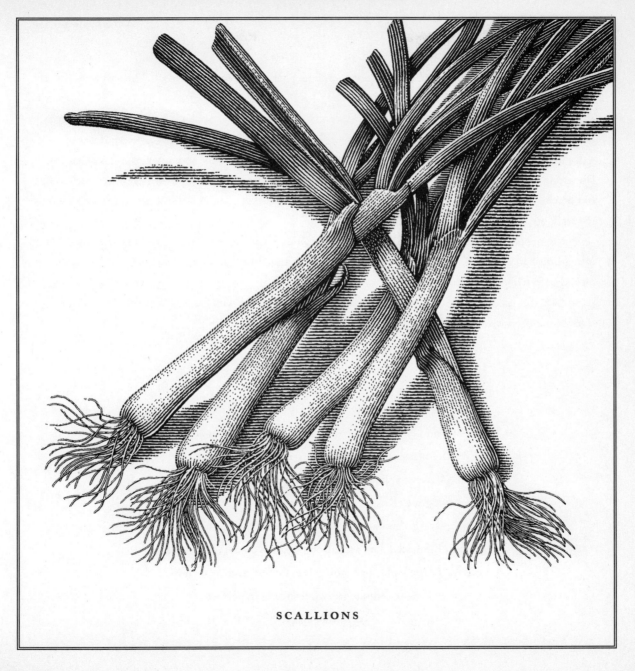

SCALLIONS

(continued from page 52)

they are pulled, tied, taken to the shed, washed, chilled, packed and sent to market. The vast majority of scallions are grown this way.

Jones reminds us that some growers still prefer to use nonbulbing varieties. The Egyptian or Tree onion, from the Proliferum Group of *A. cepa*, is still occasionally used. It produces no seed, but propagates by top-sets, or bulbils, that grow in the flower. It is pulled before the top-sets form. The Japanese Bunching onion, sometimes called the Welsh onion, is a nonbulbing variety, so farmers don't have to be too precise as to when they pull it. It occasionally comes to market. Young shallots are sometimes used for scallions.

For the cook, these distinctions really don't matter. There will be little difference in taste between an immature shallot, one of the rare Tree onions, a Japanese bunching onion, or a standard storage onion picked before it starts to grow its bulb.

In fact, if it is a green onion without a bulb, whatever its lineage, you can call it a scallion, and the clerk at the produce counter will know exactly what you mean.

In their wonderful little book called *Trucs of the Trade*,
Frank Ball and Arlene Feltmand produce five score and one trucs—
kitchen French for tricks or shortcuts—to make cooking easier and quicker.
How often have you chopped a scallion with a chef's knife only to find
that you haven't gone all the way through and the pieces are strung together
like beads on a string? Barbara Tropp, chef/owner of China Moon restaurant
in San Francisco, has a solution. Before you cut it crosswise,
says Tropp, split the scallion lengthwise, and then chop.
The technique works, resulting in perfect
scallion confetti.

Egg, Olive & Scallion Pâté

THIS SIMPLE EGG PÂTÉ of finely chopped hard-cooked eggs, minced scallions, olives and pickled jalapeño peppers has become one of our standard appetizers. People love it, and it's a nifty way to have a nibble without foundering guests' appetites. We usually pack it into a well-oiled, chilled mold, turn it out onto a bed of lettuce, decorate it with olive rings and bunches of fresh herbs and accompany it with thinly sliced pumpernickel bread. We use jalapeño-stuffed olives from the Santa Barbara Olive Company, widely available in supermarkets and specialty food shops.

MAKES 3 CUPS; SERVES ABOUT 10

6   scallions, trimmed to include 1 inch of green

6   jalapeño-stuffed olives, plus more for garnish, or 6 jumbo Spanish olives without pimientos and 1 pickled jalapeño pepper
     Leaves of 4 parsley sprigs

1   tablespoon fresh tarragon leaves

8   large eggs, hard-cooked and peeled

½   cup homemade or Hellmann's mayonnaise

1   generous teaspoon curry powder

½   teaspoon freshly ground white pepper

¼   teaspoon kosher salt
     Leaf lettuce, olive slices and fresh parsley and tarragon for garnish
     Thinly sliced pumpernickel bread, cut into triangles

In the bowl of a food processor fitted with the metal blade, combine scallions, olives, parsley and tarragon. Process until mixture is finely minced, scraping down the sides several times.

Press eggs through a ricer into a mixing bowl, or finely chop. Add scallion mixture, mayonnaise, curry powder, pepper and salt and and blend well. Taste and adjust seasonings, if necessary. Pack into a serving dish or oiled mold, cover and chill for at least 4 hours before serving. Line a serving platter with lettuce leaves, invert the pâté dish over the platter, rap the bottom sharply with a wooden spoon and remove the dish. Garnish pâté with olives and herbs and surround with bread.

Wine: Quivira Vineyards Sauvignon Blanc (California: Sonoma County)

Parma Pierogi's Potato & Onion Pierogi

WITH ONION-BUTTER SAUCE

PARMA, OHIO, is this country's pierogi capital. When candidate Bill Clinton visited Cleveland in the summer of 1992, he stopped at Parma Pierogi, which is famous for dumplings. Mary Poldruhi, the founder and president, and her sister, Anne Moore, the manager, were given just two days' notice, but when the Clinton-Gore bus pulled up, they were ready to feed 100 people and had made pierogi to go for 250 more. Months later, Mary Poldruhi was among the Faces of Hope at President Clinton's inauguration. These particular pierogi are light and delicate, and the dough is unusually easy to handle. The traditional potato filling is spiked with onions and scallions.

MAKES 30 TO 42 PIEROGI; SERVES 6 TO 8

Pierogi Dough

- 2 cups unbleached flour
- 1 large egg or 2 egg yolks
- 1 tablespoon vegetable oil
- 1 teaspoon kosher salt
  Milk and/or water (if using both, use equal amounts of each, about ½ cup total)

Filling

- 3 cups hot or warm mashed potatoes (from 2½ pounds russets, peeled)
- ¼ cup minced white onion
- 2 tablespoons minced scallions, trimmed to include 1 inch of green
- 2 tablespoons melted butter
  Kosher salt and freshly ground black pepper

Onion-Butter Sauce

- ½ cup (1 stick) unsalted butter
- ⅔ cup finely diced white onion

Sour cream, minced fresh parsley and fresh chives for garnish

To make pierogi dough: Place flour in a large bowl. In a measuring cup, combine egg, oil and salt and beat well with a fork. Add enough milk (or water and milk) to bring contents up to ¾ cup. Add liquid ingredients to flour and mix until blended. Knead dough on a floured surface until no longer sticky, about 15 minutes. (Or use the dough hook of an electric mixer to knead dough for about 15 minutes; you may need to add up to 2 tablespoons more flour.) Dough will look and feel very smooth. Cover and let rest for 15 minutes, or even overnight in the refrigerator.

To make filling: In a large bowl, combine potatoes, onion, scallions, butter, salt and pepper to taste. Blend well and taste for seasonings; set aside.

Cover a large baking sheet with wax paper and dust well with flour.

To assemble: Divide dough in half. On a generously floured surface, roll out dough ⅛ inch thick, to about a 14-inch square. With a 2½-to-3-inch cutter, carefully cut out circles of dough. (Be careful: Dough is very elastic so it is hard to cut, and you may need to use a sharp knife from time to time.) Put 1 packed teaspoon of filling in the middle of each circle—just enough to make a plump package. Fold dough over to form a half-moon shape; pinch edges closed. (You can gently stretch dough over the filling, but don't stretch it too thin.) Place pierogi on the baking sheet.

Repeat until all pierogi are made. Cover with wax paper and refrigerate until ready to cook.

To make onion-butter sauce: Melt butter in a skillet over medium heat. Add onions and sauté over high heat until tender, 3 to 5 minutes. Set aside.

To cook pierogi: Fill a large soup pot with water and add a pinch of salt. (We usually have 2 pots going at the same time.) Bring water to a rolling boil. Drop about 6 pierogi into the boiling water, cover and cook for 1 minute. Uncover, stir with a wooden spoon and cook for 3 minutes. Cover and cook for 1 minute more, or until pierogi puff up and float to the top.

Remove pierogi with a skimmer or slotted spoon, drain well and place on heated plates. Repeat until all pierogi are cooked.

Drizzle pierogi with onion-butter sauce and garnish with dollops of sour cream and a sprinkling of minced parsley and chives.

Wine: Girard Winery Dry Chenin Blanc (California: Napa Valley)

Pork & Scallion Pot Stickers

WITH CHILI-SCALLION DIPPING SAUCE

THANKS TO A CHINESE FRIEND, Kathryn King, we have been making delicate and delicious pot stickers for years. These dumplings combine ginger, scallions and cabbage with pork. We make certain to brown the bottoms nicely, then we quickly braise and steam them in a cornstarch-and-water mixture that makes the tops light gold and shiny. We serve them with a piquant dipping sauce.

MAKES ABOUT 36 POT STICKERS

Pot Stickers

¾ pound lean ground pork

¾ cup chopped Chinese cabbage (Napa)

4 scallions, trimmed to include 1 inch of green, cut into pieces

2 slices peeled fresh ginger

1 plump garlic clove, peeled

1 tablespoon soy sauce

1 tablespoon rice wine

1 teaspoon Oriental sesame oil

About ½ cup cornstarch

1 package square wonton wrappers (gyoza skins)

1 cup cold water

Dipping Sauce

3 tablespoons Chinese black vinegar

3 tablespoons rice wine

2 tablespoons red-wine vinegar

2 tablespoons soy sauce

1 teaspoon Oriental sesame oil

1 rounded teaspoon Chinese chili paste

2 finely minced scallions, green included

1 tablespoon minced fresh cilantro

About ⅓ cup peanut oil

To make pot stickers: Combine pork, cabbage, scallions, ginger and garlic in the bowl of a food processor fitted with the metal blade. Pulse until mixture is finely chopped. Add soy sauce, rice wine and sesame oil. Pulse until mixture is fairly smooth.

Sprinkle a large flat tray or plate with some of the cornstarch.

Arrange wrappers, flour side up, on a work surface. Put ½ cup water in a small bowl. Place a rounded teaspoonful of filling in the center of each wrapper. Dip your fingers into water and moisten outer edges of each filled wrapper. Fold each piece in half, using your thumb and index finger to pinch a few folds across the top of each dumpling where edges come together. Place wonton, plump side down, on the prepared tray and repeat the process until all dumplings are made. Cover well with wax paper until it is time to fry.

In a small dish, combine 1 teaspoon cornstarch and the remaining ½ cup water. Mix with a chopstick to blend thoroughly. Set aside.

To make dipping sauce: Combine all dipping sauce ingredients in a serving bowl and whisk well to blend. Set aside.

To cook pot stickers: Preheat an electric frying pan to 400 degrees F or set a 12-inch cast-iron skillet over medium-high heat. Brush the pan with enough oil to coat the bottom and heat until oil shimmers. Arrange all dumplings close together, but not touching, in the pan. Fry, uncovered, for several minutes, or until bottoms just begin to brown. Quickly pour reserved water-cornstarch mixture over tops of dumplings and cover the pan. Reduce the heat to 375 degrees and cook for 2 to 3 minutes more, or until dumplings are well browned and tops have a nice shine to them.

Carefully remove pot stickers from the frying pan and arrange on a heated serving platter. Serve with dipping sauce.

Wine: Buehler Vineyards White Zinfandel (California: Napa Valley)

Food writer Michael McLaughlin says, "Green onions are, if not my favorite, at least my most relied upon allium. For little shocks of flavor and color, scattered over the Southwestern food I love so much, or grilled to sweet tenderness as an edible garnish, they can't be beat. I cut them with a knife unless I'm pureeing them into something. Maybe I like them because they don't cause tears. As a contact-lens wearer, that's something I appreciate."

Shrimp & Scallion Spring Rolls with Plum Sauce

BITE INTO ONE OF THESE delicate, crunchy spring rolls for a complex burst of shrimp and scallion flavors. Besides the chopped cabbage and shredded carrots, there's a hint of ginger and a suggestion of hot pepper. The warm plum sauce adds a satisfying sweet-and-sour accent. The wrappers, which are readily available in Asian markets, are especially light because they are made from just water and flour. (Egg-roll wrappers, in contrast, are thicker and heartier because they are made with egg.) Despite the length of this recipe, these spring rolls take less than 1 hour to prepare.

MAKES 10 SPRING ROLLS

Spring Rolls

½ pound raw shrimp, peeled, deveined and coarsely chopped

½ cup minced scallions, white parts only

½ cup minced fresh chives

2 plump garlic cloves, minced

2 teaspoons peeled minced fresh ginger

1 dried chile pepper, crumbled

1 tablespoon cornstarch

2 tablespoons chicken stock

2 tablespoons rice wine

3 tablespoons soy sauce

2 teaspoons Oriental sesame oil

1½ cups packed finely shredded Chinese cabbage (Napa)

⅔ cup finely shredded carrots

6 scallions, trimmed to include 2 inches of green, julienned

5 tablespoons peanut oil

¼ cup minced fresh cilantro

10 spring roll wrappers

1 egg yolk, beaten

Dipping Sauce

1 teaspoon ground ginger

1 teaspoon dry mustard

1 tablespoon soy sauce

1 tablespoon rice wine

1 teaspoon fresh lemon juice

1 cup plum preserves

1 tablespoon minced scallion

2-4 cups peanut oil for frying

To make spring rolls: Combine shrimp, minced scallions and chives in a small bowl and set aside.

In another small bowl, combine garlic, ginger and chile pepper.

In a small dish, mix cornstarch with chicken stock and rice wine until well blended. Mix in soy sauce and sesame oil.

Combine cabbage, carrots and scallion in another bowl.

Heat 2 tablespoons peanut oil in a wok over high heat until hot. Quickly add shrimp mixture and toss just until shrimp turns pink, 1 to 2 minutes. Transfer mixture to a bowl.

Heat remaining 3 tablespoons peanut oil until hot. Add garlic mixture and stir-fry over medium-high heat for 15 seconds. Add cabbage mixture and stir-fry over high heat until cabbage wilts, about 1 minute. Whisk cornstarch mixture to blend and pour over cabbage; add cooked shrimp mixture. Stir-fry until sauce thickens, about 1 minute. Turn contents of the wok onto a large, cold platter and let stand for 30 minutes, or until cool. Stir in cilantro. (You can chill mixture for several hours at this point.)

Open wrappers and arrange on a large work surface with a point facing you. Place about 2 tablespoons filling in the lower third of each wrapper, leaving enough of the bottom point to fold over filling. Fold bottom up and tuck over and under filling; fold in each side. Dab some egg yolk in the middle of the remaining point, and roll up into a tight tube. The dab of egg should help the final point to seal the package. Repeat until all spring rolls are made. (You can chill spring rolls for several hours at this point.)

To make dipping sauce: In a nonaluminum small saucepan over medium heat, combine ginger, mustard, soy sauce, rice wine and lemon juice. Stir to blend; stir in plum preserves. Heat, stirring, until hot. Puree sauce in a food processor fitted with the metal blade; return sauce to the saucepan, and stir in scallion. Keep sauce warm.

To cook spring rolls: Preheat oven to warm (250 degrees F). Pour peanut oil into the wok or deep-fryer to a depth of 1½ inches and heat until hot enough to quickly brown a cube of bread tossed into it. Deep-fry 3 spring rolls at a time, without crowding, until they are properly crisp and golden brown, 1 to 2 minutes (a bit longer if they have been chilled). Drain spring rolls well on paper towels and keep warm in the oven while you fry remaining spring rolls. Quickly reheat dipping sauce, if necessary, and serve with spring rolls.

**Wine: Domaine Tempier Rosé
(France: Bandol)**

Chinese Barbecued Spareribs

WITH SCALLIONS & SHALLOTS

THE CHINESE COOKBOOK by Craig Claiborne and Virginia Lee (J.B. Lippincott Company) has been one of Linda's treasures since it was published in 1972, and it provided the inspiration for these crusty, delicious ribs. We've added a shredded vegetable salad of cabbage, carrots and onions in recent times. The salad's vinaigrette makes a splendid counterpoint to the sweetness of the ribs.

The total baking time for the ribs should be about 1 hour and 10 minutes. Because the sauce caramelizes on the pan and burns, we use disposable shallow foil pans.

SERVES 4 TO 6

Shredded Vegetable Salad

3	cups shredded Chinese cabbage (Napa)
1	cup coarsely grated carrots
1	large sweet onion, coarsely grated
1	tablespoon kosher salt
3-4	tablespoons sugar, depending on sweetness of onions
½	cup rice vinegar
2	tablespoons Oriental sesame oil

Spareribs

4	pounds pork spareribs, each rack cut in half crosswise
3	tablespoons sugar
2	teaspoons Chinese 5-spice powder
2	plump garlic cloves
1	teaspoon peeled minced fresh ginger
1	large shallot
⅓	cup soy sauce
¼	cup Chinese black bean sauce or paste
⅓	cup hoisin sauce
3	tablespoons Chinese sweet red bean sauce
3	tablespoons chicken stock
3	tablespoons fresh orange juice
2	tablespoons sesame paste
1	tablespoon fermented black beans
¼	teaspoon cayenne
3	plump scallions, minced
2	tablespoons rice wine
	About 1½ cups water
	About ½ cup peanut oil
⅓	cup finely minced scallions for garnish

To make shredded vegetable salad: Combine cabbage, carrots and onion in a large bowl and sprinkle with salt. Let stand for 15 minutes. Drain excess liquid thoroughly. Add sugar, vinegar and sesame oil and stir well. Let stand while you prepare the ribs.

To make spareribs: Place ribs on a large platter. Sprinkle with 2 tablespoons sugar and 1 teaspoon 5-spice powder; rub thoroughly and let stand 30 minutes.

Preheat oven to 450 degrees F. Fit a large baking or roasting pan with a rack.

In the bowl of a food processor fitted with the metal blade, combine remaining 1 tablespoon sugar, remaining 1 teaspoon 5-spice powder, garlic, ginger, shallot, soy sauce, black bean sauce or paste, hoisin sauce, red bean sauce, chicken stock, orange juice, sesame paste, black beans and cayenne. Pulse until smooth. Rub ½ of the sauce into spareribs; reserve remaining sauce.

Combine scallions and rice wine in a small bowl and set aside.

Pour enough water in the pan to generously cover the bottom without reaching the rack. Arrange ribs, meaty side up, close together on the rack. Roast for 20 minutes in the preheated oven.

Brush tops of ribs with some peanut oil and turn. Brush bone side with oil. Reduce heat to 350 degrees and bake for 15 minutes.

Baste tops of ribs with more oil, then with more sauce. Turn and repeat basting. Roast for another 15 minutes and turn. Quickly whisk reserved scallion mixture into remaining sauce. Baste ribs again with oil and sauce. Roast for another 20 minutes, turning ribs at least one more time, basting lightly with oil and sauce. (Total roasting time to this point is 1 hour 10 minutes.) Ribs should be very brown and tender. If not, roast for 10 minutes more.

Place racks on a carving board and cut racks into individual ribs. Pile ribs in the center of a platter, surround with shredded vegetable salad and sprinkle with minced scallion garnish.

**Wine: Georges Duboeuf Beaujolais Villages
(France: Burgundy)**

KING OF THE GREENS

NINETY-SIX MILLION green onions. A farmer who turns out that many onions from 100 acres in the course of a single season deserves a title. Bruce Buurma is Ohio's green-onion king. Altogether, Buurma Farms near Willard, Ohio, produces about 1.7 million packages of green vegetables annually, an array that includes celery, spinach, turnip greens, lettuces, and of course, all those green onions. The green-onion crop is a quickie. On March 15, they start planting White Spear, Emerald Isle and Tokyo Long White varieties. The harvest starts just three months later. Buurma Farms will send to market at least a quarter million boxes, or 12 million bunches, a total of 96 million scallions, an average of 2,500 boxes per acre. (And yes, Bruce Buurma says a green onion can be called a scallion.)

Buurma and his family partners own 700 acres of a great bog at Celeryville, Ohio. The first Buurmas, farmers from Holland, came to the region in 1896. Bruce is a fourth-generation member of the family.

As we travel the farm in his big pickup, Buurma, who runs the fields, points with pride at his equipment, all of it made right on the farm by uncles and cousins. But there is no machine that can harvest the green onions. Because they are so tender, every green onion must be picked and packaged by hand. Four hundred itinerant workers, mostly from Mexico, are necessary for this work. On an average midsummer day, as many as seven tons of green produce are taken to the packing shed every hour, where they are chilled in a hydrocooler, which takes the field heat out of them using some of the 65 tons of ice produced every day. Then the green onions are sized, graded and packed by hand.

The neat, organized farm offices are in a low brick building, full of computers, fax machines and telephones. In one office sits a television monitor linked to a weather-bureau service that shows the movements of weather systems. It provides the farmer with the same information that goes to TV meteorologists. By watching the satellite pictures of the fronts, Buurma can predict when he'll get rain and how much. Green onions need lots of water, and if the fields are dry and there is no rain in sight, he will draw irrigation water from a huge reservoir nearby. But if his monitor shows that rain is in the offing, Buurma can hold off expending his water resources.

"It's an enormous help," says the King of the Greens. "I watch it all the time. It's the best show on TV."

Fried Scallion-Shrimp Balls

THIS A VARIATION on the popular Cantonese appetizer, fried shrimp toasts. A smooth shrimp paste seasoned with ginger and scallions is rolled in bread crumbs and gently fried until golden. With their crisp exteriors and silky centers, these appetizers are easily prepared ahead and finished just before serving. They are simple to make since you can do everything but the frying ahead of time. They make fine hors d'oeuvres to precede any kind of meal.

MAKES ABOUT 20 BALLS

1	tablespoon cornstarch
1	tablespoon rice wine
¾	pound raw shrimp, peeled and deveined
2	ounces smoked ham, cut into pieces
3	scallions, trimmed to include 1 inch of green
1	teaspoon peeled minced fresh ginger
1	tablespoon packed fresh cilantro leaves
1	shallot
1	small garlic clove
2	teaspoons Oriental sesame oil
1	teaspoon soy sauce
1	tablespoon beaten egg white
2-3	cups peanut oil for frying

Chili-Scallion Dipping Sauce (see Pork & Scallion Pot Stickers, page 58)

Combine cornstarch and rice wine in a small bowl; stir well and set aside.

In the bowl of a food processor fitted with the metal blade, combine shrimp, ham, scallions, ginger, cilantro, shallot and garlic. Pulse until contents are minced; puree to a paste. Scrape mixture into a mixing bowl, blend in sesame oil, soy sauce, egg white and cornstarch mixture.

Keeping your hands wet, form shrimp mixture into balls about 1 inch in diameter; set aside on a large tray. Chill at least 30 minutes or up to 4 hours until ready to fry.

Pour oil into a wok or deep-fryer to a depth of 1½ inches and heat until hot enough to quickly brown a cube of bread tossed into it. Carefully fry shrimp balls, about 6 balls at a time, without crowding, turning often, until golden on all sides, about 2 minutes. If balls are darkening too fast, reduce heat slightly. Drain on paper towels and serve with dipping sauce.

Wine: Domaine Carneros Brut Sparkling Wine (California: Napa Valley)

Chicken Liver Pâté with Applejack, Scallions & Chives

LINDA HAS BEEN MAKING PÂTÉ this way for about 20 years. We always make more than we need so we'll have leftovers. Then we take slices of the Weller Family Bread (page 175), add some tasty greens, some thin slices of sweet onion and lots of pâté to make an unforgettable sandwich.

MAKES ABOUT 2 CUPS

½	cup (1 stick) unsalted butter
1¼	pounds chicken livers, membranes removed
1½	teaspoons freshly ground black pepper
¼	teaspoon ground cloves
¼	teaspoon freshly grated nutmeg
¼	cup applejack or Calvados
3	tablespoons chicken stock
5	scallions, trimmed to include ½ inch of green
2	teaspoons minced fresh tarragon leaves or 1 teaspoon dried
1	teaspoon fresh lemon juice
1	teaspoon anchovy paste
	Kosher salt
2	tablespoons minced fresh chives
3	tablespoons minced fresh parsley leaves
	Melba toast for serving

Melt butter in a large skillet over medium-high heat. Sauté chicken livers until just pink in middle, about 4 minutes. Add pepper, cloves and nutmeg; stir for 1 minute. Add applejack or Calvados. Quickly strike a long wooden match and, carefully averting your face, ignite liquid in the skillet. Shake the pan until the flames subside. Add chicken stock and simmer over low heat for 2 minutes.

Using a slotted spoon, transfer livers to the bowl of a food processor fitted with the metal blade. Add scallions, tarragon, lemon juice, anchovy paste and ½ of remaining liquid from the skillet. Pulse until pureed. Add salt and enough of remaining pan juices to make a creamy paste; mixture should not be too loose and usually will absorb all liquid. Pulse again.

Spoon pâté into an attractive crock. Cover and chill for at least 4 hours. To serve, allow pâté to stand at room temperature for 30 minutes. Combine chives with parsley and garnish pâté with a ring of mixed herbs. Serve with melba toast.

Wine: Iron Horse "Wedding Cuvée"
Blanc de Noirs Sparkling Wine
(California: Sonoma County, Green Valley)

Soft Cheese with Shallots

LEGEND HAS IT that this tangy soft-cheese-and-shallot spread was the favored midmorning snack of the silk workers of Lyon, France, slathered on slices of chewy fresh bread. Today, you'll still find this dish served in the old Lyon bistros, along with a hearty bread. We especially like to serve it in the summer when we have a group of friends over to eat on the terrace. We use the leftovers for *Flammekueche* (Thin Alsatian Tart, page 170).

MAKES ABOUT 4 CUPS

½ pound fresh chèvre (goat cheese)

½ pound whole-milk yogurt (available in health-food stores)

¼ cup minced shallots

2 tablespoons dry white wine

2 tablespoons white-wine vinegar

2 tablespoons extra-virgin olive oil

1 cup heavy cream, whipped into soft peaks

2 tablespoons minced chives, plus more for garnish

1 tablespoon minced fennel fronds

1½ teaspoons freshly ground black pepper

1 teaspoon kosher salt

Pumpernickel bread for serving

The night before serving, cream chèvre and yogurt together with a mixer, or blend thoroughly by hand with a wooden spoon. Scrape mixture into a large sieve lined with dampened cheesecloth placed over a deep bowl; refrigerate for the night. The next morning, let stand for 4 hours at room temperature. Discard drippings and turn cheese out into a mixing bowl.

Evenly blend shallots into cheese. Beat in wine, then vinegar and then olive oil. Gently mix in whipped cream, chives, fennel, pepper and salt. Taste and adjust seasonings as needed. Pack into a large crock, cover with plastic, and chill for at least 4 hours. Garnish with fresh chives and serve with thin slices of bread.

**Wine: Bollinger Brut Champagne
(France: Champagne)**

Pickled Lox & Onions

IN CASE YOU DON'T KNOW, lox is a salt-cured smoked salmon that is usually served in thin slices, preferably with bagels and cream cheese. A few New York City delis take lox and pickle it in a secret combination of onions, pickling spice, vinegar and lemons. When it attains just the right flavor, the liquid is removed and the pickled lox and onions are slathered with sour cream. Since pickled lox is unavailable in Cleveland, we decided to make our own. Besides being an enjoyable appetizer served on salad plates and eaten with a fork, this makes a good item for brunch when served with Kugel (Baked Noodles) with Chèvre, Scallions & Chives (page 200), some warm bagels and fresh ripe tomatoes.

SERVES 6

1   large white onion, thinly sliced

1   lemon, thinly sliced

1   cup cider vinegar

¾   cup water

¾   teaspoon kosher salt

1   bay leaf

1½   teaspoons mixed black and white peppercorns, bruised with the bottom of a heavy pan

9   allspice berries, bruised with the bottom of a heavy pan

2½   tablespoons sugar

1   tablespoon dill seeds

1½   teaspoons mustard seeds

1   pound lox, cut into 1-x-½-inch slices

1   cup sour cream
    Freshly ground black pepper

1   tablespoon minced fresh dill for garnish (optional)

Place onion and lemon slices in the bottom of a nonaluminum 2-quart bowl. Combine vinegar, water, salt, bay leaf, peppercorns, allspice, sugar, dill seeds and mustard seeds in a small nonaluminum saucepan. (If you prefer, you can tie peppercorns and allspice berries in a small cheesecloth bag.) Bring to a boil over high heat. Pour over onion mixture and let stand until cool. Remove lemons and add lox. Make certain that some onions are spooned over lox. Tightly cover bowl with plastic wrap and refrigerate for 4 to 6 days.

Use a slotted spoon to transfer fish and onions to a mixing bowl. (Remove bay leaf; some of the peppercorns and allspice will get into the mixture, but don't mind that.) Add sour cream and fold together. Stir in enough pickling liquid to make sour cream very creamy. (Add more sour cream if you like a lot of sauce.) Add more salt and freshly ground black pepper to taste. Cover and refrigerate 24 more hours before serving.

Serve on salad plates or in a shallow serving dish so guests can help themselves. If you like fresh dill, sprinkle it on before serving.

Wine: Cloudy Bay Sauvignon Blanc Marlborough (New Zealand)

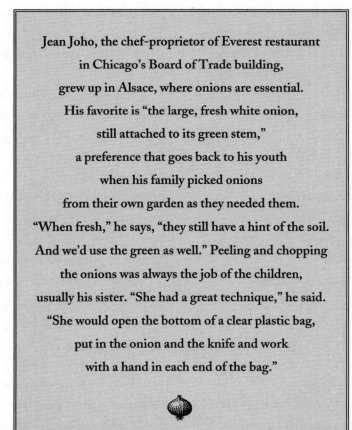

Jean Joho, the chef-proprietor of Everest restaurant
in Chicago's Board of Trade building,
grew up in Alsace, where onions are essential.
His favorite is "the large, fresh white onion,
still attached to its green stem,"
a preference that goes back to his youth
when his family picked onions
from their own garden as they needed them.
"When fresh," he says, "they still have a hint of the soil.
And we'd use the green as well." Peeling and chopping
the onions was always the job of the children,
usually his sister. "She had a great technique," he said.
"She would open the bottom of a clear plastic bag,
put in the onion and the knife and work
with a hand in each end of the bag."

Chive Crêpes with Smoked Salmon, Red Onions & Chèvre

THESE CRÊPES MAKE an elegant appetizer, but they also can be served as a main course for brunch. They are quite versatile, so feel free to use them with other fillings as well. Just select the herbs according to the kind of filling you are going to use. Whether you fill them on the browned side or not is up to you. Also, you can just roll them, or fill them and fold as a little package.

MAKES 20 6-INCH CRÊPES

Chive Crêpes

- ¾ cup unbleached flour
- ¼ cup whole-wheat pastry flour
- 1 tablespoon minced fresh chives
- ¼ teaspoon freshly ground white pepper
- ¼ teaspoon kosher salt
- 2 tablespoons unsalted butter, melted
- 2 large eggs
- 1 large egg yolk
- 1½ cups milk

Filling

- ¾ pound fresh chèvre (goat cheese) or 6 ounces chèvre and 6 ounces farmer cheese
- ½ cup low-fat sour cream
- 6 ounces smoked salmon, finely diced

- ⅔ cup finely diced red onion
- 1 tablespoon minced fresh dill or fennel fronds
- ½ teaspoon freshly ground black pepper

- 1 tablespoon unsalted butter for frying crêpes

Low-fat sour cream, salmon caviar (optional) and minced fresh dill for garnish

To make chive crêpes: Combine both flours, chives, white pepper and salt in the bowl of a food processor fitted with the metal blade. Add melted butter, eggs and egg yolk; pulse twice. With motor running, slowly add milk. Scrape down the sides of the bowl and blend for 5 seconds more.

Pour batter into a bowl, cover with plastic wrap and let stand in the refrigerator for several hours or overnight.

To make filling: Combine chèvre and sour cream in a mixing bowl. Blend with an electric mixer or by hand with a wooden spoon until mixture is light and fluffy, adding more sour cream if necessary. Add salmon, onion, dill or fennel and pepper. Mix on low, just until blended. Scrape into a small bowl and set aside.

To cook crêpes: Place butter in a nonstick or well-seasoned 6-inch crêpe pan and set over high heat. When hot, add several tablespoons of batter and quickly tilt the pan to coat the bottom. Reduce the heat to medium and cook until bottom is nicely browned, about 1 minute. (If you wish, you can lightly brown the other side at this point.) Turn out onto a tea towel; repeat until all batter is used. Add more butter to the pan only as necessary.

Shortly before serving, preheat oven to 300 degrees F. Arrange crêpes on a work surface, browned sides down or up, as you prefer. Spoon a generous tablespoon of filling into the center of each crêpe and fold in the sides. Place filled crêpes, seam sides down, on an ovenproof serving platter. Heat for 5 minutes.

Remove crêpes from the oven, garnish with dollops of sour cream and caviar, if using. Sprinkle with dill and serve.

Wine: Veuve Clicquot "Gold Label"
Vintage Champagne
(France: Champagne)

"Careful," admonished a retired pediatrician
on learning we were writing about onions.
"Make sure the nursing mothers don't eat too much
raw onion. The babies could get malodorous milk."
We don't know how he knows that, but we recall
summers in Clay County, West Virginia, when the
old Jersey cow would get out of the pasture and into the
woods and come back with an udder full of rich milk
pungently flavored by the wild mountain ramps.
Grandfather Burdick would rail at the bad fortune and
command the kids to go on fence patrol.
Modern dairy herds are so well managed that you will
never find allium-tainted milk in the market.
But if you ever taste it, you won't forget it.
It's a shock: onion milk.

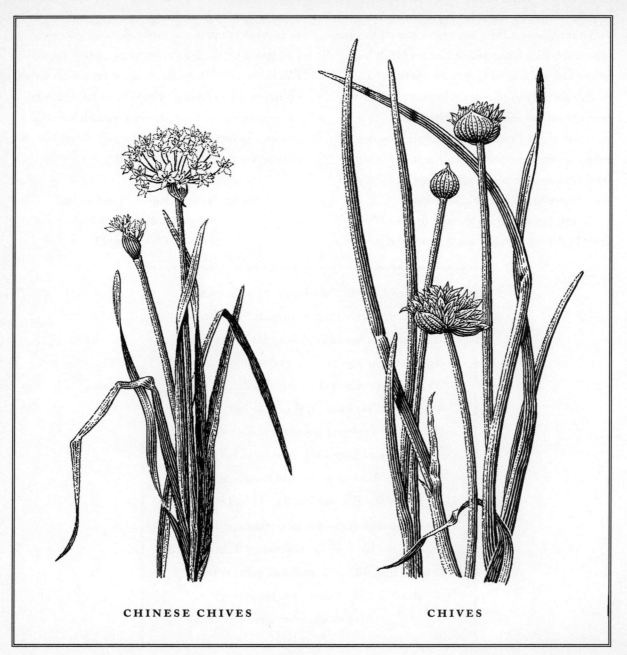

CHINESE CHIVES   CHIVES

Deep-Fried Chive Crêpes

WITH CHÈVRE, SCALLIONS & PROSCIUTTO

THIS MAY BE OUR FAVORITE. Each small, crisp golden package is filled with creamy chèvre, punctuated by the delicate flavor of scallion and salty prosciutto.

MAKES 20 TO 24 6-INCH CRÊPES

Filling

½ pound fresh chèvre (goat cheese)

⅓ cup heavy cream

3 ounces prosciutto, minced

4 scallions, trimmed to include 1 inch of green, minced

1 small garlic clove, minced
  Freshly ground white pepper

2 teaspoons minced fresh chives

Crêpes

20 chive crêpes (page 70), cooked but left unfilled

2 large egg whites, beaten with 2 teaspoons water

1 cup very fine dry bread crumbs

2-4 cups vegetable oil for frying
  Fresh edible flowers, herbs and/or watercress for garnish

To make filling: In a large mixing bowl, thoroughly combine chèvre, cream, prosciutto, scallions, garlic, pepper and chives. Set aside.

To make crêpes: Arrange crêpes, browned sides up, on a large work surface. Place a scant tablespoonful of filling in the center of each crêpe. Moisten outer edges with some egg white mixture. Fold in sides over filling. Then fold up bottom and fold down top to make a tight package about 2½ to 3 inches square. Place crêpes, seam sides down, on a large platter. Repeat until all packages are made.

Dip each package into egg white mixture, roll in bread crumbs and place on a cake rack to dry. (*Crêpes can be made ½ day ahead and kept, tightly wrapped in plastic, in the refrigerator. Bring to room temperature before frying.*)

Just before serving, pour oil into a wok or deep-fryer to a depth of 1½ to 2 inches. Heat until hot enough to quickly brown a cube of bread. Fry crêpe packages, a few at a time, turning until browned on all sides, about 3 minutes. Remove and drain well; keep warm. Serve with a garnish of flowers, herbs and watercress.

**Wine: Joseph Phelps Vineyards Sauvignon Blanc
(California: Napa Valley)**

OPERATION MAUI

MAUIS MAY BE THE MOST expensive onions in the world. They get very good press and there aren't very many of them. Although there are 8,500 acres of Vidalias and just over 1,000 acres of Walla Wallas, only 160 acres are devoted to Mauis. Nearly every one of these Hawaiian beauties is presold; many distributors have permanent orders in place, and other distributors are standing in line for what is left.

Finding Mauis isn't easy. We called Henry Koja, the general manager of the Maui Farmers' Cooperative Exchange, to ask how we could get some. "Try Chicago," he told us.

We didn't have to, as it turned out, because Jenny Crimm, a television news anchor in Cleveland, was planning a vacation to Maui and volunteered to bring some back.

Oddly, there really isn't an onion named Maui. Chinese farmers had grown ordinary onions on the Maui slopes early in the century, mainly for local consumption. In the 1930s, some of the farmers started growing the Yellow Bermuda, a sweeter and larger onion. Then, in a march of onion progress, the researchers at seed companies and agricultural colleges developed increasingly larger, hardier and sweeter varieties. The Maui onion farmers tried them out in their rich soils: the Excel, introduced in 1948; the Granex F_1, like the Excel, but bigger, in 1953; and the Granex 33 in the mid-1960s. The Granex remains the main Maui winter onion. Finally in 1984, growers brought in the Grano 1015Y, a famous Texas onion that quickly became the standard Maui summer onion.

WHAT MAKES THESE TWO FAMOUS VARIETIES, which are genetically identical to sweet onions grown in other parts of the country, different? What makes them Mauis? Henry Koja says it's a combination of rich soil, the island's weather and its latitude that make Maui's onions special. Two major environmental conditions determine how onions will grow: temperature and day-length. Maui is farther south than any other onion field in the U.S., so the days never get very long, and the temperatures are always moderate, ranging from the mid-50s to the high 80s. The young onions grow leaves until they receive the specific minimum day-length and appropriate temperature to start the bulbs grow ing. For the bulb to mature, there must be longer days and higher temperatures. But not too high: If the weather gets too warm, the bulbs won't have time to get large before the plant matures and the tops fall over. Both of the Maui cultivars respond happily to the unique environment of the little island.

B UT THERE IS A MORE ROMANTIC ANSWER to what makes a Maui, suggested by *The Maui Onion Book*: "Every onion is planted, weeded, cared for, worried over and harvested by loving hands. The Maui Onions are side-dressed with lots of hopes, best wishes and prayers all the way to maturity. They are fondled and caressed and carefully packed to be sent out into the world. No wonder Maui Onions are the sweetest. Even people react to that kind of treatment in the very same way."

Maui Salmon Mousse

THIS MOUSSE is so delicious when made with fresh salmon that we won't suggest using canned.

MAKES 4 CUPS; SERVES 10 TO 20

1¼ **pounds fresh salmon fillet, skinned**
½ **cup dry white wine**
1 **lemon, sliced**
1 **teaspoon vegetable oil**
1 **envelope unflavored gelatin**
3 **tablespoons fresh lemon juice**
¼ **cup boiling water**
⅔ **cup good-quality mayonnaise**
2 **tablespoons low-fat sour cream**
1 **medium Maui or other mild sweet onion, cut into pieces**
1 **tablespoon chopped fresh dill**
1 **tablespoon chopped fresh chives**
½ **teaspoon kosher salt**
¼ **teaspoon freshly ground white pepper**
1-2 **pinches cayenne**
1 **cup heavy cream**
  Tender lettuce, stuffed green olives, lemons and fresh herbs for garnish
  Thinly sliced pumpernickel bread for serving

One day ahead of serving, place salmon in a nonaluminum 2-quart saucepan. Add ¼ cup wine, sliced lemon and enough water to cover fish. Bring liquid to a boil over medium-high heat. Partially cover, reduce the heat to a gentle simmer and cook fish until barely done, about 5 minutes if fillet is thick. When you check the center, fish should still be rare in the middle. Remove from water with a skimmer or slotted spoon and set aside to cool.

Use oil to thoroughly coat a 4-cup fish mold; set aside. In a small bowl, combine gelatin and lemon juice. Add boiling water and stir until gelatin dissolves. Add remaining ¼ cup wine and set aside.

In the bowl of a food processor fitted with the metal blade, combine mayonnaise, sour cream, onion, dill, chives, salt, pepper, cayenne, salmon and gelatin mixture. Puree, scraping down the sides several times. With the motor running, slowly add heavy cream. Scrape sides and blend again for 15 seconds. Taste and adjust seasonings.

Pour mousse into the prepared mold, smooth top, cover with plastic wrap and chill overnight.

Just before serving, unmold on a bed of lettuces and decorate with olives, lemons and herbs. Garnish with fresh herbs and serve with bread.

Wine: Hidden Cellars "Alchemy"
(California: Mendocino)

Helofa Hot Sauce Chicken Wings

THE HEAT IN THIS RECIPE is far more subtle than that of traditional Buffalo Wings. It creeps up on you and hits you—wham—with the onions adding another layer of flavor altogether. Serve with ice-cold beer.

SERVES 4

1¼	teaspoons kosher salt
½	teaspoon freshly ground white pepper
½	teaspoon freshly ground black pepper
3	tablespoons minced fresh cilantro (optional)
24	whole chicken wings
6	tablespoons (¾ stick) butter
1	cup Helofa Hot Sauce (page 86)
2	teaspoons red-wine vinegar
2-4	cups vegetable oil for frying

In a small dish, blend together salt, white and black pepper and cilantro, if using; set aside.

Remove tips from chicken wings and discard or save for stock. Separate drumstick from wing and place all 48 pieces in a large, shallow baking dish.

Combine butter, ¼ cup hot sauce and vinegar in a small nonaluminum saucepan and heat, stirring well, over medium heat until butter melts. Pour ½ of mixture over uncooked wings and set ½ aside. Let wings marinate for 1 hour.

Pour oil into a wok or deep-fryer to a depth of 1½ to 2 inches. Heat until nearly smoking. When oil is hot enough to quickly brown a cube of bread, add a batch of wings and fry, without crowding, until golden brown on all sides, about 10 minutes.

Drain fried wings on paper towels. Keep wings warm while you finish frying the rest. At the same time, add remaining ¾ cup hot sauce to reserved butter mixture and quickly heat until hot.

Place fried wings in a large heated bowl. Toss with reserved salt mixture, add hot sauce mixture and toss well before serving.

Salsas, Spreads & Sauces

Any Season Salsa

THIS IS ONE SALSA you can enjoy even when there are no good fresh tomatoes. It's made with canned tomatoes, but you'd never guess it. A jolt of fresh lime juice and the bold, crisp flavors of white onions brighten the flavors. The soy sauce is the surprise ingredient of the originator of this dish, Cuca Ayala, the manager of the bottling line at R.H. Phillips Winery in California's Yolo Valley.

MAKES ABOUT 3 CUPS

1 28-ounce can crushed tomatoes
¾ cup finely diced white onion
1 plump garlic clove, minced
½ teaspoon freshly ground black pepper
2 teaspoons soy sauce

1 fresh jalapeño pepper, minced
2 teaspoons ground cumin
½ teaspoon dried oregano
2 tablespoons minced fresh cilantro
   Juice of 3 limes
   Kosher salt

Tortilla chips for serving

Combine all ingredients except tortilla chips and stir to mix well. Let stand for several hours, if possible. Serve with tortilla chips.

Wine: R.H. Phillips White Zinfandel
(California)

Very Fresh Salsa

YOU CAN MAKE THIS SALSA only when fresh-from-the-vine tomatoes are available Tomatoes are the stars here; the sweet onions play only a supporting role.

MAKES 1½ CUPS

1 very large vine-ripened yellow or orange tomato, finely diced

½ medium-sized sweet onion, such as Vidalia or Walla Walla, finely diced

1 pickled jalapeño pepper, minced

2 tablespoons minced fresh cilantro
Juice of 1 lime
Kosher salt and freshly ground black pepper

Tortilla chips for serving

Combine all ingredients except tortilla chips and stir gently until mixed well. Cover and refrigerate for 1 hour. Serve with tortilla chips.

Wine: Ponzi Vineyards Pinot Gris (Oregon)

Confit of Red Onions & Cherries

THIS SIMPLE AND DELICIOUS DISH is a perfect accompaniment to grilled poultry or veal. It keeps nicely in the refrigerator, but be sure to let it come to room temperature before serving. (To mail-order dried cherries, see Special Products, page 374.)

MAKES ABOUT 2 CUPS

2   large red onions
3   tablespoons olive oil
1   tablespoon minced fresh sage leaves
1   dried red chile pepper, crumbled
⅔   cup dried cherries
¼   cup dry red wine
2   teaspoons freshly ground black pepper
½   teaspoon kosher salt
1   tablespoon sugar
1   tablespoon balsamic vinegar
1   tablespoon butter

Thinly slice 1 onion; coarsely chop remaining onion. Combine sliced and chopped onions in a medium bowl and mix. Heat olive oil in a large non-stick skillet over medium heat. Stir in ½ of the onions, sage and chile. Cover and cook over low heat, stirring several times, for 6 minutes.

Stir in onions, cherries, wine, pepper and salt. Cover and cook until the onions are just tender, about 6 minutes more.

Uncover the skillet, sprinkle on sugar and cook over medium heat until syrupy, just a few minutes. Sprinkle on balsamic vinegar and add butter. Increase the heat and sauté until onions are nicely coated, 4 to 5 minutes.

Spoon confit into a clean glass jar and set aside to cool. Cover tightly and refrigerate. Confit will keep for at least 1 month.

Susan's Red Onion, Orange & Kiwi Marmalade

WITH GINGER

THIS MARMALADE of sweet orange and kiwi has nips of onion and ginger. If you've never used scented geraniums, this recipe is a good place to start. A few grindings of nutmeg will substitute.

MAKES 3 EIGHT-OUNCE JARS

6 oranges

1 lime

1 cup water

6 kiwis, peeled and diced

1 cup coarsely chopped red onion

2 cups sugar

1 tablespoon minced crystallized ginger

6 nutmeg geranium leaves plus 6 lime geranium leaves or substitute ¼ teaspoon freshly grated nutmeg and zest of 1 lime, julienned

Peel oranges and lime, reserving peel from 3 oranges and lime. Dice orange flesh into bite-sized pieces (discard membrane) and set aside in a large nonaluminum saucepan. Squeeze lime (you should have 2 tablespoons juice) and add juice to the saucepan.

In a small saucepan, combine reserved fruit peels with water. Bring to a boil over high heat. Reduce the heat to medium-low and boil for 30 minutes. Drain; cut softened peels into slivers. Add to fruit mixture in the large saucepan.

Add kiwis, onion, sugar and crystallized ginger to the saucepan. Tie geranium leaves in a cheesecloth pouch and add to the saucepan, or add nutmeg and lime zest.

Bring mixture to a boil over medium heat. Boil slowly, stirring often, until marmalade is thick and clear, 45 to 60 minutes. Remove and discard cheesecloth pouch.

Ladle marmalade into hot, sterilized jars, wipe rims, seal and process for 10 minutes in a boiling-water bath.

Remove the jars from the water bath and set aside to cool. Check the lids to make certain they are tightly sealed. Store upright in a cool, dark place; refrigerate after opening.

Onion Marmalade with Carrots & Dill

NOT TOO SWEET, this carrot and onion marmalade gets a citrus boost from lemons and oranges. It is delicious spooned on corn muffins or spread over thick slices of bread. We also like to serve it as a garnish for Maui Corn Cakes (page 370), and it makes a splendid accompaniment to a grilled chicken breast. This recipe comes from Susan Cavitch.

MAKES 4 EIGHT-OUNCE JARS

2   pounds carrots, peeled and grated

½   cup packed combined fresh lemon verbena leaves, lemon thyme leaves and dill or fresh thyme, dill and zest of 1 lemon, julienned

4   cups sugar

1   pound (1 jumbo) Vidalia onion, coarsely chopped

    Juice of 2 lemons

    Juice of 2 oranges

2   tablespoons minced crystallized ginger

In a large nonaluminum saucepan, combine carrots with just enough water to barely cover, and bring to a boil. Reduce the heat to low and simmer for 20 minutes. Drain and return carrots to the saucepan.

Tie herbs in a cheesecloth pouch and add to carrots. Add sugar, onion, citrus juices and crystallized ginger. Bring mixture to a boil over medium heat. Continue to boil slowly, stirring occasionally, until marmalade is thick and clear, about 40 minutes. Remove and discard cheesecloth pouch.

Ladle marmalade into hot, sterilized jars, wipe rims, seal and process for 10 minutes in a boiling-water bath.

Remove the jars from the water bath and set aside to cool. Check the lids to make certain they are tightly sealed. Store upright in a cool, dark place; refrigerate after opening.

Fresh Tomato-Onion Sauce

THIS SIMPLE TOMATO SAUCE is wonderful tossed with any cooked pasta. It is also good if you add some capers and a touch of vinegar and serve it with grilled fish or chicken.

MAKES 4 CUPS

3   tablespoons olive oil
1   cup finely diced yellow onions
2   plump garlic cloves, minced
4   pounds ripe tomatoes, peeled and chopped
    Juice of ½ lemon
2   tablespoons minced fresh flat-leaf parsley

1   teaspoon sugar
    Salt and freshly ground black pepper
1-2   tablespoons minced fresh basil

Heat olive oil in a heavy-bottomed nonaluminum saucepan over low heat. Add onions and cook until translucent. Add garlic and sauté, stirring often, until golden. Add tomatoes, lemon juice, 1 tablespoon parsley and sugar. Increase heat and bring sauce to a lively simmer. Cook for 15 minutes. Add salt and pepper to taste, remaining 1 tablespoon parsley and fresh basil. Serve hot.

Bourbon-Onion Chili Sauce

WHISKEY ADDS A KICK to this thick, spicy, tangy chili sauce. We serve it with meat loaf, hash, grilled pork and burgers. It holds well in the refrigerator, and your friends will love to receive it as a gift. Zack Bruell liked this sauce so much that he asked Linda to adapt it for his Cleveland-area restaurant, Z Contemporary Cuisine, where it appears on the menu as Linda Griffith's Relish. Try making it with lemon grass, lemon thyme and Thai basil.

MAKES ABOUT 8 CUPS

3 tablespoons olive oil
½ cup finely diced white onion
¼ cup finely diced shallots
¼ cup finely diced celery
1 garlic clove, minced
1 28-ounce can plum tomatoes, coarsely chopped
Juice and minced zest of 1 lemon
⅓ cup packed dark brown sugar, packed
1 teaspoon Tabasco sauce
⅓ cup mixed fresh herbs (parsley, basil, thyme, chives)
1 teaspoon kosher salt
Freshly ground black pepper
½ cup bourbon or Jack Daniels Tennessee whiskey

Heat olive oil in a heavy-bottomed nonaluminum sauté pan. Add onion, shallots, celery and garlic. Cover with a tight-fitting lid, reduce heat to very low and sweat until tender, about 5 minutes.

Stir in tomatoes, lemon juice, sugar, Tabasco, herbs and salt and pepper to taste. Increase heat to medium and bring sauce to a rapid simmer. Cook, bubbling slowly, stirring often, for 30 minutes.

Stir in whiskey and lemon zest and simmer for 10 minutes. Remove from heat and let cool to room temperature.

Chill sauce for at least 24 hours. Be sure to serve the sauce at room temperature.

Helofa Hot Sauce

EMERIL LAGASSE is one of the shining lights on the American food scene. This sauce is inspired by the recipe for piri piri in his book *Emeril's New New Orleans Cooking* (William Morrow, 1993). It's fantastic with chicken wings (see Helofa Hot Sauce Chicken Wings, page 77), and it's also good as a marinade for large shrimp that can then be skewered and grilled over hot coals, or use it as a sauce for grilled chicken breasts. Canned chipotles can be found wherever Mexican products are sold. We love their toasty, smoky flavor.

MAKES 2 CUPS

1   cup olive oil

1   large white onion, finely diced

4   red serrano or cayenne chiles, chopped (not seeded)

2   canned chipotle chiles, along with any adobo sauce that clings to them

1-2   plump garlic cloves, minced

2   tablespoons red-wine vinegar

In a medium nonaluminum saucepan over high heat, combine oil, onion, fresh chiles, chipotles and garlic. Bring mixture just to a boil; remove from the heat and set aside to cool to room temperature.

Combine chile mixture and vinegar in the bowl of a food processor fitted with the metal blade. Puree until smooth.

Pour sauce into a sterilized jar and cover tightly. Let flavors marry at room temperature for several days before using. This sauce will keep, refrigerated, for several weeks.

Onion-Pineapple Barbecue Sauce

WE LIKE THE COMBINATION of onions and pineapple in dishes and find it especially good in barbecue sauce. This thick, spicy sauce is splendid slathered on pork, chicken and brisket. If you are grilling, don't brush on the sauce until the meat is almost cooked, or it will burn. You can mince these onions in a food processor, since a release of liquid is helpful here.

MAKES 8 TO 10 CUPS

2   tablespoons vegetable oil
4   cups minced yellow onion
1   cup crushed pineapple
4   plump garlic cloves, minced
2   cups bottled chili sauce
1½ cups canned tomato sauce
⅓   cup ketchup
¾   cup pineapple juice
½   cup cider vinegar
¾   cup dark brown sugar, packed

¼   cup dark unsulfured molasses
⅔   cup bourbon
2   tablespoons dry mustard
2   tablespoons medium-hot chile powder or other chili powder
1   tablespoon ground cumin
2   teaspoons freshly ground white pepper
¼   cup Worcestershire sauce
1   bay leaf

Heat oil in a heavy 3-quart nonaluminum saucepan until hot. Add onions, pineapple and garlic and cook over medium heat, stirring often, until onions are soft but not browned, 10 to 15 minutes.

Add all remaining ingredients and stir well. Let mixture heat through slowly. Simmer over very low heat for 1 hour. Remove bay leaf. Taste and add more brown sugar, if needed. You may also wish to add more cayenne. This sauce freezes well.

Soups

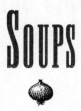

French Onion Soup au Gratin

LINDA'S FIRST TRIP TO PARIS was in winter, years before French onion soup became a cliché on North American restaurant menus. This tried-and-true recipe evolved from that trip.

SERVES 4 TO 6

¼ cup (½ stick) unsalted butter

2 pounds Spanish onions (about 2 large), finely diced

1 teaspoon sugar

10 cups (2½ quarts) beef stock

¼ cup unbleached flour

¼ cup port wine or dry sherry

3 branches fresh thyme or ½ teaspoon dried
Kosher salt and freshly ground black pepper

4-8 thick slices French bread

1 garlic clove, halved

¼ cup olive oil

1 cup grated Gruyère cheese

1 cup grated Emmenthaler cheese

In a large, heavy-bottomed soup pot, melt butter over medium-high heat. Add onions and sugar and sauté, stirring often, for 10 minutes.

Meanwhile, pour stock into a saucepan and heat until hot.

Increase the heat under onions to high and stir until quite golden, about 5 minutes. Reduce heat to medium, sprinkle with flour, and cook, stirring, for 3 minutes, to cook flour. Add port or sherry and stir briskly. Gradually add hot stock, stirring constantly. Increase the heat to medium-high and stir often until soup bubbles. Add thyme and salt and pepper to taste. Reduce heat to low, cover the pot and simmer very gently for 30 minutes. Taste and adjust seasonings; discard thyme branches, if using.

Just before serving, preheat the broiler. Heat soup until hot. Prepare croutons by rubbing bread slices with garlic halves. Using a pastry brush, paint both sides of each slice of bread with olive oil. Toast under the broiler until browned on both sides. Combine cheeses.

Place one or two croutons in each ovenproof soup bowl. Sprinkle 1 tablespoon of the cheese mixture over the top of each crouton. Ladle soup over the prepared croutons and distribute remaining cheese over tops. (The thicker the better.) Place bowls under the broiler and heat until cheese is bubbling and browned. Serve at once.

Wine: Elyse Vineyards "Nero Misto"
(California: Napa Valley)

Hearty Onion, Mushroom & Beef Soup

WITH GOUDA CROUTONS

THIS SOUP IS A beefy combination of mushrooms and onions. It's a full-flavored dish, with small chunks of beef short ribs and Gouda-and-thyme croutons. A meal in itself, this soup is especially good for a crowd after a winter afternoon of cross-country skiing.

SERVES 10 TO 12

Soup

½   pound fresh shiitake mushrooms (or a mixture of shiitakes and creminis), stems reserved, caps sliced

16   cups (4 quarts) beef stock

6   tablespoons (¾ stick) butter

2½   pounds Spanish onions (about 3 large), thinly sliced

1   plump garlic clove, minced

1   ounce dried cèpes, soaked in 1 cup boiling water for 20 minutes

6   ounces cremini mushrooms or button mushrooms, thinly sliced

1   pound boneless flanken (beef short ribs cut from the plate) or other boneless short ribs, finely diced

2   teaspoons soy sauce

3   tablespoons all-purpose flour

½   cup red wine

1   bay leaf

1   teaspoon dried thyme

   Kosher salt and freshly ground black pepper

Croutons

10-12   thick slices French bread

1   garlic clove, halved

¼   cup olive oil

1½   teaspoons dried thyme

1   cup grated Gouda cheese

   Minced fresh chives for garnish

To make soup: In a large saucepan, combine shiitake stems with stock and bring to a boil. Reduce heat to medium and simmer gently for 15 minutes. Remove stems with a slotted spoon.

Meanwhile, in a large, heavy-bottomed soup pot, melt 4 tablespoons butter over medium heat. Add onions and garlic, cover with a tight-fitting lid and cook over very low heat until onions are very limp, about 10 minutes. Remove onions and garlic from pot with a slotted spoon and set aside.

While onions are cooking, remove cèpes from soaking liquid and coarsely chop. Strain soaking liquid through a coffee filter into the beef stock. Combine soaked mushrooms with shiitakes and cremini mushrooms and set aside.

Add remaining 2 tablespoons butter to the soup pot and melt over medium heat. Add flanken and stir over medium heat until lightly browned. Add mushrooms and soy sauce, reduce heat to low and stir briefly. Tightly cover the pot, and cook for 5 minutes. Remove the lid, stir, and cover mixture with wilted onions. Simmer until you see juices bubbling around the edges, about 5 minutes.

Increase the heat to medium, sprinkle mixture with flour and cook, stirring briskly, to cook flour, about 2 minutes. Stir in stock, wine, bay leaf, thyme, salt and pepper and slowly bring to a boil. Reduce the heat to low and cook, barely simmering, for at least 1 hour. Remove bay leaf.

To make croutons: Preheat the broiler. Rub bread slices with garlic halves. Using a pastry brush, paint both sides of each slice of bread with olive oil. Toast under the broiler until browned on one side only. Combine thyme and cheese. Divide mixture among croutons, sprinkling over untoasted sides. Just before serving time, broil croutons until cheese begins to melt.

Ladle soup into warmed soup plates; be sure to include some meat, onions and mushrooms in each serving. Float a crouton on top. Sprinkle with chives.

**Wine: Vieux Télégraphe Châteauneuf-du-Pape
(France: Rhône)**

Looking for Leeks

WE HAD GONE TO LOOK FOR LEEKS at the Best of the Midwest Farmers' Market. On this fall day, the farmers had set up their stands under tents that circled the great grassy mall in Ravinia, a suburb of Chicago, Illinois.

Under the sign of Kingsfield Gardens, we saw a man wrestling some huge leeks into a bag for a buyer. It was Richard Abernethy, who, with his wife, Erika Koenigsaecker, have put the tiny town of Blue Mounds, Wisconsin, on the gastronomic map. Abernethy and Koenigsaecker bought their farm in 1989, and in five short years, they have seized the attention of everyone in the region who is looking for high-quality produce. Abernethy came to the enterprise out of a background of designing jewelry, working as a cabinetmaker, mastering the art of crafting and playing ancient musical instruments, and for a year, residing in the wilderness with no address. Koenigsaecker grew up on a farm and never lost her love for it. "If life is going to amount to anything," says Abernethy, "you have to learn, and on the farm, we do."

What struck us first was the length of their leeks. The white part didn't start to yield to the chlorophyll for 10 inches.

"We never saw a leek like that," we admitted.

"That's right, and you won't," he answered. "These are special. And they don't have dirt, either."

Traditionally, leek seeds are planted indoors in January, under the lights. In mid-March, they are hand-transplanted into a 12-inch-deep trench filled with 3 inches of compost. After a month, a little soil is added to the trench, and about every six weeks, a bit more is added to cover the growing shaft and keep it from turning green. If you are careful and lucky, you may get five inches of white. And no matter how careful you are, there will be dirt between the leaves, meaning you will have to split the leek and wash it before you can cook it.

Some growers keep the tops of their leeks cropped, not allowing the green spears to soar too high, so that the plant concentrates its growing power into the stalk rather than into the leaves. Leeks can be harvested early, when they are young, tender and slender, and used like a green onion. As they mature,

(continued on page 94)

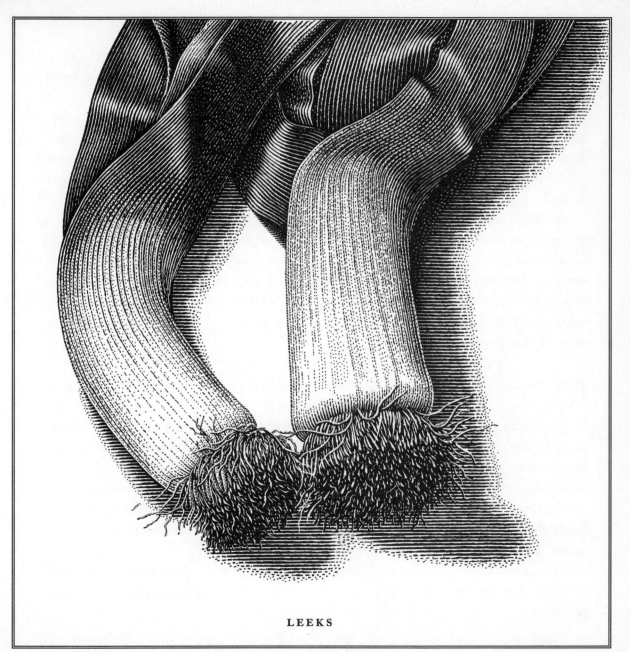

LEEKS

(continued from page 92)

they can be harvested as needed. Leeks are impervious to cold, and some growers leave them in the ground over the winter, to be harvested on a day when the ground thaws. Those that aren't picked and popped into a soup will seed in their second year of life.

Kingsfield Gardens grows eight varieties of leeks. "We've tried over 100," says Abernethy. "If they don't have the taste and aren't consistent, whether it's hot or cool, wet or dry, then they're out." Abernethy and Koenigsaecker have, from time to time, developed their own cultivars; they use the technique of hand-pollinating one variety with the pollen of another. When they get a really good one, they save the seeds.

Mainly they grow the King Richard ("Not much flavor," says Abernethy, "but clean"), Varna, French Winter, Dutch Winter, Otina and Blue Solaize, which has a "short shaft, but good flavor." They cut a lot of them early for baby leeks. Why their plants grow so long and clean turns out to be a secret, not something Abernethy wants his competitors to know. We imagine, though, that the flawless condition of the leeks has a lot to do with the way these two farmers fill the trenches and the care they take in mounding the soil high around the sides of the leeks, never allowing any to fall into the gap between the growing leaves. These are labor-intensive leeks for sure.

L IKE SHALLOTS, leeks have been slow to grab the attention of the American consumer, while in Western Europe and especially in the British Isles, they have a long and honorable history. Nero reportedly ate leek soup daily to keep his voice in shape for oratory. Shakespeare, in *Henry V*, took good note of the Welsh national passion for the leek: ". . . the Welshmen did good service in a garden where leeks did grow, wearing leeks in their . . . caps, which your majesty know to this hour is an honorable badge of the service." Ancient Pistol makes sport of the Welshman Fluellen in another scene, ordering him out of the room. "I am qualmish," he tells him, "at the smell of leeks." Even today the Welsh celebrate the leek on St. David's Day, wearing leeks in their hats, something that helped them differentiate themselves from their Saxon foes on the battlefield.

At Kingsfield Gardens, Abernethy and Koenigsaecker know the lore. What keeps them constantly working is their conviction that the leek is the noblest, tastiest, most versatile and most complex of all the alliums.

Sweet Potato & Leek Soup

WITH CRISP-FRIED SCALLIONS

WE OFTEN MAKE THIS SOUP with stock from a smoked turkey—something we prepare at least once during the year. Sometimes we'll use butternut or Hubbard squash instead of the sweet potatoes. Thick and smooth, with a crunchy garnish, this is a beautiful shade of orange.

SERVES 8 TO 10

2½ pounds sweet potatoes or yams
¼ cup (½ stick) butter
2½ cups thinly sliced leeks, white parts only
6 cups smoked turkey stock or plain chicken stock
1 cup crème fraîche (page 98) or ⅔ cup heavy cream mixed with ⅓ cup sour cream
    Salt and freshly ground white pepper
1 cup vegetable oil for frying
8 scallions, trimmed and julienned

Preheat oven to 425 degrees F. Prick sweet potatoes or yams several times and bake on a rack until very tender, about 1 hour. Remove from the oven and set aside.

Melt butter in a large nonstick skillet over medium heat. Add leeks and toss to coat. Add 1 cup stock, cover with a tight-fitting lid and cook over very low heat until leeks are very tender, about 30 minutes.

Pour mixture into the bowl of a food processor fitted with the metal blade and pulse until well pureed. Scoop sweet potato pulp out of skins and add pulp to the food processor; pulse until smooth.

In a heavy saucepan, combine puree with remaining 5 cups stock and whisk until smooth. Cook over medium heat until heated through. Add crème fraîche or heavy cream mixture, blend well and continue to simmer until heated through. Add salt and white pepper to taste. *(If you wish to serve this soup cold, chill at this point.)*

Just before serving, heat oil in a wok until it shimmers. Add julienned scallions and deep-fry until browned, about 2 to 3 minutes. Remove scallions from oil with a slotted spoon and drain on paper towels.

Divide soup among the bowls and garnish with fried scallions.

**Wine: Bonny Doon Vineyard "Clos du Gilroy"
Grenache (California) or
Joseph Phelps Vineyards Vin du Mistral
Grenache Rosé (California)**

Ali's Caramelized Onion & Leek Soup

WITH ROQUEFORT CROUTONS

ALI AND MARCY BARKER opened their beautiful restaurant, Piperade, in the spring of 1992 and Clevelanders have been raving about it ever since. This thick, rich soup appeared on their very first menu, and it continues to be one of our favorites. Because the soup is so thick, care must be taken if it is made early in the day and reheated. Add about ½ cup more chicken stock and simmering the soup, covered, over very low heat.

SERVES 6 TO 8

Soup

6-8 tablespoons (¾-1 stick) unsalted butter

2 plump leeks with tender greens, cleaned and thinly sliced

4 large Spanish onions (about 4 pounds), thinly sliced

¼ cup plus 3 tablespoons unbleached flour

1 teaspoon kosher salt

¼ teaspoon freshly ground black pepper

8 cups (2 quarts) chicken stock plus ½ cup more if needed

1 cup port wine or dry sherry

Croutons

4½ ounces Roquefort cheese, at room temperature

4½ ounces cream cheese, at room temperature

1 teaspoon Worcestershire sauce

6 drops Tabasco sauce

½ of a long French baguette, cut into 18-24 ½-inch-thick slices

To make soup: In a 3-to-4-quart heavy-bottomed saucepan, melt 4 tablespoons of butter over medium heat. Add leeks and onions and sauté, stirring often, adding butter as needed, until onions are golden brown, 20 to 30 minutes.

Add flour and stir for several minutes, so that flour and onions are evenly blended. Season with salt and pepper. Slowly stir in chicken stock. Reduce heat to very low and simmer, stirring often, for 1 hour.

Partially cover the pot and simmer for 1 hour more. Stir in port or sherry and cook, stirring often, for 30 minutes more. (This is a very thick soup that will stick to the pan if you are not careful.) It will cook down to about 6 cups.

To make croutons: While soup is cooking, combine cheeses in a bowl and mash together thoroughly with a fork. Blend in Worcestershire and Tabasco and reserve.

About 30 minutes before serving, preheat oven to 350 degrees F. Bake baguette slices until crisp on both sides, 15 to 20 minutes. Spread each crouton with a scant teaspoon of cheese mixture.

Ladle soup into heated soup plates. Arrange 3 to 4 croutons in each bowl and serve.

Wine: Benton Lane Pinot Noir (Oregon: Willamette Valley)

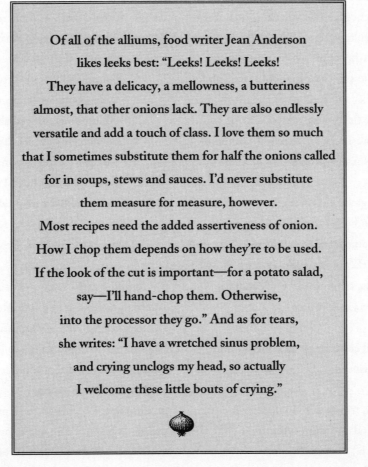

Of all of the alliums, food writer Jean Anderson
likes leeks best: "Leeks! Leeks! Leeks!
They have a delicacy, a mellowness, a butteriness
almost, that other onions lack. They are also endlessly
versatile and add a touch of class. I love them so much
that I sometimes substitute them for half the onions called
for in soups, stews and sauces. I'd never substitute
them measure for measure, however.
Most recipes need the added assertiveness of onion.
How I chop them depends on how they're to be used.
If the look of the cut is important—for a potato salad,
say—I'll hand-chop them. Otherwise,
into the processor they go." And as for tears,
she writes: "I have a wretched sinus problem,
and crying unclogs my head, so actually
I welcome these little bouts of crying."

Wonderful Wild Mushroom Soup

WITH LEEKS & SHALLOTS

THIS SILKY, RICH DISH is inspired by the extraordinary soup at Joe's Restaurant in Reading, Pennsylvania. Owner/chef Jack Czarnecki is one of the great students of mycology; his book *Joe's Book of Mushroom Cookery* (Atheneum, 1986) is a treasure trove of information and recipes for cooks of all abilities. We've added leeks and shallots to the mushrooms to increase the flavor and complexity. (If you can't get fresh wild mushrooms, double the amount of the dried wild mushrooms and the fresh cremini mushrooms instead.)

To make crème fraîche: Combine 1 cup heavy cream with 3 tablespoons buttermilk and let stand, uncovered, at room temperature for 12 hours, or until mixture begins to thicken and develop a tang. It will keep for several weeks, covered and refrigerated.

SERVES 8 TO 10

3 ounces dried cèpes or porcini mushrooms, thoroughly rinsed

5 cups water

2 plump leeks, trimmed to include ½ inch of green, cleaned and thinly sliced

8 cups (2 quarts) beef stock

7 tablespoons unsalted butter, cut into tablespoons

½ pound fresh wild or cultivated exotic mushrooms (shiitakes, portobellos or chanterelles), sliced

¼ pound cremini mushrooms, sliced

1 tablespoon soy sauce

2 tablespoons minced shallots

3 tablespoons unbleached flour
Salt and freshly ground black pepper

½ cup crème fraîche or ½ cup low-fat sour cream mixed with 3 tablespoons heavy cream

¼ cup minced fresh chives for garnish

Combine dried mushrooms and water in a saucepan and bring to a boil. Reduce the heat to low and simmer for 20 minutes. Add leeks and cook for 10 minutes. Meanwhile, place beef stock in a heavy soup pot and bring to a simmer over low heat.

Using a slotted spoon, place cooked mushroom mixture in the bowl of a food processor fitted with the metal blade. Pulse until finely chopped. Strain mushroom-cooking liquid through a coffee filter or a cheesecloth-lined sieve to remove any grit. Add some of the liquid to the processor and pulse until mixture is pureed. Whisk puree and remaining mushroom liquid into the simmering stock. Continue to simmer over very low heat.

Melt 4 tablespoons of butter in a large sauté pan over medium heat. Add wild mushrooms, cremini mushrooms and soy sauce, cover and cook for 10 minutes. Add shallots, stir and cook, uncovered, until mushrooms are tender, 5 to 10 minutes. Puree mixture in the bowl of a food processor fitted with the metal blade. Add this puree to the simmering stock mixture.

Combine flour and remaining 3 tablespoons butter in a small bowl; mix with a fork to a paste. Gradually whisk paste into simmering stock mixture and simmer for at least 30 minutes. From time to time, skim off any scum that collects on the surface, and whisk soup thoroughly to blend. Season with salt and pepper to taste.

To serve, ladle soup into bowls. Spoon some crème fraîche or sour cream mixture into the center and swirl it with a knife to make an attractive surface pattern. Garnish with minced chives.

Wine: E. Guigal Côtes du Rhône
(France: Rhône)

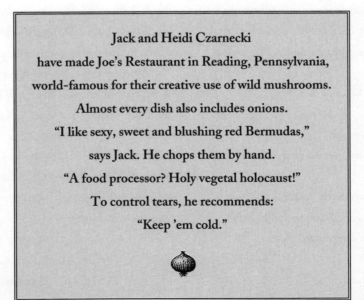

Jack and Heidi Czarnecki
have made Joe's Restaurant in Reading, Pennsylvania,
world-famous for their creative use of wild mushrooms.
Almost every dish also includes onions.
"I like sexy, sweet and blushing red Bermudas,"
says Jack. He chops them by hand.
"A food processor? Holy vegetal holocaust!"
To control tears, he recommends:
"Keep 'em cold."

Tapawingo's Wild Leek & Potato Chowder

WITH SMOKED WHITEFISH

THE WOODS OF NORTHERN MICHIGAN that shelter the wonderful morel also happen to produce the tender and flavorful ramp, or wild leek. Harlan "Pete" Peterson's May menu at Tapawingo, his Ellsworth, Michigan, restaurant, always features ramps in a dish or two during their brief, but wonderful, season. A variation of a traditional creamy leek and potato soup, this dish is one of our favorites because of the addition of delicate smoke-flavored fish. And although there is no simple substitute for ramps (it pays to make friends with some foragers), you can always use a combination of scallions and shallots instead.

SERVES 8

4½	cups chicken stock
1	pound potatoes, peeled and cut into 1-inch cubes
1½	tablespoons unsalted butter
½	cup finely chopped, cleaned wild leeks (ramps), including green parts
1	cup milk
1	cup heavy cream

	Cayenne
	Salt and freshly ground black pepper
10-12	ounces smoked whitefish or smoked trout, picked over, if necessary, and cut into pieces

In a large, heavy saucepan, bring chicken stock to a boil. Add potatoes, reduce heat to low, and simmer until potatoes are tender, 20 to 30 minutes. Meanwhile, in a small nonstick skillet, melt butter over low heat. Add wild leeks, cover with a tight-fitting lid and sweat until translucent, about 5 minutes. Add leeks to simmering potatoes.

When potatoes are tender, puree soup in a food processor fitted with the metal blade; be careful not to overprocess or potatoes will become pasty. Force puree through a medium sieve back into the saucepan. Add milk, cream and seasonings to taste. Heat until hot. If too thick, thin with more milk.

Divide fish among heated soup plates. Ladle soup over fish and serve.

Wine: MacRostie Chardonnay
(California: Sonoma, Carneros)

Three Onion & Salmon Chowder

THIS IS A LIGHTER VERSION of a traditional potato and leek soup; salmon adds a pleasing touch. While there's nothing quite as fragrant and sweet as a baby Vidalia, you can still make a good chowder with some fresh, plump green onions. By the way, when you want to serve this as a meal in itself, double the amount of salmon.

SERVES 6 TO 8

3   tablespoons unsalted butter

4   plump baby Vidalias, tough green tops discarded, chopped, or 12 scallions, trimmed and chopped

1   cup coarsely chopped white onions

½   cup finely diced shallots

1   garlic clove, minced

1   teaspoon fresh thyme leaves or ½ teaspoon dried

7   cups chicken stock

⅔   cup dry white wine

1¼ pounds Yukon Gold or red-skinned potatoes, peeled and cut into medium dice

1   cup heavy cream
    Kosher salt and freshly ground white pepper

1   pound salmon fillets, skin removed, cut into 1-inch cubes

1   tablespoon minced fresh chives

1   tablespoon minced fresh parsley

In a nonaluminum heavy-bottomed soup pot, melt butter over low heat. Add Vidalia onions or scallions, white onions, shallots, garlic and thyme. Cover the pot with a tight-fitting lid and cook over very low heat until onions are tender, about 20 minutes.

Add chicken stock and wine and cook over medium heat until mixture just comes to a boil. Add potatoes and continue to cook, stirring frequently, until soup returns to a boil. Reduce heat to a slow simmer. Add cream and salt and white pepper to taste; partially cover and simmer for 20 minutes.

Add salmon and simmer for 5 minutes. Adjust seasonings and ladle into heated bowls. Sprinkle with chives and parsley.

Wine: Honig Cellars Sauvignon Blanc
(California: Napa Valley)

Zack Bruell's Oyster & Shallot Bisque

OUR GOOD FRIEND Zachary Bruell, owner/chef of Z Contemporary Cuisine in Cleveland, is a master at creating delicious, silky bisques. This is one of his best.

SERVES 4

2 dozen oysters, scrubbed, or 1 pint shucked
2 tablespoons unsalted butter
4 shallots, finely diced
1 plump garlic clove, finely diced
½ teaspoon minced jalapeño pepper
4 cups heavy cream
2 tablespoons minced fresh tarragon or 2 teaspoons dried
   Salt and freshly ground white pepper
   Blanched fresh sweet corn, blanched diced carrots and/or diced peeled and seeded tomatoes for garnish

Shuck oysters and reserve liquor.

In a heavy saucepan, melt butter over low heat. Add shallots, garlic and jalapeño. Cover with a tight-fitting lid and sweat over very low heat until translucent, about 5 minutes. Add oyster liquor and simmer until liquids are reduced by half, about 3 to 4 minutes. Add cream and dried tarragon, if using (reserve fresh tarragon for later), and simmer until mixture is somewhat thickened, 10 to 15 minutes.

When ready to serve, reheat soup without letting it boil. Add oysters and simmer until warmed through, 1 to 2 minutes. Add fresh tarragon, if using, and season with salt and white pepper to taste.

Ladle into heated soup bowls and garnish with corn, carrots and/or tomatoes.

Wine: Kistler Vineyards Chardonnay "McCrea Vineyard" (California: Sonoma County)

Cream of Onions Soup with Stilton

IT SEEMS TO US that thick, creamy, cheesy soups are most commonly found in the Midwest, where winters are hard and long. We've created an unusual variation on the old favorite by starting with an oniony base that adds a hint of sweetness to the pungent Stilton cheese. While most cheese soups include a generous portion of beer for added complexity, we use Stilton's classic accompaniment—a glass of port wine. Generally we cook with Dow's AJS Vintage Character Port. It's easily available, richly flavored and costs just slightly more than an average port. (You can substitute an aged Cheddar for the Stilton and beer for the port.) We like to serve this soup with a red port-style wine.

SERVES 6

¼ cup (½ stick) unsalted butter

4 cups finely diced white onions

1½ cups chopped leeks, white part only

¾ cup finely diced shallots

2 plump carrots, finely chopped

3 tablespoons minced fresh flat-leaf parsley

1 tablespoon minced fresh tarragon

3 tablespoons unbleached flour

5 cups milk

¾ cup port wine

½ pound Stilton cheese, grated (2 cups)
Kosher salt and freshly ground white pepper

3 strips cooked bacon, crumbled (optional)

3 tablespoons minced fresh chives

In a large, heavy-bottomed nonaluminum saucepan, melt butter over low heat. Add onions, leeks, shallots, carrots, parsley and tarragon. Cover with a tight-fitting lid and cook over very low heat, stirring occasionally, until onions and carrots are tender, about 20 minutes. Puree vegetables in the bowl of a food processor fitted with the metal blade. Return puree to the saucepan.

Sprinkle puree with flour and stir over low heat for about 3 minutes to cook flour. Slowly add milk, stirring constantly to avoid lumps. Cook over medium heat until mixture is hot and thickened. Add port and stir until heated through. Add cheese and stir over medium-low heat until melted and evenly blended. Season to taste with salt and white pepper.

Ladle into heated soup bowls, sprinkle with bacon, if using, and chives.

Wine: Quady Winery "Starboard" (California)

Sweet Vidalia

Two big Georgia operations are known across the country for their onions: the megaproducers, Bland Farms, and G & R Farms. In the several counties that comprise the Vidalia onion district, about 8,500 acres of onions are cultivated by 250 different farmers. G & R and Bland account for 2,400 acres, or nearly 30 percent of the crop.

When we met Delbert Bland, the manager of Bland Farms, the harvest, which had been set back 14 days by a big storm, was just getting underway as thousands of people across the country clamored for onions. Five hundred workers were laboring in the fields and scores more in the huge packing shed. The sweetness of a million onions was hanging in the air. And Delbert, with both a walkie-talkie and a cellular phone in his hands, was trying to stay on top of everything.

At his elbow was Barry Rogers from Seald Sweet, the sales organization that distributes the succulent crop. He is a man hungry for a product. "We're ready," said Rogers. "Gimme them onions!"

At Bland, seeds are planted by Labor Day. About 110 acres get a sprinkling of seeds, 18 pounds per acre. After the onions are well enough established, pencil-thin and a foot high, they are pulled up from the field, their tops cropped, and replanted, by hand, a few inches apart. This operation is completed the week before Thanksgiving. Then, usually by December 10, the first of the crop, the baby Vidalias, goes to market. They are 1½ to 2 inches in diameter and are shipped with 12 to 15 inches of their greenery. The decision to ship baby Vidalias was made in the mid-1980s to allow the industry to grow a little and weather the six weeks or so before mature onions are available. When the baby Vidalias have been shipped, the packing shed is closed down, and everyone waits for the big harvest to begin.

Raymond Bland, Delbert's father, walks the farm every day. It is he who decides when to harvest, when to summon the migrant workers, who toil in the fields, run the processing and packing lines and handle the shipping. On an April afternoon, we met him near a field that was being harvested. In the back of his pickup were a hundred or more onions, with their tops. He had gathered them in the past hour from several different fields and from different parts of each field. Many had been bitten into, others had been cut with a knife. Mr. Raymond, as he is called, had been tasting.

"These uns," he said, pointing at a batch in the bed of the truck, "I think we'll use for the mail-orders.

(continued on page 106)

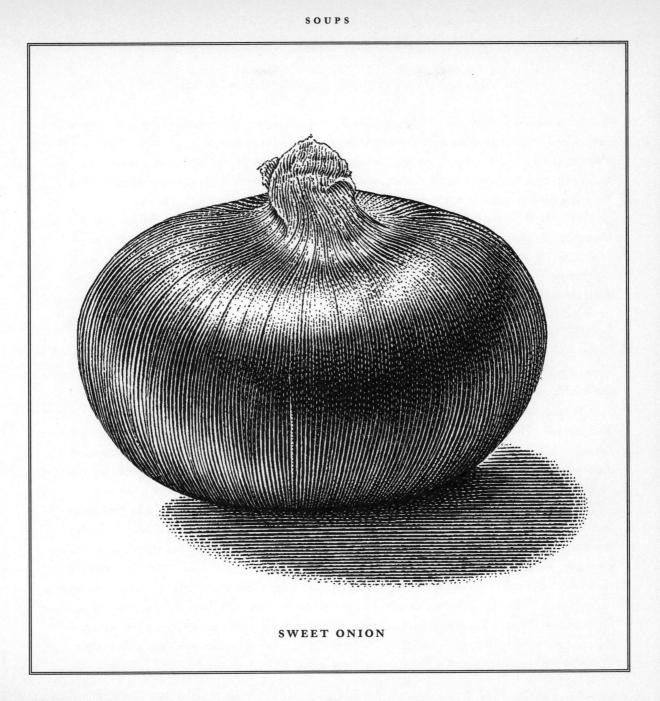

SWEET ONION

(continued from page 104)

They're the sweetest." He pointed to a nearby field. "They're from this side of that patch," he said. "And they're real good."

Like an experienced vitaculturist, Mr. Raymond knows that subtle variations in microclimate and soil conditions can have a significant effect on what he grows. So he is always tasting. He pulls an onion, cuts a wedge, tastes and spits. "You gotta spit," he says. "Otherwise you'd get sick of onions. And after you've tasted five or six, you have to eat a piece of bread or something, so you can remember what you've tasted." No notes. He just remembers. He can tell you where he got every onion and how it tasted.

When Mr. Raymond thinks a field is ready, he sends the tractor. It goes down the rows pulling sharp blades that undercut the onions, severing their roots, lifting them out of the soil and laying them on the ground, where they will dry for about three days. Then come the workers.

They pick up each onion, cut its green top an inch or so above the globe and put it into a burlap bag. After the onions are trucked to the packing shed, they are placed in dryers, enormous gas-heated bins, until their outside skin becomes papery and dry. Then they are inspected, sized, graded, stickered, packaged and shipped out.

Some of the growers of sweet onions have installed CA, or controlled-atmosphere storage. It enables them to hold the Vidalias until well into the fall without deterioration, thus providing another selling season just before the winter holidays.

"CA takes the pressure off selling," says Delbert Bland.

Bland has 14 huge climate-controlled rooms. Each costs a quarter of a million dollars to build. Each can hold 12,000 fifty-pound bags. The humidity is kept at 75 percent, the temperature at 34 degrees F. And the oxygen content of the atmosphere in the sealed room is less than 3 percent, the rest being inert nitrogen. The low-oxygen content means that no oxidation, and hence no spoilage, can take place.

The Blands, who started growing onions in 1981 and began their mail-order business in 1983, print and distribute five million catalogs per year. All the creative marketing has given the Vidalias a certain mystique, and their arrival in the market is much anticipated. Adding to their cachet, the Vidalias are a sweet, low-sulfur onion, which means that they are not good "keepers." The sulfur compounds that make most onions hot also help them resist molds, bacteria and mildew. You can hold Vidalias and other sweet onions for a while—with luck, for a month or more—if you put them into a pair of panty hose and tie a knot between the onions to keep them from touching each other. Or you can wrap them individually in foil and keep them in the refrigerator. But with fresh Vidalias, it's pretty much use them or lose them.

Baby Vidalia & Zucchini Soup

PEOPLE DON'T USUALLY think of putting onions and zucchini together in a soup. This one is fresh, light, delicate and a pretty shade of green. Baby Vidalias have plump, crisp bulbs attached to thick, but tender, green stems (called "quills" in Georgia). They're usually available between December and March, but you can make this simple soup in any season. Instead of Vidalias, we've used plump regular scallions or mixed ½ pound trimmed scallions (with about 2 inches of the green) with ½ pound of the sweetest onion available—Vidalia, Walla Walla, Arizona or even a mild Spanish onion.

SERVES 6 TO 8

2-3 tablespoons olive oil

1 pound baby Vidalias, trimmed and coarsely chopped

1 pound small zucchini, trimmed and coarsely chopped

2 large Yukon Gold or red-skinned potatoes, peeled and cut in ½-inch dice

6 cups chicken stock, heated

1 tablespoon minced fresh flat-leaf parsley

2 teaspoons minced fresh basil

1 teaspoon kosher salt

¼ teaspoon freshly ground white pepper

In a large, heavy saucepan, heat olive oil over medium-low heat. Add chopped onions and cook, stirring often, until onions soften, about 5 minutes.

Add zucchini to the pot and cook, stirring, for 2 minutes. Add potatoes and stock and bring to a boil. Reduce heat to low and simmer for 10 minutes.

Stir in parsley, basil, salt and pepper and simmer for 15 minutes. Adjust seasonings and serve.

Wine: Preston Vineyards Sauvignon Blanc (California: Sonoma County)

Grandma Weller's Hot Sweet & Sour Borscht

LINDA'S GRANDMOTHER would prepare this soup to be enjoyed during the week of Passover. She grated mounds of beets and then chopped mounds of onions, while tears coursed down her cheeks. No mild, sweet onions for her—only storage onions had the right intensity of flavor for her sweet-sour preparations.

SERVES 6 TO 12; MAKES 2½ TO 3 QUARTS

3   pounds boneless flanken (beef short ribs cut from the plate), or other boneless beef short ribs, trimmed of fat, cut into 1-inch cubes

1   beef soup bone

12   cups (3 quarts) water

2   pounds beets, trimmed, peeled and grated

1   cup canned crushed tomatoes

2   cups finely diced yellow onions

1   plump garlic clove, minced

1   teaspoon kosher salt

½   teaspoon black peppercorns, bruised with a heavy pan

½   cup packed dark brown sugar

1½   teaspoons ground ginger

     Juice of 2 lemons

     Kosher salt and freshly ground white pepper

2   large eggs

1   tablespoon matzoh meal

3   large boiled potatoes, cut into thick slices for garnish (optional)

Combine meat, soup bone and water in a large nonaluminum soup pot and bring to a boil. Cover with a tight-fitting lid and simmer briskly over low heat for 1½ hours. Skim off any foam that rises to the surface. Stir in beets, tomatoes, onions, garlic, salt and peppercorns. Cover and simmer for 1½ hours. Remove soup bone. Add sugar, ginger and lemon juice. Increase the heat and bring to a boil. Let soup boil for 5 to 10 minutes, skimming off any fat. Add salt and white pepper to taste. Adjust seasonings; soup should be a balance of sweet and sour, with a hint of ginger.

Beat eggs in a mixing bowl. Slowly whisk in matzoh meal and whisk vigorously to blend thoroughly. A bit at a time, gradually whisk hot soup into the egg mixture, until 3 cups of soup have been added. Slowly whisk mixture back into the soup pot and stir well over low heat; do not allow to boil again.

Serve in large heated soup plates. Add some of the meat, as well as a few slices of boiled potatoes, if you wish.

Wine: McDowell Valley Vineyards Grenache Rosé (California: McDowell Valley)

Cabbage, Tomato & Leek Soup

WITH CARAWAY & CHIVES

EVEN AFTER COOKING, some of the cabbage's crunch remains in this soup, an excellent partner to the robust warmth of the leeks and the smokiness of the bacon. There's also a suggestion of sweet and sour, with thyme and caraway added. If you can locate caraway thyme and garlic chives in your area, use these, or substitute regular thyme and a few more caraway seeds.

SERVES 6 TO 8

3   slices bacon, preferably smoked, diced

1   tablespoon olive oil

2   cups finely chopped leeks, whites and
    tender green parts

⅔   cup diced white onion

2   plump garlic cloves, minced

2   tablespoons dry vermouth

1   tablespoon hot Hungarian paprika

3   cups chopped cabbage

1   large baking potato, peeled and finely diced

1   28-ounce can crushed tomatoes

6   cups chicken stock

1   teaspoon caraway seeds, bruised

1   teaspoon fresh caraway thyme leaves, lemon
    thyme leaves or regular thyme leaves or
    ½ teaspoon dried thyme plus ½ teaspoon
    grated lemon zest
    Salt and freshly ground white pepper

2   tablespoons minced fresh garlic chives or
    regular chives

2   tablespoons minced fresh flat-leaf parsley

In a large nonaluminum soup pot, slowly heat bacon until some fat is rendered. Add olive oil, leeks, onion and garlic and sauté over low heat, stirring often, until leeks begin to wilt, about 5 minutes. Add vermouth and paprika and stir for 1 minute. Add cabbage and cook, stirring, until slightly wilted, about 5 to 7 minutes. Stir in potato, tomatoes, stock, caraway seeds and thyme. Increase heat to high and cook until liquid begins to bubble. Reduce the heat to low, and season with salt and pepper to taste. Cover and simmer for at least 1 hour.

Ladle soup into heated soup plates and garnish with chives and parsley.

**Wine: Chappellet Vineyard Chenin Blanc
(California: Napa Valley)**

Spanish Onion Split Pea Soup

COMBINING ONIONS, CARROTS AND POTATOES lightens the heaviness of the dried peas, while adding flavor and sweetness. We are big fans of Wigwam ham from S. Wallace Edwards & Sons in Surry, Virginia (see Special Products, page 374). It's pleasantly smoky and not as salty as other smoked hams. When it first arrives, Fred trims 4 to 6 inches off the hock, wraps it well and stores it in the freezer until we're ready to make a pot of pea soup.

SERVES 6 TO 12; MAKES ABOUT 3 QUARTS

8	cups (2 quarts) chicken stock
1½	pounds smoked ham hocks
1¼	pounds Spanish onions, finely diced
1½	pounds russet and Yukon Gold potatoes (red-skinned potatoes may be substituted for Yukon Gold), peeled and cut into medium dice
2	plump carrots, scrubbed and cut into medium dice
1	pound split peas, rinsed
½	heaping teaspoon black peppercorns, bruised with the bottom of a heavy pan
½	heaping teaspoon white peppercorns, bruised with the bottom of a heavy pan
1	teaspoon kosher salt
2	small bay leaves
1	rounded teaspoon herbes de Provence
3	cups water
¼	cup dry Marsala wine
	Freshly ground white pepper

In a heavy stockpot, combine stock, ham hocks, onions, potatoes, carrots, split peas, black and white peppercorns, salt, bay leaves and herbes de Provence. Bring to a boil. Reduce heat to low, partially cover the pot and simmer for 1 hour, stirring from time to time. Add 2 cups water and continue simmering, partially covered, for 1 hour more.

Using a skimmer or slotted spoon, remove ham hocks from the pot. Slice meat from bone and cut into small bites; set aside.

With the skimmer or slotted spoon, remove solids from pot, discard bay leaves and puree through a food mill placed over a large bowl or in a food processor. When all solids are pureed, return them to the pot and blend. Stir in remaining 1 cup water and Marsala. Season with additional salt and white pepper to taste. Stir in ham meat, partially cover, and simmer for 30 minutes. If soup is too thick, thin with a bit more water or stock. Ladle into heated bowls and serve.

Wine: Ca'de Solo Malvasia Bianca (California)

Cream of Onion & Tomato Soup

IF YOU ARE WATCHING FAT and calories, forget the bacon here, use a tad more oil if you need to and substitute yogurt for the crème fraîche. We like to garnish this with long chives and Johnny-jump-up flowers.

SERVES 6

3   tablespoons olive oil
1½ strips thick-cut bacon, preferably smoked, diced
1   jumbo sweet onion, cut into medium dice
1   plump shallot, minced
3   plump garlic cloves, chopped
3   pounds ripe tomatoes, chopped
1   cup chicken stock
1   tablespoon red-wine vinegar
1   teaspoon sugar
1   tablespoon fresh thyme leaves or 1½ teaspoons dried
¼   cup crème fraîche (page 98) or ¼ cup heavy cream mixed with 1 tablespoon sour cream
    Salt and freshly ground black pepper
    Fresh herbs for garnish

Heat oil in a heavy nonaluminum soup pot over medium-low heat. Add bacon, onion, shallot and garlic and sauté until bacon begins to brown and onion is translucent, about 8 minutes. Stir in tomatoes, stock, vinegar, sugar and thyme and bring to a boil. Partially cover and simmer for 15 minutes.

Puree soup in a food processor fitted with the metal blade. Strain puree back into the pot.

Add crème fraîche or heavy cream mixture and salt and pepper to taste. Reheat until hot, but do not boil. Ladle into soup plates and garnish with herbs.

Wine: Au Bon Climat Pinot Blanc (California: Santa Barbara)

Light Gazpacho

GAZPACHO IS REALLY a liquid salad, with some crunchy diced vegetables for garnish. Ours, of course, is a bit more oniony than others, but splendidly light and refreshing in the heat of August. Any gazpacho is best when made with a variety of tomatoes right from the garden, and we especially like to use golden tomatoes, which are low in acid, and cucumbers with seeds because they contain more water. Since we've had good luck foil-wrapping and refrigerating our Vidalias and Walla Wallas, we use those as well.

SERVES 6 TO 8

3	pounds ripe tomatoes, peeled and coarsely chopped
2	tablespoons olive oil
1	cucumber, peeled and grated
⅔	cup finely grated sweet onion, such as Vidalia, Walla Walla or Spanish
1½	cups chicken stock
2	plump garlic cloves, minced
1	teaspoon salt
1	teaspoon freshly ground white pepper
¼	cup extra-virgin olive oil
2-3	tablespoons red-wine vinegar
4	large fresh basil leaves, torn
2	tablespoons minced fresh chives
1	large ripe tomato, peeled and diced, for garnish
	Fresh flowers, such as nasturtiums or marigolds, or snipped fresh chives for garnish

Combine coarsely chopped tomatoes and oil in a heavy nonaluminum saucepan over low heat. Cover and cook until tomatoes are very soft, about 20 minutes.

Process tomatoes through a food mill into a large mixing bowl or process in a food processor. Strain and set aside to cool. Stir in cucumber, onion, stock, garlic, salt and pepper and mix thoroughly. Stir in extra-virgin olive oil, vinegar and basil. Cover and refrigerate for at least 4 hours.

Just before serving, taste and adjust seasonings. Stir in chives and diced tomato. Ladle into soup plates and garnish with flower petals or chives and serve.

Wine: Sterling Vineyards Sauvignon Blanc
(California: Napa Valley)

Chilled Cream of Sweet Onion Soup

THIS SOUP IS CREAMY and thick, yet silky, with the delicate flavor of onion ever so slightly enriched with hints of white wine, bay leaf and thyme, and a bit of lemon to brighten the flavors. We thank Pete Peterson for sharing his recipe.

SERVES 8 TO 10

¼ cup (½ stick) butter

2 pounds sweet onions, such as Vidalia, Walla Walla or Spanish, thinly sliced

4 garlic cloves, sliced

2 cups chicken stock

1 cup dry white wine

1 tablespoon fresh thyme leaves or ½ teaspoon dried

1 small bay leaf

½ cup heavy cream

½ cup sour cream

2 tablespoons fresh lemon juice

¼ teaspoon kosher salt

About 5 drops Tabasco sauce

Freshly grated nutmeg

Minced scallions and chive blossom petals for garnish

In a large, heavy nonaluminum pot, melt butter over low heat. Add onions all at once, cover and cook, stirring frequently, until onions are translucent and just at the point of caramelizing (do not let them brown), 15 to 20 minutes.

Stir in garlic, stock, wine, thyme and bay leaf and bring to a boil. Reduce heat to low, cover and simmer until onions are very soft, 20 to 30 minutes. (Onions should be fully cooked to avoid a raw taste and so they puree perfectly.)

Remove bay leaf. Puree onions with the liquid in a blender or a food processor fitted with the metal blade. Stir mixture through a medium-mesh sieve into a large bowl. Cover and chill thoroughly.

When ready to serve, whisk in heavy cream and sour cream. Season with lemon juice and salt; add Tabasco and nutmeg to taste. Garnish with scallions and chive blossom petals.

Wine: J.M. Bourgeois Pouilly-Fumé
(France: Loire Valley)
or Flora Springs Wine Company "Soliloquy"
(California: Napa Valley)

Chilled Vidalia-Asparagus Soup

IN OUR AREA, the first homegrown asparagus comes into the stores about the same time as Vidalias, so this soup seemed to be a natural combination. The asparagus works nicely with the sweetness of the onions and potato, especially with a touch of dry vermouth and some tangy yogurt. While somewhat thick, it's pleasingly smooth, with crunchy asparagus tips as a garnish.

SERVES 6 TO 8

4-6 tablespoons (½-¾ stick) unsalted butter

1 pound sweet onions, such as Vidalia or Walla Walla, thinly sliced

3 pounds fresh asparagus, tips reserved, stalks chopped

1 large Yukon Gold or red-skinned potato, peeled and diced

7 cups chicken stock

2 large fresh thyme sprigs or ½ teaspoon dried

1 fresh marjoram sprig

¼ cup dry vermouth

1 cup plain yogurt
  Salt and freshly ground white pepper

4 gratings fresh nutmeg

1 tablespoon minced fresh parsley

1 tablespoon minced fresh chives

In a heavy 3-quart nonaluminum pot, melt 4 tablespoons butter over medium heat. Stir in onions, asparagus stalks and potato. Cover with a tight-fitting lid, reduce heat to low and sweat vegetables for 5 minutes. Add more butter if needed; do not let onions brown.

Stir in stock, thyme and marjoram. Increase heat to high and bring to a boil. Reduce heat to low, partially cover and simmer briskly for at least 30 minutes. Add vermouth and simmer for 5 minutes.

Meanwhile, place asparagus tips in a small pan with salted water and cook until just tender, about 2 minutes. Plunge tips into ice water to stop the cooking; set aside.

Remove fresh herbs from soup pot. Puree vegetables in a food mill or food processor, adding liquid as necessary. Return to cooking liquid and blend well. Stir in yogurt, salt and pepper to taste and nutmeg; cover and chill until serving time. Garnish with asparagus spears and minced parsley and chives.

THE ARCTIC ALLIUM

YOU WOULDN'T THINK IT to look at them, but chives may be the toughest plant in the entire allium genus. They are able to winter tundra temperatures that drop to -40 and -50 degrees F and survive in the wild from Newfoundland to Alaska, from Lapland to Eastern Siberia. And they are hardy enough to withstand drought and heat as well.

A few years ago, we cut a wine barrel in two, filled it with some dirt from the garden and planted it with a variety of herbs. A decade later, they are still coming up. The most vigorous, the most determined and the most productive plant in the mix is the chive, and however mightily we hack at the thicket, there are always more than enough for our cooking.

Allium schoenoprasum is the skinny bulbless perennial's real name, and the plant is useful whenever a delicate hint of oniony taste is needed. Chives are best fresh, of course; their thin, hollow stalks should be snipped just before they are to be added to an omelet or a sauce.

Beyond being hardy and tasty, chives are pretty. They grow in strong, thick clumps, recover quickly after being shorn and produce usable stalks all season, and if taken inside, all year. They propagate vegetatively, and they also produce seeds. The plants grow attractive, blue, edible flowers. Chives are the allium most often found in the home garden.

Pat Bourdo, who operates a beautiful commercial herb garden in Northport, Michigan, uses chives decoratively as well as for cooking. Around her sign, along the walkways and bordering a small pond, she has planted curly chives. "A little bit bitter-tasting," she says, "but it makes up for that with its beauty." Bourdo sells chives for her customers' gardens, and she also dries them to sell in her store.

Most chives come from small growers rather than large commercial farms. Only since the dairy industry began selling cottage cheese with chives has there been any real acreage devoted to the crop. And that isn't much. In San Mateo County, near San Francisco, as many as 20 acres of chives are grown for freezing or freeze-drying and shipping to creameries across the country.

But nowadays, at almost any supermarket, thanks to growers like Pat Bourdo, you can find fresh chives, even in winter.

Linda's Chicken Soup

WITH ONION-CHIVE MATZOH BALLS

IT IS LINDA'S BELIEF that if chicken soup has curative powers, they must come from the onions. Why not add onion matzoh balls, too? These are fairly weighty, just like the ones Grandma Weller used to make.

SERVES 8 TO 10

Chicken Soup

12 cups (3 quarts) chicken stock

2 large yellow onions, peeled and halved

1 parsnip, peeled and halved

6 carrots, trimmed, scrubbed and cut into chunks

½ bunch fresh parsley

 Several large sprigs fresh lemon thyme or regular thyme or ½ teaspoon dried

8-10 chicken thighs

Matzoh Balls

2 tablespoons chicken fat

⅓ cup minced yellow onions

2 tablespoons minced fresh chives

2 large eggs

1 tablespoon water

⅔ cup matzoh meal

½ teaspoon kosher salt

 Freshly ground black pepper

½ cup chopped fresh parsley

To make chicken soup: In a large, heavy-bottomed soup pot, combine stock, onions, parsnip, carrots, parsley, thyme and chicken thighs. Bring to a boil. Reduce heat and simmer very briskly for 1 hour. Using a skimmer or tongs, remove and discard onions, parsnip, parsley and thyme. Carefully remove chicken from the pot and set aside to cool. Cut meat from bones in chunks; cover and reserve.

To make matzoh balls: Prepare matzoh balls 1½ hours before serving. In a small skillet, heat chicken fat over medium heat. Add onions, and sauté, stirring constantly, until translucent, about 5 minutes. Set onion mixture aside to cool for 10 minutes. In a small bowl, combine onion mixture with chives, eggs and water; beat thoroughly. Stir in matzoh meal and salt and pepper to taste. Beat with a fork until thoroughly blended. Cover and chill for 1 hour.

Bring soup to a very brisk simmer. With wet

hands, make matzoh balls about 1 inch in diameter and place on a large plate. (There should be enough for 14 to 16 balls.) Drop matzoh balls into simmering soup, cover pot and simmer briskly for 20 minutes.

Add reserved chicken and parsley to soup and heat until warmed through. Adjust seasonings and serve in heated bowls.

Wine: Kistler Vineyards "Sonoma County" Chardonnay (California: Sonoma County)

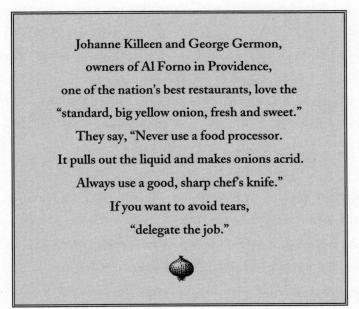

**Johanne Killeen and George Germon,
owners of Al Forno in Providence,
one of the nation's best restaurants, love the
"standard, big yellow onion, fresh and sweet."
They say, "Never use a food processor.
It pulls out the liquid and makes onions acrid.
Always use a good, sharp chef's knife."
If you want to avoid tears,
"delegate the job."**

Salads

Wild Leek Salad with Paprika Vinaigrette

TAPAWINGO, Pete Peterson's great restaurant, sits on the edge of a small lake in Ellsworth, Michigan. This is the far northern part of the Lower Peninsula, where every spring, foragers bring Peterson ramps (wild leeks), morels and fiddleheads. This particular salad, created by Peterson, uses sweet paprika in the vinaigrette, where it adds its smoky note to the flavor and its rosy hue to the color. We often use this vinaigrette when we're combining leftover chicken with a variety of lettuces as a dinner salad.

SERVES 6

¼ cup tarragon vinegar

2 teaspoons sweet paprika

1 teaspoon Dijon mustard

½ teaspoon cayenne

1¼ teaspoons kosher salt

¾ cup extra-virgin olive oil
  About 1 teaspoon sugar

½ pound wild leeks (ramps), white part only, cleaned and trimmed

3 cups watercress sprigs

Combine vinegar, paprika, mustard, cayenne and ¼ teaspoon salt in a small bowl. Very slowly, whisk in olive oil; whisk in sugar to taste. Set aside.

Fill a medium saucepan with water. Add the remaining 1 teaspoon salt and bring to a boil. Add wild leeks and cook until just tender (the tip of a sharp knife will penetrate), 3 to 5 minutes. Drain, rinse with cold water and drain again. Place leeks in a medium bowl and toss with ¼ cup vinaigrette. Marinate at room temperature for 2 to 3 hours.

When ready to serve, drain vinaigrette from leeks and whisk into remaining vinaigrette. Distribute watercress among 6 chilled plates. Arrange 6 to 8 leeks on top of each. Drizzle 2 to 3 tablespoons paprika vinaigrette on watercress and around the perimeter of the plate.

**Wine: Qupé Marsanne
(California: Santa Barbara)**

Frisée Salad with Poached Egg
& WARM BACON-SHALLOT VINAIGRETTE

THE FRENCH CITY OF LYON is one of the great culinary treasures of the world. This is our variation of a traditional salad we first had in a wonderful bistro in Vieux Lyon. We grow frisée, fine curly endive, all summer long, and thanks to our friend, hydroponic grower Patrick McCafferty, we can enjoy it in the winter, too. This salad is a frequent feature at our table.

SERVES 4

½ pound (4-6 cups) frisée or young curly endive, washed and spun dry

1 small head tender lettuce, washed and spun dry

4 large eggs

4 thick slices bacon, preferably smoked, cut into medium dice
  Pinch kosher salt

2 tablespoons cider vinegar

3 tablespoons extra-virgin olive oil

3 tablespoons minced shallots

1 garlic clove, minced

¼ cup red-wine vinegar

2 teaspoons Dijon mustard
  Freshly ground black pepper

Tear both types of greens into bite-sized pieces and place in a large bowl.

Break eggs into separate small cups and place near the stovetop.

Sauté bacon in a heavy skillet over medium heat until crisp; remove with a slotted spoon and drain. Set aside. Reserve skillet and bacon fat.

Fill a large, deep sauté pan with water, add a pinch of salt and cider vinegar; bring mixture to a rolling boil.

While water is coming to a boil, pour bacon fat into a measuring cup. Add enough olive oil to measure ½ cup; return oil mixture to the bacon skillet. Heat mixture over medium heat until warm. Add shallots and garlic and sauté over low heat, stirring often, until shallots wilt, about 2 minutes. Pour mixture into a small bowl. Add wine vinegar to the skillet and cook over medium heat, scraping the bottom of the pan to loosen any particles. Whisk in mustard, then slowly whisk in oil mixture. When vinaigrette is warmed through, crumble in cooked bacon and season with salt and pepper to taste. Toss warm vinaigrette with salad greens just before cooking eggs.

One at a time, quickly slip eggs into gently boiling water, using a slotted spoon to coax whites into a nice shape. Poach in simmering water until done, 2 to 3 minutes. Remove from water (you can trim the whites, if you wish).

Quickly divide salad among 4 large plates. Garnish each with a poached egg. Add a few grinds of pepper over eggs and serve.

Wine: George Vernay Condrieu (France: Rhône)

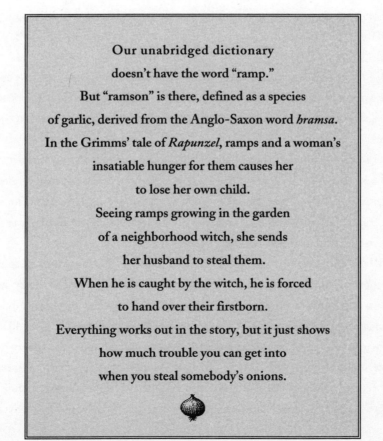

Our unabridged dictionary
doesn't have the word "ramp."
But "ramson" is there, defined as a species
of garlic, derived from the Anglo-Saxon word *hramsa*.
In the Grimms' tale of *Rapunzel*, ramps and a woman's
insatiable hunger for them causes her
to lose her own child.
Seeing ramps growing in the garden
of a neighborhood witch, she sends
her husband to steal them.
When he is caught by the witch, he is forced
to hand over their firstborn.
Everything works out in the story, but it just shows
how much trouble you can get into
when you steal somebody's onions.

ONION CAKE

"TALK TO MARGUERITE," said Craig Christensen, president of the Onion Growers Association. "She won the prize at the Walla Walla Onion Festival with a German chocolate sweet-onion cake." Though we feared it was inevitable, we heard no hint of a cake made with onions during our long visit to Vidalia. No Texan that we talked to about their fabled 1015Ys ever mentioned an onion dessert. Even Linda's creative cousin Susan Cavitch, who had made a red onion-lemon verbena sorbet, never entertained the notion of singing "Happy Birthday" to one of her kids over a cake made with onions.

We located Marguerite Daltoso in her office at the Agricultural Extension Service.

"Yes," she said. "It's true."

But she decided not to call it an onion cake—it would sound oxymoronic, perhaps even frighten the judges. Her prize-winning effort, the best recipe in the 1991 festival, is listed as "Chocolate Coconut-Pecan Surprise Cake." You can guess what the surprise is. (With her kind permission, we are reprinting the recipe.)

Along with her recipe, Daltoso sent us Walla Walla onions, just harvested from her own farm. They were enormous—a boxful of the biggest we had seen. And they were the sweetest onions we had ever eaten. Here, at last, was an onion that you really could eat as you would eat a peach, an onion so crisp and moist that it could quench your thirst. There was not a scintilla of heat in the taste—cooler than the Vidalia, cooler than the Maui, cooler than the Texas Sweet.

In the Walla Walla onion region, which includes one county in Washington and another across the river in Oregon, there are scarcely more than 1,000 acres of sweet onions grown every year—only about one-eighth of the acreage given to sweets in south Georgia. While some megafarms there grow 1,000 acres or more, the average of the 30 or so Walla Walla sweet onion growers is 35 to 40 acres.

Still, that is enough to keep a farm going successfully. Ben and Marguerite Daltoso grow 50 acres of sweets, 40 acres of storage onions and 10 acres of wheat. Their history in the valley goes back to the earliest onion times. Ben's father came from northern Italy in 1921 to work on a friend's farm, growing onions. Marguerite's father, Eugenio De Luca, came from southern Italy in the same year to work on his brother's farm, growing onions. Both men married, and while they raised onions, they also raised families.

The two onion families came together when Ben and Marguerite met in church, fell in love and, after college, married and started a family of their own. They have six children, all of whom grew up helping in the onion fields and selling bags of onions at their roadside stand.

THEIR PROGENY ARE ALL GROWN NOW and only one has yet to finish college. Only one is in the onion business. There are 13 grandchildren who visit the farm but who will never really know the pleasures—and the toil—of coaxing giant sweet onions from the rich Walla Walla soil. They may not grow onions, but when they come for dinner at their grandparents' house, they eat them. "I never cook without onions," says Marguerite. "How about some Chocolate Coconut-Pecan Surprise Cake?"

This is Marguerite Daltoso's prize-winning recipe:

1   18.25-ounce box devil's food cake mix
¾   cup Walla Walla sweet onion, finely diced
1   16-ounce can prepared coconut-pecan frosting
1   16-ounce can prepared chocolate frosting
    Slivered almonds for garnish (optional)

Preheat oven to the temperature recommended on the box. Prepare 2 nine-inch round cake pans according to instructions on cake-mix package; follow directions for preparing cake mix, but reduce water by 2 tablespoons and add diced onion. Pour into prepared cake pans; bake as directed on package.

When cool, spread ⅔ of the coconut-pecan frosting on the first layer; top with the second cake layer. Frost top with remaining coconut-pecan frosting. Frost sides with chocolate frosting and, if desired, garnish the top with slivered almonds.

Grilled Salad of Onions, Peppers & Squash

WITH LEMON-MINT VINAIGRETTE

IN THE SUMMER, we like to grill a variety of vegetables and treat them as a warm salad. The combined flavors and textures, bathed in a vinaigrette, make a pleasing accompaniment to meat, fish, poultry or even beans and rice. Mint gives a refreshing surprise to any vinaigrette; if you are lucky enough to have lemon verbena or lemon balm in your garden, be sure to add some as well.

SERVES 6 TO 8

Dressing

10	mint leaves, bruised
	Juice of 1 lemon
1	tablespoon white-wine vinegar or white-wine fruit vinegar
⅓	cup extra-virgin olive oil
1	garlic clove, minced
1	tablespoon minced fresh chives
2	teaspoons minced fresh mint
	Kosher salt and freshly ground black pepper

Salad

2	large sweet onions, such as Vidalias or Walla Wallas, or 4 red onions
3	young yellow squash, halved lengthwise
3	young zucchini squash, halved lengthwise
3	medium-hot chile peppers, halved lengthwise and seeded
2	red bell peppers, halved lengthwise, seeded and quartered
1	plump head radicchio, halved lengthwise
¼	cup olive oil

To make dressing: A few hours before serving, combine mint leaves, lemon juice and vinegar in a small bowl and mix. Let stand for 10 minutes; discard mint. Slowly whisk in olive oil. Add garlic, chives, mint and salt and pepper to taste. Blend well, and set vinaigrette aside.

To make salad: Cut onions lengthwise, then into quarters, keeping some of the root end on each piece in order to hold each wedge together. Combine all vegetables in a large bowl and gently toss with olive oil.

Clean a charcoal or gas grill well and coat grill rack with vegetable oil. Preheat until hot. Arrange vegetables on the grill, cover, and grill, turning vegetables often, until done, about 10 minutes. Remove from the grill and return vegetables to the large bowl. Break radicchio and onions into pieces. Pour on vinaigrette and toss well. Adjust seasonings and serve.

Wine: Georges Burrier Pouilly-Fuissé "Cuvée Clair-Marie" (France: Burgundy)

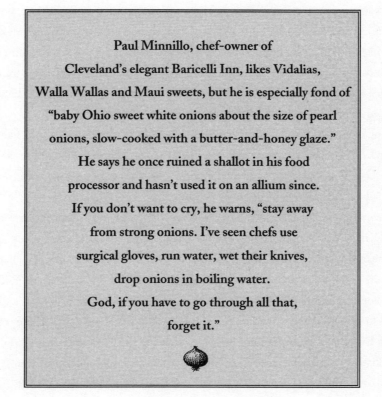

Paul Minnillo, chef-owner of
Cleveland's elegant Baricelli Inn, likes Vidalias,
Walla Wallas and Maui sweets, but he is especially fond of
"baby Ohio sweet white onions about the size of pearl
onions, slow-cooked with a butter-and-honey glaze."
He says he once ruined a shallot in his food
processor and hasn't used it on an allium since.
If you don't want to cry, he warns, "stay away
from strong onions. I've seen chefs use
surgical gloves, run water, wet their knives,
drop onions in boiling water.
God, if you have to go through all that,
forget it."

The Mighty Pearl

MARTINI STANDING," you tell the bartender. "With an onion." And there it is, cold as ice, and with any kind of luck, the bartender will have put two onions—small, white and translucent—in your drink. And when you reach the bottom of the glass, you get your real reward.

If you are having this drink in an American bar, the onions probably came from Hollister, California, or perhaps from an onion field in Idaho.

According to some growers, the delicious pickled pearls are not a specific cultivar, but the result of a style of cultivation. In the rich muckland of central Ohio, a good grower can sometimes get 40,000 pounds of big storage onions from one acre, the product of about 3.68 pounds of onion seed. (There are about 120,000 seeds per pound.) The growers in the pearl trade, however, will use a minimum of 65 pounds of seed per acre and some Idaho producers will use from 80 to 110 pounds. That means the onions are destined to be crowded and, with no room to grow, will remain small.

Another way of keeping the bulbs small is to use a short-day or southern cultivar like Crystal Wax, Eclipse or Barletta. They will start growing bulbs when the day-length is 10 to 12 hours, while the plant is still immature. Darrell Bolz, an agent of the University of Idaho Cooperative Extension System, confirmed that that is how Idaho growers get their pearls.

Erica Koenigsaecker and her husband, Richard Abernethy, who grow pearl onions on their little Wisconsin farm, Kingsfield Gardens, take vigorous exception to these approaches.

"You grow a pearl for taste," Koenigsaecker says. "You want something with real character. It's little, so it has to be really good. It has to be a special cultivar." She grows Snow Baby and Purplette.

According to botanist and onion expert Henry A. Jones, American pearls are just a diminutive *Allium cepa* cultivar held to small size by cultivation practices, and not a true pearl at all. The real pearl onion, long cultivated in Europe, is, according to Jones, a member of the Great-Headed Garlic group, an *A. ampeloprasum*, a kissing cousin of the leek. Its bulb is formed from one thickened leaf. It is the pearl traditionally pickled in Holland, Germany and Italy and sold in specialty food stores.

Any of these onions, however, will work in your martini.

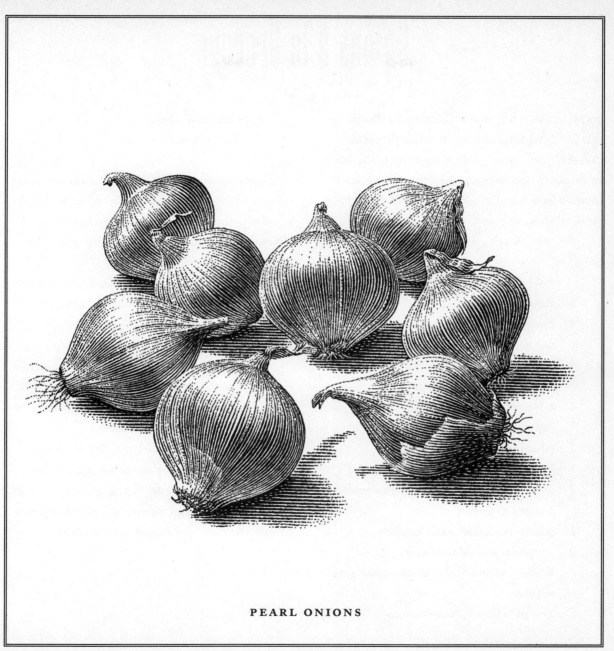

PEARL ONIONS

Onions à la Grecque

WHETHER THIS IS REALLY Greek in origin, or just Mediterranean, it is a terrific preparation that grew out of our frequent visits to the south of France. These onions make a great accompaniment to food from the grill or as part of a medley of small salads as an hors d'oeuvre.

MAKES ABOUT 4 CUPS

Marinade

1   cup chicken stock
½   cup olive oil
¾   cup dry white wine
2   tablespoons fresh lemon juice
3   tablespoons red-wine vinegar
1   tablespoon tomato puree or paste
½   cup dried currants
1   tablespoon chopped fresh parsley
1   bay leaf
2   teaspoons minced fresh thyme leaves or
    1 teaspoon dried
1   tablespoon fennel seeds, crushed
2   teaspoons ground coriander
    Kosher salt and freshly ground black pepper
    to taste
    Zest of ½ lemon, cut into strips

2   pints pearl onions
    Boiling water

To make marinade: Combine all marinade ingredients in a small nonaluminum saucepan and bring to a boil over medium heat. Reduce the heat to low and simmer for 10 minutes. Remove from the heat and discard lemon zest.

Meanwhile, place pearl onions in a large saucepan and cover with boiling water. Boil for 2 minutes. Quickly drain onions and plunge into cold water; drain again.

Peel onions and check for doneness. They should be crisp-tender. Place peeled onions in marinade. If they need more cooking time, you can cook them in the marinade for a few more minutes.

Place onion mixture in a large, clean container, cool to room temperature and cover. Let stand at room temperature for a day before serving. These will keep in the refrigerator for several weeks. We prefer to serve them at room temperature, however.

Watercress Salad with Raspberries & Red Onions

P EPPERY WATERCRESS is perfect with red onions and raspberries. We've also made this full-flavored salad with some sweet onions (Vidalia, Walla Walla, Maui, or 1015Ys) and strawberries. The salad is best served by itself, following the main course.

SERVES 6

3 tablespoons balsamic vinegar
1 tablespoon rich raspberry or black raspberry vinegar (or use ¼ cup balsamic vinegar in all)
1 teaspoon Dijon mustard
⅓ cup extra-virgin olive oil

3 large bunches watercress, thick stems discarded
1 large red onion, thinly sliced and separated into rings
1 pint fresh raspberries
1 tablespoon minced fennel fronds
   Kosher salt and freshly ground black pepper

In a large salad bowl, combine both vinegars with mustard. Gradually add olive oil, whisking vigorously to make a thick emulsion. Add watercress, onion rings and raspberries. Season with fennel and salt and pepper. Toss gently and serve on large chilled plates.

Marinated Beets & Onions

WITH SHALLOT-POPPY SEED DRESSING

THIS SWEET-AND-SOUR beet salad is outstanding made with golden beets, but be sure to experiment with varieties of beets and onions. When baking your beets, remember that small ones will cook more rapidly than large ones. Finally, find a good source for fruit vinegars; they are splendid additions to a salad repertoire.

SERVES 6

1-2   tablespoons olive oil

1½-2   pounds beets, trimmed (2-2½ pounds untrimmed)

⅓   cup peach, pear or berry vinegar or white-wine vinegar mixed with 1 tablespoon fruit juice

1   tablespoon honey

1   teaspoon Dijon mustard

2   shallots, finely minced

½   cup extra-virgin olive oil

1   tablespoon poppy seeds

1   tablespoon minced fresh chives

1   tablespoon minced fresh lemon verbena or lemon balm or 1 teaspoon grated lemon zest
    Kosher salt and freshly ground white pepper

1   medium-sized red onion, thinly sliced

Salad greens for lining serving platter
Minced chives and/or chive blossom petals for garnish

Preheat oven to 375 degrees F. Coat a large baking dish with olive oil and rub excess oil on beets. Add enough water just to cover the bottom of the dish. Cover the baking dish with foil and bake in the preheated oven until beets are tender when pierced with a knife, about 1 hour for large beets. Remove from the oven, uncover and let beets cool.

In a large mixing bowl, mix together vinegar, honey, mustard and shallots. Slowly whisk in olive oil to make a thick emulsion. Whisk in poppy seeds, chives, lemon verbena or lemon balm or zest and salt and white pepper to taste. Add onion and toss thoroughly. Let dressing stand until beets are cool.

Carefully peel beets; cut into ¼-inch-thick slices. Gently toss beets with onions. Cover the bowl with plastic and chill at least 2 hours before serving.

To serve, line a shallow serving bowl with salad greens. Adjust seasonings in beet salad. Spoon salad in the center of the prepared serving dish. Sprinkle with minced chives and chive flower petals and serve.

Tomato & Onion Salad

THE FIRST THING you notice about this salad is its heady basil fragrance. We first made it one very hot summer when every one of the nearly dozen tomato varieties we planted produced copiously. We love the contrast of the slightly acidic tomatoes with sweet, crisp onion. Even when you only have one variety of tomato, you can enjoy this classic salad.

SERVES 4

1½   pounds various ripe tomatoes, including red, yellow and orange

6-10   teardrop tomatoes (red and yellow) or cherry tomatoes

¾   cup finely diced sweet or red onion

10   basil leaves, finely julienned

⅓   cup extra-virgin olive oil
     Freshly ground black pepper

3   tablespoons red-wine vinegar
     Kosher salt
     Edible flower petals, such as marigolds, borage and nasturtiums for garnish (optional)

Coarsely dice all but teardrop or cherry tomatoes and place in a bowl. Slice teardrop or cherry tomatoes and add to others. Add onion, basil, olive oil and pepper to taste. Mix and let stand for 30 minutes. Just before serving, add vinegar and season with pepper and salt to taste. Stir gently, sprinkle with edible flower petals, if using, and serve.

Salad of Fennel, Smoke-Cured Ham & Red Onions

WE THINK THERE IS NOTHING more delicious than crisp fennel with a good vinaigrette. Smoky, slightly salty ham plays against licorice-flavored fennel and tender lettuces. If you don't have any smoke-cured, aged Virginia ham, good prosciutto makes an excellent substitute.

SERVES 6

2   large fennel bulbs, trimmed
¼   pound thinly sliced smoked ham, preferably Virginia ham, julienned
1   medium-sized red onion, thinly sliced
3   cups torn mixed tender lettuces
¼   cup red-wine vinegar
½   teaspoon Dijon mustard
½   cup extra-virgin olive oil
    Kosher salt and freshly ground black pepper
1   tablespoon minced fresh fennel fronds
2   tablespoons minced fresh chives
2   ounces Parmesan cheese, shaved, for garnish

Slice fennel crosswise as thinly as possible and place in large salad bowl. Add ham, onion and lettuces.

In a small bowl, combine vinegar and mustard and whisk thoroughly. Slowly whisk in oil until mixture forms a thick emulsion. Blend in salt and pepper to taste, fennel fronds and chives.

Pour dressing over fennel mixture and toss well. Taste and adjust seasonings. Garnish with cheese shavings and serve.

Wine: Codorniu Napa Valley Sparkling Wine (California: Napa Valley)

RED ONIONS

Broccoli Salad with Red Onions, Raisins & Pine Nuts

WE FIRST HAD a chilled broccoli salad at the West Point Market in Akron, Ohio. Off we went to our own kitchen to add red onion, orange and a few herbs. The sweetness of the raisins is a counterpoint to the zip from the red onions, and the orange zest and fennel taste good with the balsamic vinegar. If you happen to have a good fruit vinegar, such as peach or cherry, use it instead of orange juice, and if you have access to orange mint, use it instead of ordinary mint.

SERVES 6

1 pound broccoli, trimmed and cut into florets
2 teaspoons kosher salt
1 cup medium-diced red onion
½ cup finely diced fennel (optional)
1 cup golden raisins
⅓ cup toasted pine nuts

Zest of 1 orange, minced
3 tablespoons balsamic vinegar
2 tablespoons fresh orange juice
3 tablespoons extra-virgin olive oil
Freshly ground black pepper
1 tablespoon minced fresh tarragon leaves
1 teaspoon minced fresh mint leaves

Place broccoli in boiling water to cover and add salt; cook for 1 minute. Drain and refresh in ice water until cold; drain again.

In a large bowl, combine broccoli, onion, fennel (if using), raisins, pine nuts and orange zest.

In a small bowl, combine vinegar and orange juice. Slowly whisk in oil, beating until a thick emulsion forms. Season with salt and pepper to taste and stir in herbs. Pour over broccoli mixture and toss well. Let stand for 1 hour before serving.

ONION BREATH

SOMETIMES AN ONION EATER unknowingly telegraphs the nature of his dinner to those who happen to be near. In some of its publications, the National Onion Association offers suggestions for dealing with onion breath:

- *Rinse your mouth with equal portions of lemon juice and water.*
- *Chew a citrus peel after eating onions to sweeten the breath.*
- *Chew on aniseed or dill seed.*
- *Suck on a small piece of cinnamon or a whole clove to get rid of the odor.*
- *Eat a freshly washed apple.*
- *Eat a sprig or two of parsley—one of the best solutions.*
- *Munch on roasted coffee beans.*

Food writer Craig Claiborne told us that if you are worried about onion on your breath, try the parsley—not just a sprig, but a large amount. Chase it by chewing whole cloves and coriander seeds. But maybe the best thing to do is avoid the society of people who do not eat onions.

Roasted Red Potato Salad

WITH RED ONIONS, HERBS & BACON

WE MAKE THIS SALAD quite frequently in the spring and summer. While we vary the variety of onions, our current favorite is red. When there are salad leftovers, we'll use them in a frittata, such as Ramps Gallimaufry Frittata (page 154).

SERVES 8 TO 10

3   pounds small red-skinned potatoes, scrubbed and quartered
¼   cup olive oil
3   tablespoons red-wine vinegar
2   teaspoons Dijon mustard
¼   cup extra-virgin olive oil
    Kosher salt and freshly ground black pepper
⅔   cup finely diced red onion
1   tablespoon minced fresh parsley
1   tablespoon minced fresh chives
2   teaspoons minced fresh thyme leaves
1   teaspoon minced fresh rosemary leaves
3   strips crisp cooked bacon, crumbled

Preheat oven to 450 degrees F. Combine potatoes and olive oil in a shallow roasting pan and toss. Arrange potatoes in a single layer. Roast until brown and tender, about 40 minutes.

Meanwhile, pour vinegar in a small bowl and whisk well with mustard. Gradually add extra-virgin olive oil and whisk to form a thick emulsion. Set aside.

When potatoes are done, remove them from the pan with a slotted spoon and place in a large bowl. Toss with vinaigrette and let stand for at least 15 minutes.

Add onion, fresh herbs and bacon just before serving. Serve salad warm or at room temperature.

Iceberg Lettuce Salad

WITH TOMATOES, RED ONIONS & BLUE CHEESE

CHOPPED, CRISP ICEBERG LETTUCE, diced red onion, chunks of blue cheese and diced red tomatoes: Add a cup of chopped mixed fresh herbs and a balsamic vinaigrette, and you have the best summer salad you'll ever taste. Clevelander Zack Bruell created this colorful salad that is at its peak of flavor in summer when the tomatoes are lush and the herbs are right from the garden.

SERVES 6

¼ cup balsamic vinegar

½ cup plus 1 tablespoon extra-virgin olive oil

1 head iceberg lettuce, trimmed and coarsely chopped

1 large red onion, cut into medium dice

3-4 ounces blue cheese, crumbled

1 cup mixed coarsely chopped fresh herb leaves and/or flowers, such as tarragon, basil, marjoram and/or thyme

2 large ripe tomatoes, cored and cut into medium dice

Kosher salt and freshly ground black pepper

Long chives for garnish

In a small bowl, whisk together vinegar and oil; set aside. In a large mixing bowl, combine lettuce, onion, cheese and herbs. Gently toss to blend. Add tomatoes, vinaigrette and salt and pepper to taste. Toss gently.

Garnish with chives and serve on large, chilled plates.

A Name to Remember

WHO WAS IT, really, who first discovered the botanical or geological aberration that led to a sweet, tearless onion? Some say it was Mose Coleman, a Vidalia farmer, who, back in the 1920s, planted a few onions on his truck farm, only to discover to his horror at harvesttime that the product had no power, no clout, no fire—was instead as sweet as an apple. An onion without character. Who would want it? He bagged them up, so the story goes, and carried them to market. "A sweet onion," he told the shoppers, and they bought, and they enjoyed. And that, according to local legend, is how it started.

In 1945, the late Walter Dasher, a farmer in Glennville, about 30 miles from Vidalia, was raising similar sweet onions. (It turned out that every onion grown in the region was, to one degree or another, sweet and without heat.) Dasher's sons, Gerald and Robert, stayed close, learned the business and transformed their father's little farm into the G & R Farms, a huge operation based primarily on those odd, acid-free sweet onions. Now they grow over 1,000 acres of them, 30 to 40 million pounds, marketing them cooperatively with the other Vidalia growers. They have a big mail-order business, too, using handsomely designed boxes to ship the onions, and they also have controlled-atmosphere storage for 6½ million pounds.

The G & R ranch is in Glennville in Tattnall County. Actually more sweet onions are grown there than in Toombs County, where Vidalia is located. For a long time, the growers in Tattnall County, including the Dashers, marketed under the Glennville name. They had their own association, selected their own onion queen, had their own onion festival.

But in the late 1960s, a new executive with the Piggly Wiggly grocery chain bought some onions at a roadside stand. He was astonished at their sweetness. The Piggly Wiggly started buying the onions and putting them in their stores. The bag said Royal Brand Onions, but it was also marked Vidalia, Georgia. And somehow it was Vidalia that the customers remembered.

The farmers got the Georgia legislature to proclaim that only onions grown in 13 counties and parts of 7 others—all within about 30 miles of Vidalia—could be called Vidalia. It was a brilliant marketing move that became the envy of the entire onion world.

Molded Salad of Vidalias, Cucumbers & Gorgonzola

ONIONS COMBINE WITH CUCUMBERS in this smooth, creamy molded salad made with Gorgonzola cheese. It's marvelous with poultry and ham. With thin slices of pumpernickel bread, it makes a nifty appetizer.

To make scallion brushes: Carefully trim scallions, leaving several inches of the green attached to the bulb. Make a fringe of the bulbs by cutting many close-together thin slices through them. When chilled for several hours in ice water, the fringes curl back into green-handled scallion brushes.

MAKES ABOUT 6 CUPS; SERVES 10 TO 12

2	teaspoons olive oil
½	pound Vidalias or other sweet onions, thinly sliced
1	English cucumber, thinly sliced
½	cup fresh lemon juice
6-7	ounces Gorgonzola cheese, crumbled and at room temperature
2	envelopes unflavored gelatin
3	tablespoons fresh lime juice
2	tablespoons hot water
2	tablespoons minced fresh chives
½	cup low-fat sour cream
	Salt and freshly ground white pepper
¾	cup heavy cream, whipped until stiff
	Tender lettuce, cucumber slices, scallion brushes and herbs for garnishes

Thoroughly coat a 6-cup mold with olive oil; chill until needed.

Combine onions and cucumber in a medium-sized nonaluminum pot and add water to cover. Add ¼ cup lemon juice and bring to a boil over high heat. Boil for 30 seconds; remove the pot from the heat. Let stand for 3 minutes. Drain thoroughly.

Transfer mixture to the bowl of a food processor fitted with the metal blade. Add cheese and process until smooth. Scrape mixture into a large mixing bowl and let stand until cool.

In a small bowl, soften gelatin in lime juice. Stir in hot water. Stir in remaining ¼ cup lemon juice. Add to onion-cheese mixture and blend thoroughly. Fold in chives and sour cream. Season with salt and white pepper to taste. Fold in whipped cream. Spoon mixture into the prepared mold; cover and chill overnight.

Unmold on a bed of lettuce and garnish with cucumber slices, scallion brushes and fresh herbs.

Wine: Trimbach Pinot Blanc or Tokay Pinot Gris (France: Alsace)

Italian Bread Salad

WITH RED ONIONS, TOMATOES & FRESH BASIL

BREAD SALAD, a traditional Tuscan dish, is only as good as the bread and tomatoes you use. In Italy, it is made with a full-flavored, rough-textured peasant bread. Linda has discovered that Onion-Olive Bread (page 179) works wonderfully, but you can also use a toothsome sourdough bread. Be sure to use a bread with a coarse, rough crumb so that it keeps some texture after soaking, draining and marinating. (A delicate white bread will turn to paste.) As far as onions go, use red ones, as the Tuscans do. The tomatoes are key; there is no substitute for fresh vine-ripened tomatoes, so the season for this dish is short.

SERVES 8

¾   pound day-old Onion-Olive Bread (page 179), lightly toasted, torn into ½-inch pieces

1   medium-large (¾-pound) red onion, thinly sliced

3-4   ripe tomatoes, cut into medium dice

⅔   cup loosely packed snipped fresh basil leaves

½   cup loosely packed snipped fresh flat-leaf parsley

¼   cup red-wine vinegar

⅓   cup extra-virgin olive oil

Kosher salt and freshly ground black pepper

Place bread in a large bowl and cover with cold water; let soak for 20 minutes.

Drain bread well, carefully pressing to eliminate all water. Crumble bread into a large bowl. Add onion, tomatoes, basil, parsley and vinegar. Toss gently. Add olive oil and salt and lots of pepper to taste. Toss again. Let stand for 5 to 10 minutes and serve.

Wine: Bonny Doon Vineyard "Vin Gris de Cigare" (California)

Red Onion Sorbet

THIS RECIPE IS INSPIRED by a sorbet we once tasted made by the great French chef André Daguin at his restaurant in Auch. We serve this often following a rich duck dinner. It is also good after lamb.

MAKES ABOUT 4 CUPS

1¼ cups water

¾ cup sugar

1 5-inch branch fresh tarragon

2 cups dry white wine or Champagne (Chef Daguin uses Sauvignon Blanc)

1 tablespoon minced fresh tarragon leaves

⅓ cup minced red onion

Combine water, sugar and tarragon branch in a small nonaluminum saucepan over medium heat. Stir well and bring to a boil. Boil for 30 seconds; remove from heat and cover. Let stand at room temperature until sugar syrup is completely cool. Remove and discard tarragon.

Combine sugar syrup with wine. Freeze in an ice cream maker according to the manufacturer's directions. Just before mixture is frozen, add minced tarragon and onion.

Light Meals

French Toast Sandwiches with Onion, Prosciutto & Cheese . . . 143

White Onion Soufflé with Zucchini Sauce . . . 144

Huevos Rancheros Gratins . . . 146

Omelet of Three Cheeses with Red, White & Green Onion Salsa . . . 148

Scrambled Eggs with Ramps . . . 153

Ramps Gallimaufry Frittata . . . 154

Potato, Asparagus & Red Pepper Frittata . . . 155

Yellow Grits with Sausage, Green Chiles & Red Onions con Queso . . . 157

Creamy Onion Polenta . . . 159

Red Onion & Spinach Risotto . . . 160

Risotto of Leeks, Zucchini & Chard . . . 161

Leek Tart (Flamiche) . . . 162

Onion & Gouda Tart with Sun-Dried Tomatoes . . . 167

Alsatian Onion Quiche . . . 168

Flammekueche (Thin Alsatian Tart) . . . 170

Tracy's Breakfast Quiche of Scallions, Ham & Cheese . . . 171

Onion & Cheese Quesadillas with Red Onion & Black Bean Salad . . . 172

French Toast Sandwiches

WITH ONION, PROSCIUTTO & CHEESE

THE INSIDE of this lightly battered and fried "ham and cheese with onion" is creamy and yummy, with just a touch of heat from the onion. You can make this with any onion and any toothsome bread. We like to use red onion and Weller Family Bread (page 175) or Vidalia onions and Egg Bread with Vidalia Onions & Cheddar (page 178). The sandwich is good made with Saga, Fontina, Port Salut or Muenster.

SERVES 4

3	large eggs
1	cup milk
8-10	ounces tasty semisoft cheese, cut into ⅛-inch-thick slices
4	thin slices large red onion
4	large, thin slices prosciutto (2-4 ounces)
8	slices homemade bread, each cut ¼ inch thick
4	tablespoons (½ stick) unsalted butter or margarine

Beat eggs and milk together in a shallow soup plate. Set aside.

Place 1 slice cheese, 1 slice onion and 1 slice prosciutto on each of 4 slices of bread. Top each with remaining sliced cheese and finally with another slice of bread. Carefully dip sandwiches into egg mixture and soak bread well.

Heat 2 tablespoons of the butter or margarine in a large nonstick skillet over medium heat. When the skillet is hot, add 2 sandwiches. Reduce the heat to low and fry until bottoms brown, about 5 minutes. Carefully turn with a spatula and fry the other side until browned, about 5 minutes.

Keep these warm while you repeat with remaining sandwiches.

Wine: De Loach Vineyards White Zinfandel (California: Sonoma County)

White Onion Soufflé with Zucchini Sauce

ONCE YOU'VE MADE a successful soufflé, you'll make them often. This scrumptious combination makes a terrific supper for four or an appetizer for six. We like to use Loomis Cheese, a Welsh-style Cheshire cheese, made in Ann Arbor, Michigan (see Special Products, page 374). It has a pleasant tartness that works well with white onions. But this soufflé is also excellent with a good, sharp Cheddar. It is served with a simple, colorful and tasty zucchini sauce.

SERVES 4

Soufflé

7½	tablespoons unsalted butter
2	tablespoons freshly grated Parmesan cheese
2½	cups finely diced white onions
1⅔	cups milk
¼	cup plus 1 tablespoon unbleached flour
2	teaspoons dry mustard
5	large egg yolks, beaten
½	teaspoon kosher salt
½	teaspoon freshly ground white pepper
¼	pound Cheshire cheese or sharp Cheddar cheese, shredded (about 1 cup)
2	tablespoons minced fresh chives
6	large egg whites

Sauce

4	cups grated unpeeled zucchini
1	cup chicken stock
2	tablespoons heavy cream
½	teaspoon kosher salt
½	teaspoon freshly ground white pepper
	Pinch cayenne
2	teaspoons minced fresh tarragon leaves

To make soufflé: Prepare a 2-quart soufflé dish. Butter well with 1 tablespoon of butter; dust evenly with Parmesan. Butter a foil "collar" and tie it around the soufflé dish so that the top extends 2 inches above the rim of the dish.

Place an oven rack in the middle of the oven and preheat oven to 400 degrees F.

In a heavy saucepan, melt 1½ tablespoons butter over low heat. Add onions, and cook over very low heat, stirring from time to time, until onions are tender, about 10 minutes. If liquid collects in the saucepan, continue to cook until liquid evaporates, about 3 to 5 minutes. Do not let onions burn. Set aside.

Scald milk and set aside. Melt remaining 5 tablespoons butter in a heavy nonaluminum saucepan over medium-low heat. Whisk in flour and mustard, blending well; slowly whisk in scalded milk until a very thick béchamel sauce is made. Reduce the heat to low and cook, whisking constantly, for 2 minutes to cook flour. Remove sauce from the heat and slowly whisk a little hot milk mixture into beaten egg yolks until yolks are thoroughly heated. Whisk beaten yolks back into milk mixture; add salt, pepper and all but 1 tablespoon of shredded cheese, stirring constantly over very low heat until cheese melts. Add onion mixture and chives, blend well; remove from the heat and set aside.

Beat egg whites with a pinch of salt just until they hold stiff peaks. Stir ¼ of egg whites into cheese mixture to lighten it; gently fold in remaining egg whites. Spoon into the prepared soufflé dish and sprinkle with reserved 1 tablespoon cheese.

Place soufflé on the middle rack of the preheated oven. Reduce the oven temperature to 375 degrees.

Bake soufflé for 40 minutes, or until nicely browned, firmly set, yet slightly creamy in center.

To make sauce: While soufflé is baking, combine zucchini and stock in a small saucepan. Cover and cook over medium heat until zucchini is very tender, about 15 minutes. Puree mixture in a food processor fitted with the metal blade. Add cream, salt, pepper and cayenne and pulse to combine. Return mixture to the saucepan and cook briskly over medium-high heat until mixture thickens, about 10 minutes. Stir in tarragon.

Heat 4 serving plates. Just before serving, spoon a generous portion of sauce on the surface of each heated plate. Place a portion of soufflé on top of sauce and serve.

Wine: Paul Cotat Chavignol Sancerre "La Grande Côte" (France: Loire)

Huevos Rancheros Gratins

IN MEXICAN CUISINE, "rancheros" means something served with a rustic, spicy sauce that features tomatoes, onions and chiles. These rancheros-style eggs baked in sauce make a super brunch dish. Use plump white onion bulbs that still have their quills—the ones that look like very fat scallions, such as baby Vidalias—or you can use any type of onion or even some leeks. For added indulgence, serve these with Yellow Grits with Sausage, Green Chiles & Red Onions (page 157).

SERVES 6 TO 8

4	tablespoons vegetable oil
⅔	cup finely diced fresh white onion, trimmed to include 1 inch of green
⅓	cup finely chopped celery
2	plump garlic cloves, minced
2	teaspoons medium-hot chile powder or other chili powder
1	teaspoon dried oregano
½	teaspoon ground cumin
6	cups canned crushed tomatoes
3	scallions, including tender green, thinly sliced
1	pickled jalapeño pepper, chopped
1	tablespoon fresh lime juice
½	teaspoon Tabasco sauce
¼	cup chopped fresh flat-leaf parsley leaves
¼	cup chopped fresh cilantro leaves
	Kosher salt and freshly ground black pepper
6-8	corn tortillas
6-8	large eggs
1	cup shredded jalapeño Jack cheese (¼ pound)
	Chopped fresh chives, cilantro and parsley for garnish

Thoroughly butter 6 to 8 individual gratin dishes or one 13-x-9-inch baking dish. Cut a piece of foil to cover each dish. (If using a 13-x-9-inch baking dish, butter the dish thoroughly and cut 1 large sheet of foil to cover the dish securely.)

Heat 2 tablespoons oil in a large nonaluminum saucepan over medium heat. Add onion, celery and garlic and sauté until onions are translucent but not brown, about 5 to 7 minutes. Stir in chile powder, oregano and cumin and sauté for 1 minute to release the flavors. Add tomatoes, scallions, jalapeño, lime juice and Tabasco. Reduce heat to low and cook, stirring occasionally, for 30 minutes. Stir in parsley, cilantro and salt and pepper to taste. Keep sauce hot. Meanwhile, preheat oven to 375 degrees F.

Heat remaining 2 tablespoons oil in a large skillet over heat. Quickly fry each tortilla for about 5 seconds per side; drain well. Place a tortilla in each gratin dish. (If using a 13-x-9-inch baking dish, cover the bottom thoroughly with tortillas, overlapping as needed.) Divide hot tomato mixture among the prepared dishes or among tortillas, if using a baking dish, and make a slight indentation in each mound of sauce for egg. Break 1 egg into each indentation. Cover the dishes with foil and bake for 12 minutes.

Remove the foil, distribute cheese evenly over each and bake, uncovered, for 1 to 2 more minutes, depending upon how soft you like your eggs. Sprinkle with fresh herbs and serve at once.

**Wine: Roederer Estate Sparkling Wine
(California: Mendocino)**

Rick Bayless, chef-owner of Topolobampo, Frontera Grill and Zinfandel restaurants in Chicago, uses lots of onions in his Mexican food "to add crunchy vibrancy when raw, to add slow-cooked sweetness and depth when browned." His favorite onion is the white: "It has a crisp, clean taste. If carefully chopped, then quickly rinsed in cold water, it adds a sharp fresh crunch to salads and guacamole without the ugly lingering 'oniony' taste. Because the juices of cut onions sour so quickly and because machines always create/extract so much juice, I always chop onions by hand." But he allows that onions sliced in a food processor, then cooked immediately, are passable to him. As for the tears, "Work in a well-ventilated place."

Omelet of Three Cheeses

WITH RED, WHITE & GREEN ONION SALSA

THIS IS SUCH A GOOD SALSA that we often serve it as an appetizer on its own, with tortilla chips, but it's also a fine counterpoint to a very cheesy omelet. We struggled for years to make a light, delicate omelet—one that is just barely runny. It's important to have a well-seasoned omelet pan, one that you use only for that purpose, or one that is nonstick. The bottom of ours is 7 inches in diameter with sides that slope out to about 10 inches. Once you are comfortable with the process, you can make a good omelet in less than a minute. Experiment with a variety of cheeses.

SERVES 2

Salsa

¼ cup finely diced red onion

¼ cup finely diced white onion

¼ cup finely chopped scallions, including 1 inch of green

1 medium-sized tomato, finely diced

1 tablespoon minced pickled jalapeño pepper
Juice of 1 lime

1 tablespoon minced fresh cilantro
Kosher salt and freshly ground black pepper

Omelet

2 rounded tablespoons shredded jalapeño Jack cheese

2 rounded tablespoons freshly grated Parmesan cheese

2 rounded tablespoons fresh chèvre (goat cheese), crumbled

4 large eggs

4 teaspoons water
About 2 tablespoons unsalted butter

To make salsa: In a small bowl, mix together both onions, scallions, tomato, jalapeño, lime juice and cilantro. Season with salt and pepper to taste. Set aside.

To make omelet: In a bowl, combine cheeses.

In a small bowl, beat 2 eggs with 2 teaspoons water and salt and pepper to taste. In another small bowl, beat remaining 2 eggs and 2 teaspoons water with salt and pepper to taste. Place cheese and egg mixtures near the stove.

Warm 2 serving plates.

Heat a well-seasoned omelet pan over medium-high heat. Add ½ to 1 tablespoon butter and swirl the skillet to coat the sides and bottom with melted butter. Quickly pour in egg mixture from one bowl, and with one hand, rapidly shake the skillet over the heat. Once bottom begins to set, sprinkle egg with ½ of cheese mixture and rapidly jerk the skillet toward you until omelet begins to roll over on itself. Tilt the skillet with one hand, while using the fork with your other hand to roll omelet over once more. Tilt it out on a heated plate.

Repeat with remaining butter, egg mixture and cheese to make a second omelet. Using a slotted spoon, garnish omelets with onion salsa and serve.

Wine: Sanford Winery Sauvignon Blanc (California: Santa Barbara)

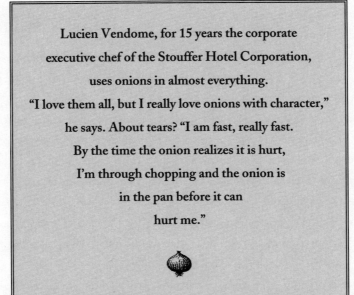

Lucien Vendome, for 15 years the corporate executive chef of the Stouffer Hotel Corporation, uses onions in almost everything. "I love them all, but I really love onions with character," he says. About tears? "I am fast, really fast. By the time the onion realizes it is hurt, I'm through chopping and the onion is in the pan before it can hurt me."

The Feast of the Ramson

ALLIUM TRICOCCUM, the ramp or wild leek, grows all over the hills of Appalachia and from New England to the Carolinas, appearing like a crocus out of the spring snow. In mid-April every year, the people of Richwood, West Virginia, celebrate the Feast of the Ramson, to mark the return of spring. Sometimes snow lingers in the hollows as the foragers tramp over the hillsides searching for this most pungent of alliums. The season isn't a very long one. The ramps spring up, grab the sun until the trees grow leaves and shade them, and then, if they are not eaten, they die back, and the bulbs remain dormant until the next spring.

The celebration features an arts-and-crafts show, a weekend of folk music, a parade that includes the high school band and some antique cars, and of course, a day-long feast highlighting ramps—every dish but the apple pie has ramps in it.

The town of Richwood, located about 75 miles east of Charleston, got its name in an era when timbering flourished and hundreds of families earned their daily bread by working in the sawmills, paper mills and clothespin and handle factories.

Jim Comstock, an old-time Richwood newspaperman, was active in starting the festival, writing often about the ramps and helping to create their mystique. Indeed, he once drew national attention to the ramp when he mixed ramp juice into the printer's ink at his newspaper and printed an edition of *The Hillbilly* that was sent through the mails to expatriate West Virginians all across the nation. They say that the aroma of ramps lingered in post offices for days. And it was said that the Post Office got an injunction to prohibit West Virginians from ever trying that trick again. (Comstock once cautioned us to be careful in handling ramps on television since they are the only known substance whose aroma can be broadcast.)

We arrived in Richwood on the eve of the feast, our tickets to the event already in hand, ordered by mail a month earlier. Eight dollars each, for all you could eat. Those tickets would give us an advantage the next morning; we would not have to wait in the long line to get into the high school gym, where the feast was held.

(continued on page 152)

RAMPS

(continued from page 150)

When we sought out dinner that night, our quest took us to Gale's Restaurant, a Richwood spot popular for the past 35 years.

"Any ramps?" we asked the proprietor.

"I won't allow them in here," he said with a laugh. "Once you do, your carpet and drapes smell like ramps 'til Christmas." But the next day at the feast, there he was, and his wife, too, working with the ramps on the serving line.

In fact, dozens of volunteers toil to put the event together. Perhaps the major chore is cleaning 2,500 pounds of freshly picked ramps—about 75 garbage bags full.

The ramp feast that causes so much fuss is the same every year. There is ham and bacon, both crisply fried. The fat rendered from the pork is used to fry the potatoes, with ramps chopped into them. The pinto beans are soaked all night and cooked for half of the day with ham bones and ramps and served like a rich soup. Other ramps are boiled briefly or steamed and served as a side dish with salt and pepper. Some festival-goers prefer their ramps sautéed in bacon fat or butter and anointed at the table with a little vinegar. And there are always raw ramps on the tables as a garnish. The bread of choice is inevitably old-fashioned corn bread, cut into chunks as big as a brick. The old-timers like to drink sassafras tea with such a dinner.

So everyone has some ramps, which makes them immune to the aroma, and outside, they buy a peck to take home, ensuring that when they try to trade in their pickup, the salesman will ask, "What's that funny smell?"

Chicago is said to have gotten its name from the
Chippewa word for the wild onions growing around Lake Michigan.
Wrong, says John Swenson, student of the onions.
There was a fraudulent translation from the French.
"She-gau-gawnish" is really the word for the wild leek, the ramp.

Scrambled Eggs with Ramps

LEGENDS ABOUND concerning the strong smell and flavor of West Virginia's ramps. We bought a half bushel of them at the Feast of the Ramson in Richwood, West Virginia. Worried about ruining our fine car, we wrapped our fragrant treasures in three layers of garbage bags. The ramps made it to Cleveland in perfect shape—and so did the car. We had ramps for days. While the traditional West Virginia method for cooking ramps is to boil them and fry them in bacon fat, we find that they look better and taste better without the boiling. This dish is really simple and absolutely delicious.

Ramps clean easily, by the way, if you soak them a bit in cold water, slice off the very end at the roots, and carefully slip off the outer layer of skin. After all of the ramps are cleaned this way, soak them again in clean water to get rid of any soil at the base of the leaves. Dry them with paper towels, put them into plastic bags, seal the bags, and store in the refrigerator. If they were fresh to begin with, they'll keep for several weeks.

SERVES 2

⅓   pound thick-sliced bacon, preferably smoked

½–⅔   pound cleaned ramps, leaves attached (about 1 pound dirty)

2-3   teaspoons cider vinegar
     Kosher salt and freshly ground black pepper

4   large eggs, lightly beaten

In a large cast-iron skillet, slowly cook bacon until very crisp. Remove bacon, drain on paper towels and crumble into a small bowl; reserve. Add ramps to bacon fat in the skillet and sauté over medium heat, turning often with tongs, until bulbs are tender, about 5 minutes.

Quickly remove ramps from the skillet with tongs and remove the skillet from the heat. Place ½ of the ramps in a salad bowl, chop the remaining half on a cutting board and set aside. Dress whole ramps with vinegar and salt and pepper to taste.

Pour off all but 1 tablespoon bacon fat. Reheat the skillet over medium-high heat until hot. Add eggs, chopped ramps and bacon. Scramble until done. Season with salt and pepper. Serve on heated plates with ramp salad on the side.

Ramps Gallimaufry Frittata

A GALLIMAUFRY IS A HASH or hodgepodge. This frittata grew out of a bunch of delicious leftovers in our refrigerator. "Waste not, want not," Fred always says. It was a few days after the Ramps Festival; we had made only a small dent in our half bushel of ramps. We had leftover Roasted Red Potato Salad with Red Onions, Herbs & Bacon (page 136) in the refrigerator, as well as a nice piece of Wigwam ham (see Special Products, page 374).

SERVES 3 TO 4

6   large eggs, beaten
    Kosher salt and freshly ground black pepper
2   tablespoons vegetable oil
1   tablespoon minced ham fat or minced bacon
⅔   cup julienne strips of aged smoked ham or prosciutto
12 clean ramps, trimmed to include 3 inches of green, diced (scallions can be substituted)
1   tablespoon olive oil
2   cups leftover Roasted Red Potato Salad (page 136) or leftover hash browns, coarsely chopped
1   tablespoon butter

Preheat the broiler.

In a small bowl, thoroughly whisk together eggs and salt and pepper to taste.

In a 9-to-10-inch cast-iron or other ovenproof skillet, combine vegetable oil and ham fat or bacon, and cook over medium heat until fat begins to darken. Add ham or prosciutto strips and ramps and sauté over medium-low heat until ramps begin to soften, about 5 minutes. Add olive oil, stirring until hot. Add potato salad or hash browns and sauté, 4 to 5 minutes more, until mixture browns.

Add butter and stir until melted. Distribute mixture evenly over the pan. Pour in eggs, reduce heat to low and cook, without stirring, until bottom of egg is set and only surface is wet, about 5 minutes. Place the skillet under the hot broiler and broil until surface of frittata sets. Turn frittata out onto a heated platter and cut into wedges.

**Wine: Havens Sauvignon Blanc
(California: Napa Valley)**

Potato, Asparagus & Red Pepper Frittata

A FRITTATA IS THE substantial Italian cousin to an omelet. Generally, the eggs and fillings are cooked together, often begun on the stovetop and finished in the oven or under the broiler. The frittata is served flat, usually cut into wedges. This one is not particularly eggy, with potatoes that are fried until crisp on both sides and then topped with a stew of onions and peppers. After the cheesy eggs are added, the frittata is baked in the oven. You might want to serve it with Fresh Tomato-Onion Sauce (page 84). Add some bread and a salad for a hearty supper.

SERVES 4 TO 6

9   large eggs
⅓   cup freshly grated Parmesan cheese
4   fresh basil leaves, julienned
1-2 teaspoons minced fresh oregano or
     1-1½ teaspoons dried
     Kosher salt and freshly ground black pepper
6   asparagus spears
5   tablespoons olive oil
1   large (1 pound) white onion, thinly sliced
1   plump garlic clove, minced
1   large red bell pepper, cut into medium dice
4   tablespoons (½ stick) unsalted butter

1½   pounds Yukon Gold or red-skinned
     potatoes, thinly sliced
2   tablespoons minced fresh chives

In a small mixing bowl, beat together eggs, cheese, basil and oregano. Season with salt and pepper to taste; set aside.

Cook asparagus in boiling water until tender but still firm, 3 to 4 minutes; dice and set aside.

In a medium skillet, heat 3 tablespoons olive oil over medium heat. Add onion, reduce heat to low, cover, and cook until quite wilted, about 10 minutes. Remove cover, increase heat to medium and add garlic. Cook, stirring constantly, until mixture is golden, about 5 minutes. Add bell peppers and cook, stirring, over medium heat, until peppers are slightly tender, about 5 minutes. Remove mixture from the skillet with a slotted spoon and combine with asparagus in a medium bowl. Season with salt and pepper.

Preheat oven to 350 degrees F.

In an 11-to-12-inch cast-iron or other ovenproof skillet, combine remaining 2 tablespoons olive oil with 3 tablespoons butter over medium heat. When hot, add sliced potatoes in even, overlapping layers. Reduce heat to medium-low and sprinkle potatoes with salt and pepper. Cover and cook until potatoes are golden on the bottom, 15 to 20 minutes. With a large spatula, carefully turn potatoes over in the pan so browned ones are on top, adding remaining 1 tablespoon butter. Increase the heat to medium and cook for 5 minutes over medium heat.

Scatter onion-asparagus mixture over potatoes and pour eggs over top. Place the skillet in the hot oven and bake until set, about 15 minutes.

Invert frittata onto a heated serving platter, sprinkle with chives, cut into wedges and serve.

Wine: Mazzocco Vineyards Zinfandel (California: Sonoma County, Dry Creek)

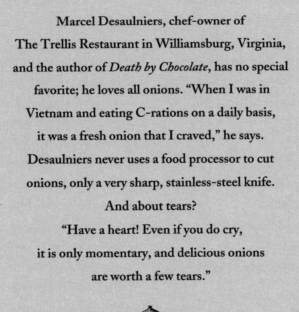

Marcel Desaulniers, chef-owner of
The Trellis Restaurant in Williamsburg, Virginia,
and the author of *Death by Chocolate*, has no special
favorite; he loves all onions. "When I was in
Vietnam and eating C-rations on a daily basis,
it was a fresh onion that I craved," he says.
Desaulniers never uses a food processor to cut
onions, only a very sharp, stainless-steel knife.
And about tears?
"Have a heart! Even if you do cry,
it is only momentary, and delicious onions
are worth a few tears."

Yellow Grits

WITH SAUSAGE, GREEN CHILES & RED ONIONS

THIS CASSEROLE made of grits and Cheddar has a layer of onions, sausage and chiles in the middle. While folks in the South tout the glories of white grits, here in the Midwest, thanks to our friends at Fowler's Mill in Chardon, Ohio, we get fresh and flavorful stone-ground yellow grits. But if you prefer, use white. We like the smoked Virginia sausages from S. Wallace Edwards and Sons (see Special Products, page 374), but you can use chorizo or even hot Italian sausage.

SERVES 6 TO 8

2 tablespoons freshly grated Parmesan cheese
4 cups (1 quart) chicken stock
1 teaspoon kosher salt
1 cup yellow or white stone-ground grits
1 cup shredded sharp Cheddar cheese (¼ pound)
1 tablespoon minced fresh cilantro leaves
½ teaspoon Tabasco sauce
⅓ cup evaporated milk
  Freshly ground black pepper
2 tablespoons vegetable oil
1 pound spicy sausage, cut into ¾-inch slices
½ cup minced red onions
4 ounces canned mild green chiles, julienned
½ cup shredded jalapeño Jack cheese (2 ounces)

Thoroughly butter a 1½-quart casserole. Add Parmesan and toss well to coat.

Combine chicken stock and salt in a heavy-bottomed saucepan and bring to a boil. Very slowly stir in grits and cook, stirring, over medium-low heat until mixture begins to boil. Cover and reduce heat to very low. Cook, stirring from time to time, for 10 to 12 minutes, or until liquid is almost completely absorbed. Remove cover and stir grits thoroughly, being certain to scrape the bottom and sides of the pot. Cook for 3 minutes more, or until mixture is very thick. Remove from the heat and stir in Cheddar, cilantro and Tabasco until cheese is evenly blended. Beat in evaporated milk and pepper to taste. Set aside.

In a heavy skillet over medium-high heat, heat 1 tablespoon oil until hot. Add sausage and fry until nicely browned on all sides, about 4 to 6 minutes, adding more oil if necessary. Add onions and chiles and cook over low heat, stirring often, until chiles are tender, about 5 minutes. Tilt the skillet to separate fat from sausage mixture, and scoop sausage mixture into a small bowl.

Spoon ½ of grits mixture into the casserole and spread evenly. Add sausage mixture; cover with remaining grits. Chill for at least 2 hours or overnight.

Preheat oven to 375 degrees F.

Sprinkle casserole with shredded Jack cheese. Bake in the preheated oven for 40 minutes, or until golden brown.

**Wine: Sanford Winery Vin Gris
(California: Santa Barbara)**

Creamy Onion Polenta

POLENTA IS ONE OF those hearty, heavenly dishes that warms the soul, especially in winter. We make it the old-fashioned way, stirring, stirring, stirring. While it is traditionally made with water, we prefer to use chicken stock. Onions and shallots add another nice fillip. For a special supper, make sautéed chicken livers and onions (See Farfallette with Chicken Livers & Onions, page 201) for a sauce. Any polenta leftovers can be cooled, wrapped as a block, chilled, sliced and fried in olive oil.

SERVES 4

6   cups (1½ quarts) chicken stock
1   cup minced yellow onions
2   shallots, minced
2   cups medium-ground yellow cornmeal
    Kosher salt and freshly ground black pepper
2   tablespoons unsalted butter
    About 1 cup freshly grated Parmesan cheese
2   tablespoons minced fresh chives

In a large, heavy-bottomed saucepan, bring stock to a boil. Add onions and shallots. Very gradually add cornmeal (you can pour it through a sieve), whisking constantly, to incorporate it evenly into stock. Whisk vigorously to eliminate all lumps. Reduce the heat to very low and stir with a wooden spoon, scraping bottom and sides very thoroughly, until polenta pulls away from the sides of the pan when you stir and is the consistency of thick oatmeal, 30 to 45 minutes. Season with salt and pepper to taste.

If you are not quite ready to serve, you can keep polenta warm, covered in a double boiler, for a short while. You may need to thin it with more stock just before serving.

To serve, stir in butter and ⅓ cup cheese. Spoon into warmed soup plates. Divide remaining ⅔ cup cheese among portions, sprinkling it over the tops. Sprinkle with minced chives and serve.

Wine: Le Sang des Cailloux Vacqueyras (France: Rhône)

Red Onion & Spinach Risotto

THERE IS NO SHORTCUT to making good risotto. You must cook it over low heat and stir most of the time. We love this combination; even though the red onion doesn't stay very colorful in this dish, we like it with the spinach. We serve risotto as a course by itself and like to follow it with a roasted chicken and a simple vegetable. Arborio rice, a short-grain Italian rice that is ideally suited for risotto, can be found in Italian grocery stores and many supermarkets.

SERVES 6 TO 8

5	cups chicken stock
3	tablespoons butter
2	tablespoons olive oil
¼	cup finely diced shallots
1	plump garlic clove, minced
¾	cup red onion, coarsely diced
2	cups Arborio rice
½	pound trimmed spinach leaves, well washed
½	cup freshly grated Parmesan cheese
	Pinch freshly grated nutmeg
	Kosher salt and freshly ground white pepper

Put stock in a small saucepan and bring to a boil; reduce heat and keep hot.

In a heavy-bottomed nonaluminum pot over medium-low heat, combine 2 tablespoons of butter and olive oil. When butter melts, add shallots and garlic and sauté until shallots are translucent, 1 to 2 minutes. Add onion and rice and sauté, stirring often, until rice is well-coated with oil, about 3 minutes.

Begin adding hot stock to rice, a ladleful at a time, stirring constantly and scraping bottom and sides. Keep heat at medium to medium-low. As liquid is absorbed, add another ladleful of stock. Add spinach after the third ladleful and keep stirring. Resume adding stock; this process will take 20 to 25 minutes. When rice is quite creamy and firm to the bite, stir in remaining 1 tablespoon butter, cheese, nutmeg and salt and pepper to taste. Stir thoroughly and serve.

Wine: Calera Wine Company Chardonnay "Central Coast" (California: Central Coast)

Risotto of Leeks, Zucchini & Chard

LEEKS AND CHARD COMPLEMENT one another quite nicely in this stirred-rice preparation.

SERVES 6 TO 8

5   cups chicken stock
3   tablespoons butter
2   tablespoons olive oil
¾   cup chopped leeks, white parts only
1   plump garlic clove, minced
2   cups Arborio rice (see previous page)
2   small zucchini, diced
6   ounces Swiss chard, thick veins discarded, coarsely chopped (1½-2 cups)
½   cup freshly grated Parmesan cheese
    Pinch freshly grated nutmeg
    Kosher salt and freshly ground black pepper

In a small saucepan, bring stock to a boil; reduce heat and keep hot.

In a heavy-bottomed nonaluminum pot over medium-low heat, combine 2 tablespoons butter and olive oil. When butter melts, add leeks and garlic and sauté until leeks are tender, about 5 minutes. Add rice and zucchini and stir over medium heat until rice is well coated with oil, about 3 minutes.

Begin adding hot stock to rice, a ladleful at a time, stirring constantly and scraping bottom and sides. Keep heat at medium to medium-low. As liquid is absorbed, add another ladleful of stock. Add chard after the third ladleful and keep stirring. Resume adding stock; this process will take 20 to 25 minutes. When the rice is quite creamy and firm to the bite, stir in remaining 1 tablespoon butter, cheese, nutmeg and salt and pepper to taste. Stir thoroughly and serve.

Wine: Acacia Winery "Marina Vineyard" Chardonnay (California: Napa Valley, Carneros)

Leek Tart
(Flamiche)

TENDER, MELLOW LEEKS, slowly cooked in butter, are the filling for this simple quiche. French in origin, the *flamiche* has been made in a variety of ways over the centuries. This pastry recipe makes enough for a 12-inch tart shell, so if you have leftovers, make some miniature shells and fill them with berries and ice cream—or freeze them for later use.

MAKES AN 11-INCH TART; SERVES 10 TO 12

Pastry Shell

1⅓	cups unbleached flour
¼	teaspoon kosher salt
½	cup (1 stick) cold unsalted butter, cut into pieces
3-4	tablespoons ice water

Filling

¼	cup (½ stick) unsalted butter
2½	pounds leeks, trimmed to include tender greens, cleaned and thinly sliced
3	large whole eggs
1	large egg yolk
1½	cups heavy cream
½	cup milk

Generous pinch freshly grated nutmeg
Kosher salt and freshly ground white pepper

1	egg yolk, beaten with 1 teaspoon water, for egg wash

To make pastry shell: Combine flour and salt in a shallow bowl. Using a pastry blender or your fingers, quickly cut butter into flour until mixture is the texture of cornmeal. Sprinkle evenly with 3 tablespoons ice water. Using a fork, gather mixture together into a ball, adding a little more ice water, if necessary.

Place pastry ball on a lightly floured work surface. Using the heel of your hand, quickly push away small amounts of dough across the work surface until all dough has been worked. With the help of a pastry scraper, gather dough together. If it seems to need more blending, repeat the process one more time. Form dough into a disk about 4 inches in diameter, wrap in wax paper, and chill for at least 20 minutes.

Lightly flour a work surface and rolling pin. Roll out pastry into a 13-to-14-inch circle and carefully fit it into an 11-inch tart pan with a removable bottom. Trim edges to 1 inch above the top of the rim. Fold overhanging edge back to form a firm ½-inch rim above the edge of the pan. Prick bottom and sides of pastry with a fork. Chill shell for at least 30 minutes.

Preheat oven to 400 degrees F. Line pastry shell with foil and fill with pie weights or raw rice. Bake for 15 minutes. Remove weights and foil, and bake for 10 minutes. Take shell from the oven and place on a rack to cool.

To make filling: Melt butter in a large nonstick skillet over medium heat. Stir in leeks and cover with a tight-fitting lid. Reduce heat to very low and sweat leeks until very tender, about 20 minutes. Using a slotted spoon, remove leeks from the skillet to a large plate and cool.

While leeks are cooking, place eggs and egg yolk in a large mixing bowl and beat thoroughly. Gradually whisk in cream and milk. Season with nutmeg and salt and white pepper to taste. Let filling rest for 30 minutes.

Preheat oven to 400 degrees F. Lightly brush sides of shell with egg wash. Fill shell with cooked leeks and pour on filling. Bake for 30 to 35 minutes, or until top is puffed and browned and filling is set. Let cool on a rack for a few minutes before serving hot or at room temperature.

**Wine: Girard Winery Chardonnay
(California: Napa Valley)**

THE ONIONS OF CELERYVILLE

CHARLES HANLINE welcomed us to his little office. We had driven down to Celeryville to see Stambaugh Farms, Ohio's biggest onion farm. Hanline spotted the small green-backed book we were carrying from across the table.

"Is that Donald Comin's book?" he asked. In fact, it was. We had borrowed *Onion Production* from the Cleveland Public Library. Published in 1946, it was the standard text for a generation of farmers. The last time it had been taken out was March 8, 1947. (Who grows onions in the city?)

It turned out that Hanline and Comin had worked together for years. They were involved in the development of a spectacular patch of central Ohio—3,000 acres of what they call muck—a peat bog, rich in organic matter. "Comin," said Hanline, "had a creative understanding of the muckland's potential and helped develop ways to maintain it. He had a lot to do with how good this land is today."

Hanline, who is president of Stambaugh Farms, began working on the farm as a college student in the 1930s. After the war, he went to work as a civil engineer for the Standard Oil Company in Cleveland, but in 1946, John Stambaugh, the owner, summoned the young man and sold him on the idea of using his engineering skills to improve the farm. The chance to return to this rich area seemed challenging and appealing, so Hanline took the opportunity. Now he raises mainly storage onions—457 acres of them—plus some potatoes, and in his nonmuck fields, tomatoes.

While his onions are growing, his son, Chuck Hanline, keeps the packing shed and the workers busy by bringing in bulk quantities of Texas, New Mexico and Arizona sweet onions and packaging and distributing them to East Coast customers.

Hanline shakes his head in wonder at the mention of Vidalia. "They are marketing wizards," he says. "While that cultivar might be $6.50 a bag in Texas, at the same time they'll be selling the same bag of onions in Vidalia at $22.50."

Hanline believes it's the water that makes a mild onion. A sweet onion has thick rings and is much higher in water content, which dilutes the onion's heat. Hanline asked his son to bring us some of the sweets that were being repackaged. Chuck returned with a 1015Y, the Texas sweet, and Hanline cut into it with a pocket knife. Crisp, juicy, with lots of sugar, it had enough heat so you knew it was an onion. Then Hanline cut into an Arizona, a Y33. It was equally crisp, but with a bite that had a longer reverberation. "Arizona," Hanline said, waving his knife for emphasis, "is the best-kept secret in the onion industry." We washed them down with Diet 7-Up.

"Try to help the general public understand the benefits of onions," said the onion man. "They'll keep your cholesterol in check. And remember what Grant said: 'I won't move my army until I get my onions.'"

The Hanlines plant mainly Spartan Banner and Spartan Banner 80 onions, sowing the seeds by March 25. They are long-day yellow storage onions, which do not have to be transplanted, as many southern varieties do. The harvest begins in late summer and concludes in the early fall. The onions Hanline raises provide a high yield, can be mechanically harvested and can be stored in 8-foot-high piles without being harmed. Not too pungent, the onions have single centers, making them attractive for the onion-ring trade. The Hanlines also raise some Norstars, a fast-growing Japanese cultivar that they plant close together to make a smaller bulb, and a new cultivar called Hustler, another fast-growing storage onion. In 1992 the Hanlines raised and packed 386,000 fifty-pound bags of onions.

On a hot day in mid-August, we went back for the harvest. At this latitude in northern Ohio, after their March planting, the juvenile storage onions march smartly through their youth, impervious to peril. Then, assuming there has been the right amount of heat, the long days of summer signal that it is time for the onions to form bulbs. If it has been too cool, some may invest their energy in forming a seed stalk instead, but most will bulb. And one day in mid-August, the tops of an entire field will collapse almost simultaneously. As they fall, the right angle the stalks form seals off the neck, and the onions are allowed to dry there for two or three weeks, remaining undisturbed in the soil until the machines come for them.

"It's very important," says Hanline, "that the tops be completely dry. Otherwise botrytis [a common mold] will invade the bulb and ruin it."

On this morning, the workers at Stambaugh farms had started, as they usually do, at about 10 o'-clock, late enough for the dew to have evaporated; the less moisture the better, for it is better to put a dry onion in the drying shed than a wet one.

(continued on page 166)

(continued from page 165)

One crew of workers was gathering the early Norstars. Another crew was harvesting the test patch of Hustlers. The Spartan Banners were growing strongly, still days away from their harvest.

The machines, with their big rubber paddles, scooped the onions onto the conveyor belts, which transported them to giant, tractor-drawn wagons. In Georgia, the sweet Vidalias are harvested by hand, one at a time, their green tops lopped off by the workers as they put them in bags or baskets. But these tougher, long-day storage onions can be machine-handled and shed their dry tops in the process. At the storage shed, the onions are piled high on wooden pallets. Big fans drive dry air into the pallet slats and through the onions, until they are cured enough for packing.

After two or three weeks in the shed, the bagging begins, and off the onions go to market. They will keep through the winter and well into spring. Most of the storage onions on Stambaugh Farms are yellows, and they are always packed in red-mesh bags.

"No accident," said Charles Hanline. "The red bags make those yellow onions look good. The white onions—they'll be put in a blue-mesh bag. It brightens their whiteness. We want our onions to look pretty."

Onion & Gouda Tart with Sun-Dried Tomatoes

GOUDA, a mild, buttery cheese, is excellent in combination with onions. Serve this dish with a big salad for a nice supper meal or as a tasty brunch.

MAKES AN 11-INCH TART; SERVES 10 TO 12

Pastry for tart shell (see Leek Tart, page 162)
1   egg white, lightly beaten

Filling

2   tablespoons butter
1½ pounds yellow onions, thinly sliced
1   tablespoon minced fresh tarragon leaves or 1½ teaspoons dried
1   teaspoon minced fresh thyme leaves or ½ teaspoon dried
4   sun-dried tomatoes, softened in boiling water, drained and minced, or 4 oil-packed sun-dried tomatoes, drained and minced
4   large eggs, beaten
1   large egg yolk, beaten
1½ cups milk
1   cup heavy cream
½   teaspoon freshly ground white pepper
¼   teaspoon freshly grated nutmeg
6   ounces aged Gouda or regular Gouda cheese, shredded (about 1½ cups)

2   tablespoons dry bread crumbs
2   tablespoons freshly grated Parmesan or aged Jack cheese

Prepare tart shell. When cool, lightly brush shell with beaten egg white to seal bottom and prevent it from getting soggy.

Preheat oven to 400 degrees F.

In a nonstick skillet, melt butter over low heat. Add onions, tarragon and thyme and cook until tender, about 10 minutes. Stir in sun-dried tomatoes and cook for 2 minutes. Scoop mixture into a strainer and drain until ready to use.

In a mixing bowl, combine eggs, egg yolk, milk, cream, pepper and nutmeg. Whisk thoroughly and strain into a large bowl. Stir in shredded Gouda. Spread onions over bottom of tart shell. Pour in egg and cheese mixture. Sprinkle with bread crumbs and grated cheese.

Bake for 30 to 40 minutes, or until top is lightly browned and filling is set. Let cool on a rack for a few minutes before serving. This is best served hot, but it is quite tasty served warm as well.

Wine: Domaine de la Solitude
Châteauneuf-du-Pape (France: Rhône)

Alsatian Onion Quiche

IT TOOK US MANY YEARS of travel to France to visit Alsace. When we finally did, we found ourselves in food heaven. This is our version of a very traditional Alsatian dish, a creamy, slightly tangy tart of onions and bacon held together by a custard. We first tasted it in a little restaurant in Riquewihr as the guest of the charming Johnny Hugel, whose family has been producing wine in that town since 1639.

MAKES AN 11-INCH TART; SERVES 10 TO 12

	Pastry for tart shell (see Leek Tart, page 162)
½	**pound thinly sliced lean bacon, cut into ½-inch pieces**
¼	**cup (½ stick) unsalted butter**
1½	**pounds white onions, thinly sliced**
3	**large eggs**
1½	**cups crème fraîche (page 98)**
2	**pinches freshly grated nutmeg**
	Kosher salt and freshly ground white pepper

Prepare tart shell.

Preheat oven to 400 degrees F. Place a rack in the top third of the oven.

In a large skillet, fry bacon over medium heat until crisp. Drain thoroughly on paper towels and reserve.

In a large nonstick skillet, melt butter over medium-low heat. Add onions and sauté, stirring often, until very soft and slightly golden but not browned, about 20 minutes. Drain onions in a strainer.

In a large mixing bowl, beat eggs thoroughly, then slowly beat in crème fraîche, nutmeg and salt and white pepper to taste. Scatter bacon and onions evenly over bottom of tart shell. Pour egg mixture over onions.

Bake for 30 to 40 minutes, or until quiche is browned and puffed. Cool quiche on a rack for 5 minutes before serving.

Wine: Hugel Gewürztraminer (France: Alsace)

WHITE ONION

Flammekueche

(THIN ALSATIAN TART)

OUR FIRST VISIT to the Alsatian village of Ribeauvillé happened to be on the first Sunday of September, a day that for more than 600 years has been Pfifferdaj, the Piper's festival. The narrow, winding streets were packed with viewers. Twenty-seven bands and floats paraded through this stunning medieval town. The sights and sounds were extraordinary, and so were the *flammekueche*, the traditional paper-thin tarts covered with a mixture of fromage blanc (a tart, cream-like cheese), onions and bacon and baked in wood-fired ovens. *Flammekueche* can be cooked crisp and cut into wedges, or it can be cooked for a shorter time so that the bottom remains pliable. The slices can then be rolled into a cylinder and eaten.

MAKES 2 TARTS; SERVES 4

Pissaladière Dough (page 191)
About ½ cup unbleached flour
2   **cups Soft Cheese with Shallots (page 67) or 1 cup heavy cream mixed with either 1 cup farmer cheese or with 1 cup whole-milk ricotta cheese**

½   **pound bacon, preferably smoked, finely diced**
2   **cups finely diced white onion**
     Freshly ground black pepper

Prepare Pissaladière dough and let rise until doubled in bulk.

Place a baking rack in the top third of the oven. Preheat oven to 475 degrees F.

After dough has risen, knead for a moment on a lightly floured surface. Divide in half. Add a bit more flour to the surface and pat out ½ of the dough into a large rectangle. Transfer it to a large baking sheet and roll out to a very thin 13-x-14-inch rectangle. Spread 1 cup cheese over whole surface. Scatter ½ of the bacon and onions on top; sprinkle with some grindings of pepper.

Repeat using remaining dough and ingredients to make a second *flammekueche*.

Bake tarts until topping is bubbling, bacon is crisp and onions are cooked, 12 to 14 minutes.

Wine: Mure Riesling (France: Alsace)

Tracy's Breakfast Quiche of Scallions, Ham & Cheese

THIS QUICHE made without pastry is exceptionally easy to prepare. It comes from our daughter-in-law, Tracy Myers, and has become one of the family's favorites, especially when served with Blue Corn Sticks with Bacon, Scallions & Chives (page 189).

SERVES 6 GENEROUSLY

1 tablespoon unsalted butter, softened

2 tablespoons fine dry bread crumbs

9 large eggs, beaten

2 cups creamed cottage cheese

½ pound sharp Cheddar cheese, shredded (2 cups)

½ pound jalapeño Jack cheese, shredded (2 cups)

¼ cup unbleached flour

1 teaspoon baking powder

¾ cup finely diced ham, preferably smoked (6 ounces)

⅓ cup finely chopped scallions, including tender green part

1 tablespoon chopped pickled jalapeño pepper
Sour cream, salsa and pickled jalapeño peppers for garnishes

Preheat oven to 375 degrees F. Butter a 10-inch round glass or ceramic baking dish or deep pie plate. Coat with bread crumbs; invert the dish to discard excess crumbs.

In a large mixing bowl, combine eggs, cottage cheese, shredded cheeses, flour, baking powder, ham, scallions and chopped jalapeños. Blend gently but thoroughly.

Pour into the prepared baking dish and smooth top. Bake for 45 minutes, or until golden brown and firm to the touch. Cut quiche into generous portions and serve immediately. Pass bowls of sour cream, salsa and jalapeños at the table.

Wine: Gloria Ferrer Brut Carneros Cuvée (California: Carneros)

Onion & Cheese Quesadillas

WITH RED ONION & BLACK BEAN SALAD

FLOUR TORTILLAS filled with a combination of cheeses, onions, jalapeños and cilantro are folded and gently fried until they become golden outside and creamy inside. A zesty black bean salad with crunchy red onions is served on the side.

MAKES 8 TORTILLAS; SERVES 8

Black Bean Salad

3 cups cooked black beans

1 cup finely diced red onion

¼ cup extra-virgin olive oil

¼ cup fresh lime juice

1 garlic clove, minced

1 pickled jalapeño pepper, minced

2 tablespoons minced fresh cilantro leaves

1 tablespoon minced fresh oregano leaves or 1 teaspoon dried

   Zest of 1 orange, minced

   Kosher salt and freshly ground black pepper

1 large yellow or red tomato, diced (optional)

Quesadillas

1¼ cups finely chopped plump white bulbs from creaming onions or white onions

¼ cup minced fresh cilantro leaves

1 large fresh jalapeño pepper, minced

8 large (10-inch) white flour tortillas

½ pound Monterey Jack cheese, cut into 16 thin slices

½ pound farmer cheese, cut into 16 thin slices

1 egg white, lightly beaten

1½ cups vegetable oil for frying

   Low-fat sour cream, crumbled aged goat cheese, thinly sliced rings of white onion and chopped fresh cilantro for garnishes

To make black bean salad: Combine all salad ingredients except tomato in a large bowl. Mix well, cover and chill for several hours. Just before serving, fold in tomato, if using.

To make quesadillas: Combine onions, cilantro and jalapeño in a small bowl. Mix well and set aside.

Arrange tortillas on a clean work surface. Fold each tortilla in half, crease it and open it up again. Place a slice of Jack cheese on the upper part of the right half and a piece of farmer cheese on the lower part of the same side, leaving at least a ¼-inch border around the edge and leaving the left half of tortilla empty. Sprinkle about ¼ cup onion mixture over cheeses. Moisten borders of tortilla all around with egg white. Fold left side over cheese to meet right side; press edges to seal. Fold crescent in half and press edges together (it will not seal well); set aside. Repeat with remaining tortillas until all are filled.

Pour oil into a heavy 10-inch skillet and heat over medium until hot. Slip 2 to 3 quesadillas into hot oil, reduce heat slightly, and fry until golden, about 1½ minutes per side. Drain on paper towels and keep warm until all quesadillas are fried.

Serve quesadillas garnished with a dollop of sour cream, crumbled cheese, fresh onion rings and cilantro. Serve black bean salad on the side.

Wine: A. Charbaut Brut Rosé Champagne NV (France: Champagne)

BREADS

Weller Family Bread

THIS IS THE ONLY RECIPE in the book that doesn't include onions. It is one of our most treasured recipes, a bread Linda has been making for nearly 35 years. It has a flavor similar to challah (Jewish egg bread), with a hint of yeasty sweetness and a dense and slightly silky texture. (We've always made this bread with fresh yeast because we believe that it gives a particularly pleasing fragrance and texture, but dry yeast works well too, if that is what you have on hand.) Since this is our favorite buffet bread, we like to make it large and round, so we use a springform pan. Then we serve it on a large wooden board and let guests cut their own slices. It's also the perfect bread for sweet (unsalted) butter and raw onion sandwiches as well as for French Toast Sandwiches with Onion, Prosciutto & Cheese (page 143).

MAKES A 9-INCH ROUND LOAF

1   cake (0.6 ounce) fresh yeast or
    1 tablespoon active dry yeast
¼   cup lukewarm water
1   cup milk, scalded
1   cup boiling water
½   cup (1 stick) butter
2   large eggs, beaten
6   cups sifted unbleached flour
¼   cup sugar
2   teaspoons kosher salt
1   egg yolk, beaten, for egg wash

In a small bowl, combine yeast and lukewarm water and blend well; set aside until foamy, 10 to 15 minutes.

In a medium bowl, combine milk, boiling water and butter; stir until butter melts. When mixture is cool, add eggs and yeast mixture.

Mix flour, sugar and salt in a large bowl. Put ½ of the flour mixture and all milk mixture into the bowl of an electric mixer (if mixing by hand, use a wooden spoon). With motor running at medium speed, mix well. On low speed, gradually add remaining flour. Add more flour if mixture is too wet to knead.

When dough is stiff enough to knead, remove the bowl from the mixer, cover with a towel and set aside to rest for 10 minutes.

Turn out dough onto a lightly floured surface and knead for 15 minutes, until silky. Turn into a lightly oiled bowl, cover with plastic, and let rise in a warm place until doubled in bulk, 2 to 3 hours.

Oil a 9-inch springform pan. Knead dough until smooth, at least 5 minutes. Let rest, covered with a towel, for 10 minutes.

Divide dough in half. Flatten first half into a circle and fit into the bottom of the pan. (It does not have to fit all the way to the edges.) Divide remaining dough into 3 pieces. Shape each piece into a ball and place dough balls near each other on top of prepared dough circle. Cover with a damp towel and let rise in a warm place until bread rises to the top of the pan, about 1 hour.

About 15 minutes before baking, preheat oven to 400 degrees F. Brush some beaten egg wash on surface of bread. Bake for 45 minutes. Tap to see if done (bread should sound hollow), or test by sticking a toothpick in the middle; it should come out clean.

Remove from the oven and cool on a rack for 5 minutes. Release the sides of the pan, remove bread from the pan, slip off the bottom and return bread to the rack to cool completely.

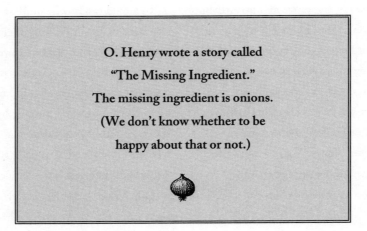

**O. Henry wrote a story called
"The Missing Ingredient."
The missing ingredient is onions.
(We don't know whether to be
happy about that or not.)**

GOING TO ONION SCHOOL

YOU'RE JUST IN TIME," said Robin Raiford, excitedly. "You're really in luck. The Vidalia Onion Cooking School is just about ready to start." We had just driven into town and the manager of the Vidalia Onion Committee had met us at our motel. No time to unpack. She took us directly to the elementary school, the site of one of the town's most popular annual events.

Outside, a giant onion was walking about, greeting students as they arrived. "Mr. Onion," said a young boy, "will you sign my shirt?" And Mr. Onion did, one of the great green leaves producing a black magic marker for the assignment.

Standing room only. There were 300 seats and 100 standees. We were able to find a patch of wall to lean against. A big sign above the stage proclaimed, "Vidalia Onions . . . Yummeee Year Round."

Piggly Wiggly Supermarkets, which had a little something to do with getting Vidalia named the onion capital, was a sponsor, along with Bryan Foods and the gas company. The emcee, Mark Boone, the meat man from Bryan's, was cherubic, unrepentantly Southern in his speech, and funny. "They don't pay me to do this," he said, on finding that he had lost his notes, "so they can't hurt me."

There were lots of door prizes: bags of onions, a grill, a dishwasher and a sack full of Piggly Wiggly treasures for every attendee. But there was also a caveat. "If y'all work at Piggly Wiggly," said Boone, "y'all ain't gonna win. You dead in the watta."

The three teachers, all home economists, were referred to variously as "gals" and "girls" to no one's discomfort, although once the emcee did display a little awareness of the potential political incorrectness of those labels and called them "ladies."

Michele Jones, the second teacher, representing the gas company, made everyone stand up, stretch and put a finger in one ear so that "what I teach you about Vidalia onions won't go in one ear and out the other."

As the lesson progressed, onion bran muffins, an egg-onion stir-fry, pastry shells filled with a mixture of onion, crabmeat and Swiss cheese, Vidalia chicken phyllo, Vidalia party bread (made from canned refrigerated biscuits, onion, peppers, cheese and bacon) and half a dozen other oniony concoctions were put before us by the chatty and enthusiastic home economists. Not a soul left early.

Egg Bread with Vidalia Onions & Cheddar

ONCE BAKED, the flavors of cheese and onion merge together into a subtle and softly toasty bread. If you use yellow onions, the onion flavor will be more assertive.

MAKES 2 LOAVES

1	tablespoon active dry yeast
¼	cup lukewarm water
1	tablespoon sugar
1½	cups cool water
¼	cup honey
2	large eggs
¼	cup vegetable oil
6-8½	cups unbleached flour
1	teaspoon kosher salt
1½	cups shredded sharp Cheddar cheese (6 ounces)
1¼-1½	cups coarsely grated Vidalia or other sweet onions, well drained
1	egg yolk, beaten with 2 teaspoons water for egg wash

In a warm bowl, combine yeast, lukewarm water and sugar. Mix well and set aside until foamy, 10 to 15 minutes.

In the bowl of an electric mixer, combine cool water and honey and turn the motor on low. Add eggs and oil (if mixing by hand, use a wooden spoon), and mix. Add yeast mixture. Gradually add 6 cups flour. Add salt, cheese and onions; if dough is too wet, gradually add up to 2½ cups more flour. Change to a dough hook, if available, and knead for 10 minutes, adding a bit more flour, if needed, or knead by hand until a slightly sticky dough forms. Place dough in a well-oiled bowl, cover with plastic, and let rise in a warm place until doubled in bulk, about 2 hours. Punch down dough and let rise for 40 minutes longer.

Thoroughly oil two 9½-x-5½-inch bread pans. Divide dough into 2 equal balls. Divide first ball in half. Shape 1 piece and fit it in the bottom of the pan. Divide other piece in half, form into 2 balls and place them over piece in the pan. Repeat, using second ball and the second pan. Place the pans in a warm place, cover loosely with plastic wrap and let rise until balls come slightly above the top of the pans, about 1 hour.

Meanwhile, place a rack in the top third of the oven. Preheat oven to 400 degrees F.

When loaves are risen, brush tops with egg wash. Bake for 40 to 50 minutes, or until loaves sound hollow when tapped on bottoms. Let loaves cool in the pans on a rack for 2 to 3 minutes, remove from the pans and finish cooling on a rack.

Onion-Olive Bread

OLIVE OIL, chopped oil-cured black olives and red onions give a pungent flavor to this hearty bread. In winter, it can accompany a soup or stew. In summer, it goes well with almost anything cooked on the grill. When it's a few days old, it makes a splendid participant in our version of Italian Bread Salad with Red Onions, Tomatoes & Fresh Basil (page 140).

MAKES 1 ROUND LOAF

1	tablespoon active dry yeast
½	teaspoon sugar
1	cup lukewarm water
4½	cups unbleached flour
1	teaspoon kosher salt
¼	cup olive oil
¾	cup pitted oil-cured black olives, coarsely chopped
¾	cup medium-diced red onion
1	tablespoon cornmeal
1	scant tablespoon butter

Combine yeast, sugar and ¼ cup lukewarm water in a medium bowl. Mix well and set aside until foamy, 10 to 15 minutes.

Combine flour and salt in the bowl of an electric mixer (if mixing by hand, use a wooden spoon). Add oil, olives and onion. With motor running on medium, add yeast mixture and remaining ¾ cup water. Mix until dough is evenly blended, about 3 minutes. Change to a dough hook, if available, or continue to mix and knead by hand until olives and onions are thoroughly broken apart and dough feels elastic, about 10 minutes. Add more flour if dough is too sticky.

Knead dough for a few minutes on a lightly floured surface. Place dough in a large, well-oiled bowl, cover with plastic wrap, and let rise in a warm place until doubled in bulk, about 2 hours.

Sprinkle a pizza pan or baking sheet with cornmeal. Shape dough into a large round and place it on the prepared pan. Loosely cover with plastic and let rise for 1 hour. Meanwhile, place a rack in the top third of the oven. Preheat to 400 degrees F.

Bake until bread sounds hollow when rapped on bottom and top is golden brown, 40 to 45 minutes. Place loaf on a rack and rub top with butter to make it shiny. Let cool on the rack.

A Hot in Sweet's Clothing

JON ROWLEY, Seattle's fish guru, had found a "burn" in a batch of Walla Wallas he had planned to use for dinner. His public complaint to a Seattle newspaper about the fire in a sweet onion found its way to Craig Christensen, the president of the Walla Walla growers. The onion, Craig explained, was undoubtedly a "pseudo sweet," a hot storage onion that had been falsely labeled.

We asked Bill Dean, a horticulturist at the Washington State University Research Center who is an onion Ph.D. steeped in the history of the Walla Walla, whether the hot onion could have been a real Walla Walla gone astray. Had the farmers lost control of their product? Dean agreed with Christensen that the hot onion had probably been a storage onion in a sweet-onion bag. He thinks the association could do what the Vidalia growers did—get a law that makes it a crime to mislabel an onion.

Today's Walla Walla sweet is a direct descendant of a variety brought from Corsica to the Northwest in the late 1800s. Since it is always sweet and grows well in the region and since the microclimate and the soil agree with it, experimentation has focused on improving it, rather than bringing in something new. Most of the other American sweets are recent cultivars created for a specific place; Grano, Granex and the 1015Y are examples.

AS GOOD AS THE WALLA WALLA IS, Dean is always at work on a possible next step, working for a better yield, an onion that is more pest-resistant and easier to handle. The growers feel that the microclimate and the soil make for a sweet onion.

"Sure they like to believe that," says Dean. "Because this is where they are. The soil is good, low in sulfur. But I think it's the onion. The Walla Walla would be sweet grown anywhere."

Zucchini & Sweet Onion Quick Bread

WHILE THIS PARTICULAR BREAD is not especially sweet, it is light and filled with delicate flavors. When baked, the onion becomes subtly toasty. Use any sweet onion; if Vidalias are available, they are perfect. You can grate the onion in a food processor. Scrape all of the juices into the measuring cup along with the grated onion.

MAKES 2 LOAVES

2	cups unbleached flour
1	cup whole-wheat pastry flour
1	cup sugar
¼	cup packed dark brown sugar
1	tablespoon baking powder
1	teaspoon baking soda
1	teaspoon ground cardamom
1	teaspoon ground coriander
2	teaspoons finely minced crystallized ginger
1	teaspoon ground cinnamon
8	gratings fresh nutmeg
	Zest of 1 orange, finely minced
½	cup vegetable oil
3	large eggs
2	cups grated zucchini, undrained
1	cup grated sweet onion, undrained

Thoroughly grease two 8½-x-4½-x-2½-inch loaf pans. Place a rack in the upper third of the oven. Preheat oven to 350 degrees F.

In the bowl of an electric mixer, combine both flours, both sugars, baking powder, baking soda, cardamom, coriander, crystallized ginger, cinnamon, nutmeg and orange zest (if mixing by hand, use a wooden spoon). Beat on low speed for 30 seconds. Add vegetable oil and eggs and beat thoroughly, scraping down the sides of the bowl once. Add zucchini and onion and beat until thoroughly combined.

Divide batter between the prepared pans. Bake for 50 to 60 minutes, or until a toothpick inserted into middle of breads comes out clean.

Cool on racks for 5 minutes. Slip breads from pans and continue to cool on the racks.

Corn Rye Bread

WITH WALLA WALLA ONIONS, DILL & CARAWAY

THIS IS A WINTER BREAD, hearty and full-flavored, seasoned with caraway, dill and onion. We especially like it with tomato-based soups and stews. You can make it with any kind of onion. Whatever you use, Susan Cavitch, who tested this bread, encourages you to serve it warm. "All four of my children loved it that way," she wrote. "The entire loaf disappeared in a flash."

MAKES I LOAF

1½   tablespoons active dry yeast

½   cup lukewarm water

¼   cup honey

1   cup plus 1 tablespoon cornmeal

1   cup boiling water

½   cup milk, warmed

¼   cup vegetable oil

    About 4 cups unbleached flour

1   cup rye flour

2   teaspoons kosher salt

1   cup medium-diced Walla Walla or other sweet onion

1   tablespoon caraway seeds

3   tablespoons minced fresh dill or 1 tablespoon dried

1   tablespoon olive oil

1   tablespoon milk

Combine yeast, lukewarm water and honey in a small bowl. Mix thoroughly and set aside until foamy, 10 to 15 minutes.

In the bowl of an electric mixer, combine 1 cup cornmeal and boiling water (if mixing by hand, use a wooden spoon). Allow to stand until mixture cools to lukewarm. Stir in warm milk, oil and yeast mixture, mixing well. With the motor running on low, or by hand, gradually add 2 cups unbleached flour. Add rye flour, 1 cup more unbleached flour, salt, onion, caraway and dill.

Coat a large bowl with olive oil; let stand in a warm place until dough is ready for rising.

Turn dough out onto a well-floured board and knead, gradually adding remaining 1 cup flour, until elastic and smooth, about 15 minutes.

Place dough in the prepared bowl, cover with plastic wrap and let rise in a warm place until doubled in bulk, about 2 hours.

Turn out dough onto a lightly floured surface and knead for 5 minutes. Sprinkle a pizza pan or a large flat baking sheet with remaining 1 tablespoon cornmeal. Form dough into a large, round loaf and place on the pizza pan or baking sheet. Cover loosely with

plastic and set aside in a warm place until doubled in bulk, about 1 hour.

Meanwhile, preheat oven to 400 degrees F. Brush top of bread with milk. Bake until golden on top and bottom sounds hollow when rapped, about 50 minutes. Cool on a rack.

Jimmy Schmidt, chef-owner of
Detroit's Rattlesnake Club, Très Vite and other
restaurants, loves Vidalias, Walla Wallas and Mauis.
"The sweet flavor allows for brief cooking, resulting
in a crisp texture without a strong onion bite.
Also, caramelized, they are the sweetest."
He uses a sharp knife, never a food processor.
About the tears? He claims none of the usual
suggestions work. He dismisses the idea of
cutting an onion under water or putting
a slice of bread in your mouth as you cut as
"old wives' tales."

Focaccia with Rosemary & Onions

YOU CAN MAKE this popular Italian flat bread with all kinds of herbs and toppings. We made focaccia for years but improved the results after reading Carol Field's marvelous book *The Italian Baker* (Harper and Row, 1985). That's where we learned about "dimpling" the shaped dough and letting it rest before the second rising. The dimples catch the wonderful oil from the topping, making an infinitely better focaccia. Serve warm with Zack's Roasted Onion Tapenade (page 45) as an appetizer. Or, serve as an accompaniment to vegetable soup, roasted chicken, an omelet or a frittata.

MAKES AN 11-INCH ROUND BREAD

Bread

1 tablespoon active dry yeast
1 cup lukewarm water
About 3 cups unbleached flour
1 teaspoon kosher salt
1 rounded teaspoon freshly ground black pepper
3 tablespoons extra-virgin olive oil
1 rounded tablespoon minced fresh rosemary leaves or 2 teaspoons dried

Topping

½ cup olive oil
2½ pounds yellow onions, thinly sliced
2 plump garlic cloves, minced
1 tablespoon minced fresh rosemary leaves or 1½ teaspoons dried

To make bread: Dissolve yeast in ¼ cup lukewarm water and set aside until foamy, 10 to 15 minutes. In the bowl of an electric mixer, combine 3 cups flour, salt and pepper (if mixing by hand, use a wooden spoon). Add yeast mixture, olive oil and remaining ¾ cup lukewarm water. Run the motor on low until mixture is well blended or continue to mix by hand.

Turn out dough onto a floured surface and knead until smooth, gradually adding rosemary and only enough additional flour to keep dough from sticking. When dough is smooth and shiny, place it in a large, well-oiled bowl, cover with plastic wrap and let rise in a warm place until doubled in bulk, about 1 hour.

Meanwhile, make topping: Heat olive oil in a large, heavy skillet over medium heat. Add onions, garlic and rosemary and sauté for 1 minute. Cover with a tight-fitting lid and cook over very low heat for 40 minutes. Stir mixture, add more oil if needed, and cook until onions fall apart and caramelize, about 20 minutes. Set aside.

Lightly coat a 12-inch pizza pan with olive oil.

After dough has doubled, turn out onto a lightly floured surface and roll into an 11-inch circle. Lift it onto the prepared pan and gently stretch dough until it covers the pan; it should be about ½ inch thick. Using the tips of your fingers, vigorously press "dimples" all over surface of dough. Cover lightly with a towel and let rest for 20 minutes. Spread cooked onion mixture evenly over surface of dough. Lightly cover top with the towel again and let focaccia rise for 1 hour.

Place a rack in the top third of the oven. Preheat oven to 425 degrees F. Spray the bottom of the oven with water. Bake focaccia for 15 minutes, spraying several times more. Reduce heat to 400 degrees and bake until top and edges are golden, 10 to 15 minutes. Cool slightly on a rack, but cut into wedges and serve soon after baking.

Food writer Carol Field is a champion
of the red onion. "I love its sweetness."
She is a knife person, except when she is making
a quantity of chopped vegetables for minestrone, for
example. Does she have a special way to deal with tears?
"Don't I wish! I've tried matches in my mouth,
wetting the onion under cold water—forget it!
I haven't tried goggles, though."

WHY WE CRY

Mine eyes smell onions, I shall weep anon.

—*Shakespeare*

FACE IT: If you are going to chop the ordinary onion, you are going to cry. There are all kinds of strategies for avoiding the tears, but with close to 80 years of combined experience at the onion cutting board, we feel that there is nothing you can do that really will help.

Cut onions under water, if you like, but you can't chop them under water without washing a lot of the oniony character away. We have heard of holding a slice of bread between your teeth. It didn't work for us. Some say you should chill onions in the refrigerator before you cut. Or chop them in one of those little closed chopping jars, or in a food processor, but the onions may become too juicy for some preparations. Some experts tell us to keep the root intact until the very end because the tear-causing substances are concentrated there.

The coveted sweet onions—from Maui, Walla Walla, Vidalia, Texas or California's Imperial Valley—don't make you cry. But they don't keep very well. The very chemicals that cause the tears make possible the long-term storage of hot onions. These compounds fight bacteria and molds. If a bug bites a hot onion, it gets a jolt.

An enormous amount of research has gone into the chemistry of the hot onion, and scientists have discovered that organic sulfur compounds are the villains in the drama. But there still is no general agreement as to how the complex chemical constituents work in creating taste and odor. The gas enzymatically formed when an onion is cut is unstable and short-lived, making its chemistry difficult to study. But as every cook knows, it lives long enough to react with the moisture on the eye, creating minute amounts of attention-getting sulfuric acid.

The good part is that the burning stops after a few seconds, and the onion's wonderful pungency does not carry over through cooking or processing.

Red Onion & Dill Soda Bread

IN COMBINATION WITH onion, dill creates a perfect bread for a wintertime hearty soup or summertime salad supper. Feel free to experiment with different onions and different herbs.

MAKES I LOAF

About 4½ cups unbleached flour

1   tablespoon baking powder

1   teaspoon baking soda

1   teaspoon kosher salt

¾   cup minced red onion

1   tablespoon minced fresh dill

1   large egg

2   tablespoons vegetable oil

1½ cups buttermilk

1   tablespoon unsalted butter

Preheat oven to 375 degrees F. Lightly oil a baking sheet. In the bowl of an electric mixer, combine 4 cups flour, baking powder, baking soda and salt (if mixing by hand, use a wooden spoon). Add onion and dill and mix on low speed for 1 minute. Add egg and oil. With motor running on low speed, gradually add buttermilk. Mix until thoroughly blended.

Sprinkle some of remaining ½ cup flour on a work surface and knead dough, adding flour as necessary, until only slightly sticky. Form into a round loaf, place on the prepared baking sheet, and cut a deep X into top of loaf.

Bake loaf for 55 to 60 minutes, or until it sounds hollow when bottom is rapped. Brush top of bread with butter. Let bread cool on a rack for several hours before serving.

Skillet Scallion & Chile Corn Bread

WE PREFER TO MAKE CORN BREAD in a cast-iron skillet; it gets brown on the bottom and has a toasty flavor that is not achieved in a regular cake pan. Buttermilk, scallions and chiles give this bread extra punch. Another secret to good corn bread is the cornmeal. We either use organic cornmeal from Arrowhead Mills or a slightly coarser meal from Fowler's Mill in Chardon, Ohio (see Special Products, page 374). Any whole-grain cornmeal that is stone-ground will have a fuller, sweeter flavor than mass-produced cornmeal, which is made from degerminated corn to ensure long shelf life.

MAKES A 9-INCH-ROUND LOAF

1½ cups stone-ground cornmeal, fine grind preferred

1 cup unbleached flour

2 tablespoons sugar

1 tablespoon baking powder

½ teaspoon baking soda

1 teaspoon kosher salt

1⅔ cups buttermilk

6 tablespoons (¾ stick) butter, melted

¼ cup vegetable oil

2 large eggs, beaten

1 red serrano or jalapeño pepper, stemmed, seeded and minced

⅓ cup minced scallions

3 tablespoons minced fresh cilantro leaves

1 tablespoon minced fresh chives

Thoroughly oil a 9-inch cast-iron skillet.

Combine cornmeal, flour, sugar, baking powder, baking soda and salt and sift into the bowl of an electric mixer. Combine buttermilk, melted butter, oil and eggs in another mixing bowl. With the motor running on low or with a wooden spoon, add buttermilk mixture to dry ingredients and mix well. Scrape the sides of the bowl once. Add chile pepper, scallions, cilantro and chives; mix briefly.

Let batter rest for 15 minutes. Preheat oven to 400 degrees F. Heat the skillet in the preheated oven for 5 minutes. Pour batter into the hot skillet. Bake for 30 minutes, or until a toothpick comes out clean. When done, turn corn bread out of the pan onto a rack and let cool slightly before serving.

Blue Corn Sticks

WITH BACON, SCALLIONS & CHIVES

BLUE CORNMEAL isn't essential to the success of this recipe, but it gives the sticks a distinctive blue-lavender tinge. We use antique cast-iron corn-stick pans for this recipe, a favorite around the Griffith household for many years. When we prepared it on television, the requests for recipes were overwhelming.

MAKES ABOUT 20 CORN STICKS

1	cup finely ground blue cornmeal
1	cup unbleached flour
2	tablespoons sugar
1	tablespoon baking powder
½	teaspoon baking soda
1½	cups buttermilk
2	large eggs, lightly beaten
3	tablespoons butter, melted
¼	cup minced scallions, white parts only
1	tablespoon minced fresh chives
2	tablespoons minced fresh thyme leaves or 2 teaspoons dried
3	thick slices bacon, preferably smoked, cut into ¾-inch pieces

Place a rack in the top third of the oven. Preheat oven to 450 degrees F. Combine cornmeal, flour, sugar, baking powder and baking soda in a large mixing bowl; set aside.

Combine buttermilk and eggs in a medium-sized bowl. Slowly whisk in melted butter. Add scallions, chives and thyme and blend well. Slowly whisk buttermilk mixture into dry ingredients, blending thoroughly. If batter is too dry, add more buttermilk. (Batter should spread out by itself when spooned into the molds.)

Prepare cast-iron corn-stick pans by placing a piece of bacon in each indentation. Place the pans in the oven and bake until bacon is crisp, about 3 minutes. Quickly remove the pans and brush accumulated fat all over the surface of each indentation. Spoon batter over crisp bacon, filling each indentation about ¾ full. Return the pans to the oven and bake until sticks are browned and pull away from the sides, 12 to 15 minutes.

Remove the pans from the oven and let cool on racks for 3 minutes. Turn the pans over to release corn sticks. Serve warm.

Pizza & Pasta

Pissaladière

THE FRENCH VERSION of pizza, pissaladière, is sold by the piece in bakeries and food shops and is eaten at room temperature. A few slices of oniony pissaladière, a glass of a chilled Bandol rosé, and you have a memorable summer meal.

MAKES AN 11-INCH ROUND BREAD; 10 TO 12 SLICES

Dough

1   tablespoon active dry yeast
1   tablespoon honey
¼   cup lukewarm water
    About 2 cups unbleached flour
½   teaspoon kosher salt
3   tablespoons cold unsalted butter, cut into pieces
1½ tablespoons olive oil
1   large egg, beaten
2   tablespoons cornmeal

Topping

⅓   cup olive oil
2½ pounds sweet onions, such as Vidalia or Spanish, thinly sliced
2   plump garlic cloves, minced
1   teaspoon minced fresh rosemary leaves or ½ teaspoon dried
1   teaspoon minced fresh thyme leaves or ½ teaspoon dried
1   teaspoon minced fresh basil leaves or ½ teaspoon dried
1   teaspoon minced fresh lavender flowers (optional)
2   medium-sized ripe tomatoes, sliced ½ inch thick
1   2-ounce tin flat anchovy fillets, drained
18-20 niçoise olives, pitted

To make dough: In a small bowl, combine yeast, honey and lukewarm water. Stir well and set aside in a warm place until foamy, 10 to 15 minutes.

In a medium-sized mixing bowl, combine 1½ cups flour, salt and butter. Quickly cut in butter with a pastry blender until mixture is the texture of coarse cornmeal. Stir in yeast mixture, oil and egg.

Turn out dough onto a lightly floured surface and knead, adding 1 tablespoon flour at a time, until smooth and elastic, about 15 to 20 minutes. Form into a ball, place in a lightly oiled bowl, cover with plastic wrap and let rise in a warm place until doubled in bulk, about 2 hours.

To make topping: Meanwhile, heat olive oil in a large skillet over medium heat. Add onions, garlic and herbs and sauté for 1 minute. Cover with a tight-fitting lid and cook over very low heat for 40 minutes, stir well, cover and cook for 20 minutes more, stirring from time to time, until onions are falling apart. Set aside.

Preheat oven to 375 degrees F. Sprinkle a baking sheet with cornmeal. When dough has risen, roll out on a floured surface to fit an 11-inch tart pan with a removable bottom, or shape into a rectangle and put on the prepared baking sheet.

Spread onion mixture over dough. Arrange tomato slices over onions. Distribute anchovies and olives in an attractive pattern in the spaces between tomatoes.

Bake until top is browned but not dried, 50 to 60 minutes. Let cool slightly on a rack. Remove from the pan and continue cooling. Serve at room temperature.

Wine: Domaine Tempier Rosé (France: Bandol)

Red Onion Pizza with Mashed Potatoes

ONE OF THE BEST PIZZAS of our lives was topped with mashed potatoes and served at Al Forno restaurant in Providence, Rhode Island. We've been experimenting ever since. We bake ours in a conventional oven on a pizza tile; if you don't have one, use a pizza pan or large baking sheet. This mashed-potato topping, flavored with red onions, shallots and rosemary, becomes crusty outside but soft within in the hot oven. The dough recipe yields enough for 2 pizzas; make one right away, the other will keep for at least a week in the refrigerator.

MAKES A 12-INCH PIZZA; SERVES 2 TO 4

Pizza Dough

¾ cup lukewarm water
1 tablespoon honey
2½ tablespoons active dry yeast
2½ cups unbleached flour
½ cup whole-wheat flour
1 teaspoon salt
¼ cup milk
2 tablespoons olive oil

Topping

1 pound Yukon Gold or red-skinned potatoes, scrubbed and quartered
4 tablespoons (½ stick) unsalted butter
1 medium-large red onion, coarsely chopped
2 garlic cloves, minced
2 rounded tablespoons minced shallots
1 rounded tablespoon chopped fresh rosemary leaves or 2 teaspoons dried
3 tablespoons dry white wine
5 tablespoons olive oil
½ cup milk
3 tablespoons minced fresh chives
Salt and freshly ground white pepper

2 tablespoons cornmeal
¼ cup freshly grated Parmesan cheese

To make dough: In a small bowl, combine ¼ cup lukewarm water, honey and yeast. Set aside in a warm place until foamy, 10 to 15 minutes.

Combine both flours, salt, milk and olive oil in the bowl of an electric mixer (if mixing by hand, use a wooden spoon). With motor running on high speed, pour in yeast mixture and most of remaining ½ cup lukewarm water. Beat just until dough leaves the sides of the bowl and forms a ball; dough should be elastic. If it is too dry, add a bit more water. If too moist, knead in more flour by hand.

Lightly flour a board and knead dough for 5 minutes. Place in a lightly oiled bowl, cover with plastic wrap and let rise in a warm place until doubled in bulk, about 1 hour. *(If preparing ahead, place dough in a plastic bag, seal tightly and refrigerate for up to a week. Cut dough in half and bring to room temperature before stretching.)*

Meanwhile, make topping: Cover potatoes with cold water in a large saucepan and bring to a boil. Simmer briskly until tender, about 15 minutes.

While potatoes are cooking, melt 3 tablespoons butter in a large nonstick skillet over low heat. Add onion, garlic, shallots and rosemary. Cover the skillet with a tight-fitting lid and cook, stirring occasionally, until onions are tender, 7 to 10 minutes. Uncover, increase the heat to medium, add wine and stir until liquid evaporates. Set onions aside.

When potatoes are tender, drain well and return them to the saucepan. Over very low heat, thoroughly mash potatoes with a masher. Beat in remaining 1 tablespoon butter and 3 tablespoons olive oil. Add enough of the milk to make a fairly creamy potato mixture that will spread easily. Remove from the heat, blend in chives and salt and pepper to taste. Set aside.

To assemble: Preheat oven and pizza tile, if using, to 500 degrees F. Sprinkle a pizza pan, baking sheet or pizza peel, if using a tile, with cornmeal. Punch down dough and divide into 2 balls. Place 1 ball in a large plastic bag, seal tightly and store in the refrigerator for later use with another topping (see pages 191, 195, 198 or 199).

On a lightly floured surface, roll out dough into a large round. Begin stretching dough over closed fists to make a thin 12-inch round. Place round on the prepared pan or peel. Coat surface with remaining 2 tablespoons olive oil. Spread surface with potato mixture. Top with onion mixture, followed by grated cheese. Bake until bottom of crust is nicely browned, 12 to 15 minutes. Serve at once.

**Wine: Marietta Cellars NV "Old Vine Red"
(California: Sonoma County)**

Roasted Sweet Onion Pizza

WITH TELEME CHEESE & VIRGINIA HAM

W E FIRST MADE THIS pizza in the midst of a horrible blizzard. With the storm swirling about, we scanned the refrigerator for something hearty to eat. We combined leftover roasted onions in a sweet-and-sour glaze with a creamy white cheese called Teleme (see Special Products, page 374) and some strips of leftover ham to make a pizza topping. While there is a slight difference in flavor, Monterey Jack can be substituted for Teleme; it melts nicely.

MAKES A 12-INCH PIZZA; SERVES 2 TO 4

1 12-inch pizza shell (pages 193-194)
2 tablespoons cornmeal
2 tablespoons olive oil
¼ pound Teleme cheese
2 cups loosely packed Roasted Sweet Onions (page 340)
¼ pound aged Virginia ham or prosciutto, thinly sliced and cut into strips
2 tablespoons freshly grated Parmesan cheese

Prepare pizza shell.

Preheat oven and pizza tile, if using, to 500 degrees F. Sprinkle cornmeal evenly over a 12-inch pizza pan, baking sheet or pizza peel, if using tile.

Place pizza shell on the prepared pan or peel. Spread oil evenly over dough. Crumble cheese and distribute evenly on top. Scatter with roasted onions and ham. Sprinkle on grated cheese. Bake until bottom of pizza is nicely browned and top is browned and bubbling, 12 to 15 minutes.

Wine: Ridge Vineyards "Lytton Springs" Zinfandel (California: Sonoma County)

ONION GENIUS

I F WE COULD PUT FLASHING LIGHTS at the top of this page, we would, because no development in the history of onion cultivation is more important than a discovery made by a botanist in a California onion field in the summer of 1925.

In the fall of the previous year, Henry Alfred Jones, a scientist at the University of California at Davis, planted 63 Italian Red onions. They grew through the mild winter, and in the spring, when the onions flowered, Jones placed small paper bags over them to ensure self-pollination, so that no pollen from other onions could get to them. He wanted seed that would precisely replicate the onions he had planted.

In August, the seed heads of the 63 onion plants were harvested. Some had produced as many as 6,000 seeds. But one plant had no seeds at all. It turned out that because of a developmental aberration, that plant's pollen contained no genetic material. The pollen had fallen from the stamens onto the stigmas of the onion flower, but it could not fertilize the ova and make seeds.

While the plant made no seeds, to Jones' astonishment, it grew head-sets instead—tiny bulbils growing among the flowers in the head of the onion—miniature replicas of the onion bulb from which it started. The forming of head-sets is a rare event, but it is one of the techniques that the species sometimes uses for self-perpetuation, one that does not require pollination. In this single plant, Jones saw a remarkable opportunity. From the 136 bulbils the plant produced, he could guarantee the survival of this line, which was male-sterile. He would grow onions from these bulbils and then use the plants as female parents, fertilizing them with the pollen from other plants that had a desirable characteristic—perhaps a larger bulb, a top resistant to mildew, a sweet taste or a specific color or shape. The result: seeds that would yield a plant with a specific desirable feature.

Jones's botanical breakthrough revolutionized the onion field, making possible the rapid development of thousands of onion cultivars, one for virtually every climate, every latitude, every culinary purpose. The man who made the discovery and understood its significance was a phenomenon in the academic world. Jones grew up on a Nebraska farm and attended country schools. He was still in high school when his father died, and he had to drop out to assume the responsibilities of running the farm and helping to raise his brothers and sisters. He was finally able to resume high school by correspondence and then went to the University of Nebraska, where he completed requirements for his degree in 2½ years. His performance was good enough to get him into a graduate program at the University of Chicago. If he dazzled them at Nebraska, he blew them away in Chicago, completing a Ph.D. in just a year and a half. His academic career took him to West Virginia University, the University of Maryland and finally to the University of California at Davis, where he made his now-famous discovery.

The United States Department of Agriculture recruited Jones and made him head horticulturist in charge of research on onions, potatoes, spinach and other crops. Among other things, his work saved the melon industry in the Imperial Valley when it was threatened by disease in the 1930s.

Retirement was required by the government in those days, and in 1953 at the age of 67, Jones was out of a job. It was then that he joined Archie Dessert at the Dessert Seed Company in El Centro, California, as director of research, a post he held until he was 90.

"Was Henry Alfred Jones the Luther Burbank of onions?" we asked Dessert.

"Smarter than Luther Burbank," he answered emphatically. "Jones was a complete genius."

Dessert told us that Jones could do the scientific work of half a dozen well-trained researchers, and that at one time, he had over 2,000 breeding lines at The Dessert Seed Company. Most of the important onions under cultivation in the world owe something to the work Jones did in the onion fields.

"He was a great scientist," said Dessert. "But he was also a wonderful guy." After his second retirement, Jones went to live in Phoenix with a grandson. He died there at the age of 91.

His book, *Onions and Their Allies*, co-written with his colleague Louis K. Mann, is still a standard work—a summation of a lifetime of research. Dessert was one of the technical editors.

What Jones set down in his books and papers was all science. But once in a while, one could find some clue to the passion for his work that kept him at it.

"The more we know about a plant or crop," he wrote, "the more we tend to be attracted to it. So it is with the onion. Watching the seed sprout, the seedling unfold, the plant grow, and the parts differentiate into highly specialized organs, until seeds are formed again, is a fascinating experience."

"That's why he couldn't quit," said Dessert. "That's why he worked until he was 90. He just couldn't give up the thrill of learning something new, of watching that happen again and again."

Smoked Gouda, Shrimp & Broccoli Pizza

WITH RED ONION-TOMATO SAUCE

THIS IS A COLORFUL PIZZA: rosy shrimp, red sauce, green basil and broccoli under a sprinkling of melted smoked Gouda. If you cannot find smoked Gouda, experiment with other smoked cheeses or even regular Gouda.

MAKES A 12-INCH PIZZA; SERVES 2 TO 4

1	12-inch pizza shell (pages 193-194)
¼	cup olive oil
¼	teaspoon dried red pepper flakes
1	garlic clove, minced
2	tablespoons cornmeal
1	cup Fresh Tomato-Onion Sauce (page 84)
4	fresh basil leaves, julienned
¾	cup broccoli florets, blanched
¾	pound medium-sized raw shrimp, peeled and deveined, left whole
⅓	cup finely diced red onion
1	cup grated smoked Gouda cheese
	Minced fresh basil leaves and snipped fresh chives for garnishes

Prepare pizza shell.

Combine olive oil, pepper flakes and garlic in a small saucepan over medium heat. Sauté for 2 minutes; let stand off the heat for 5 minutes. Sprinkle a pizza pan, baking sheet or pizza peel, if using a baking tile, with cornmeal. Place pizza shell on the prepared pan or peel. Generously coat pizza shell with warm oil mixture; reserve remaining oil.

Spoon sauce over pizza shell. Scatter basil and broccoli over sauce; add shrimp and onion. Sprinkle evenly with Gouda, and drizzle with remaining seasoned oil.

Place the oven rack and the pizza tile, if using, in the top third of the oven. Let pizza rest while preheating the oven to 500 degrees F. Bake pizza until 12 to 15 minutes, or until cheese has melted and top is browned and bubbly. Remove and sprinkle with minced basil and chives.

Wine: Joseph Phelps Vineyards Vin du Mistral Viognier (California: Napa Valley)

Pizza with Caramelized Red Onions & Prosciutto

OUR FRIEND Merrilyn Siciak had us salivating one night as she described her very favorite pizza— one with caramelized red onions and prosciutto. We couldn't wait to get into our kitchen and make it.

MAKES A 12-INCH PIZZA; SERVES 2 TO 4

1	12-inch pizza shell (pages 193-194)
¼	cup (½ stick) unsalted butter
3	tablespoons olive oil
1	jumbo red onion, thinly sliced
½	teaspoon kosher salt
½	teaspoon freshly ground black pepper
2	tablespoons cornmeal
¼	pound prosciutto, very thinly sliced
3	fresh basil leaves, julienned
¼	cup freshly grated Parmesan cheese

Prepare pizza shell.

In a heavy-bottomed skillet over low heat, combine butter and 2 tablespoons oil. Add onion, cover, and cook, stirring often, until onion caramelizes; about 1 hour. Season with salt and pepper.

Place oven rack and pizza tile, if using, in the top third of the oven. Preheat oven to 500 degrees F. Sprinkle a pizza pan or peel, if using a tile, with cornmeal.

Place pizza shell on the prepared pan or peel. Coat shell with remaining 1 tablespoon olive oil.

Scatter prosciutto over surface, sprinkle with basil, distribute caramelized onions and sprinkle evenly with cheese.

Bake until bottom of crust is nicely browned and top is golden, 12 to 15 minutes.

Wine: Bonny Doon Vineyards "Clos du Gilroy" Grenache (California)

Kugel (Baked Noodles)

WITH CHÈVRE, SCALLIONS & CHIVES

THIS IS A DELICIOUS VARIATION on Linda's mother's traditional kugel, or noodle pudding. Besides being a wonderful accompaniment to chicken, this kugel sits well on the brunch buffet table along with some smoked salmon.

SERVES 10 TO 12

1	pound wide egg noodles
¾	pound creamed cottage cheese
½	pound fresh chèvre (goat cheese), crumbled
1	cup sour cream
1	cup finely chopped scallions, including some green
1-2	tablespoons minced fresh chives
2	teaspoons kosher salt
1	teaspoon freshly ground black pepper
½	cup (1 stick) unsalted butter, melted
6	large eggs, beaten

Bring a large pot of salted water to a brisk boil. Add noodles and cook just until tender, about 10 minutes. Drain thoroughly and cool.

Preheat oven to 350 degrees F. Thoroughly butter a 12-x-9-inch baking dish.

In a large mixing bowl, blend cottage cheese, chèvre and sour cream. Add scallions, chives, salt, pepper, melted butter and beaten eggs; blend thoroughly. Fold in noodles and blend well. Pour into the prepared baking dish.

Bake in the preheated oven for 1 hour, or until a knife inserted into center comes out clean. Let stand for 5 minutes before serving.

Wine: Edna Valley Vineyard Chardonnay (California: Edna Valley)

Farfallette with Chicken Livers & Onions

LIVER AND ONIONS go together perfectly in any dish but are especially good for a sauce over farfallette, which look like little bow ties. This particular dish is one of Linda's favorites. If we're serving this as a first course, we'll follow it with chicken and asparagus.

SERVES 4

¾-1   pound chicken livers, trimmed and
        membranes removed

2   tablespoons unsalted butter

2   tablespoons olive oil

1   cup medium-diced yellow onions

2   plump garlic cloves, minced

1   small dried red chile pepper, crumbled

¼   pound bacon, preferably smoked, diced

¼   pound shiitake or cremini mushroom caps,
        sliced (6 ounces with stems)

1   teaspoon minced fresh sage leaves or
        ½ teaspoon dried

½   cup dry red wine

2   tablespoons tomato paste

½   cup fresh or frozen peas
        Kosher salt and freshly ground black pepper

1   pound farfallette pasta (little bow ties)
     Freshly grated Parmesan cheese for serving

Carefully quarter each liver and set aside. Fill a soup pot with salted water and bring to a boil.

Meanwhile, in a large nonaluminum skillet, melt butter with olive oil over medium heat. Add onions and stir until wilted, 3 to 5 minutes. Add garlic and chile and stir for 2 minutes. Add bacon, mushrooms and sage and cook, stirring often, until bacon is slightly crisp and mushrooms are somewhat tender, about 5 minutes. Add chicken livers and sauté until livers lose their red color, 3 to 4 minutes. Stir in wine, tomato paste, peas and salt and pepper to taste. Simmer over very low heat until peas and mushrooms are tender, 2 to 3 minutes.

Cook farfallette until tender but still firm to the bite, 10 to 12 minutes. Drain thoroughly.

Stir pasta into simmering sauce and blend. Divide pasta among 4 heated soup plates. Sprinkle generously with Parmesan and serve.

Wine: R.H. Phillips EXP Syrah (California)

Baked Fusilli

WITH RED ONIONS, TOMATO & SMOKED SAUSAGE

You'll love the crisp crust of this baked pasta casserole filled with mushrooms, sausage, cheese and tomato sauce. We use quark (see Special Products, page 374), an old-fashioned cottage cheese that is smooth and tangy. If you don't have it, substitute 1 cup whole-milk ricotta cheese mixed with ¼ cup low-fat sour cream.

SERVES 6

	Kosher salt
3-4	tablespoons olive oil
6-8	ounces fresh wild mushrooms, such as shiitakes, portobellos or cremini, thinly sliced
1	pound smoked or hot Italian sausage links, cut into 1-inch lengths
1	jumbo red onion (about 1¼ pounds), thinly sliced
2-3	garlic cloves, minced
1	dried red chile pepper, crumbled
4	cups canned tomato puree
1	pound tricolored fusilli pasta
1	cup quark
½	cup sour cream
½	cup freshly grated Parmesan cheese
	Freshly ground black pepper
4	fresh basil leaves, julienned

Preheat oven to 500 degrees F. Lightly oil a shallow 3-quart oval baking dish.

Fill a soup pot with water, add salt and place over medium-high heat.

Meanwhile, in a large nonaluminum sauté pan, heat 3 tablespoons oil over medium heat. Add mushrooms and cook, stirring, for 1 minute. Cover and cook for 4 minutes. Remove the cover, add sausage, and cook, stirring often, until sausage is heated through and lightly browned, about 5 minutes. (If using Italian sausage, cook thoroughly.) Add more oil, if needed, and stir in onion, garlic and chile. Cook, stirring often, until onions are tender, about 10 minutes. Add tomato puree and cook until sauce is heated through and very hot.

Meanwhile, cook fusilli in boiling water for about 12 minutes, or for about 4 minutes less than package instructions suggest; pasta should still be tough. Drain and reserve.

Add quark, sour cream and ¼ cup grated Parmesan to sauce. Stir until blended. Stir in fusilli, a generous amount of pepper and the basil. Pour into the prepared baking dish and sprinkle evenly with remaining ¼ cup Parmesan. Bake for 15 minutes in the preheated oven, or until top is crusty. Serve immediately on heated plates.

Wine: Cafaro Cellars Merlot
(California: Napa Valley)

Part of what you get when you have dinner
at the East Side Grill in Northampton, Massachusetts,
is a splendid house salad. Some decent tender lettuce,
a nice vinaigrette with just the right amount of blue
cheese, topped with big rings of a gorgeous red onion.
A handsome man had come to the adjacent table
with two beautiful women, all so attractive and deeply
attentive to each other that they drew our
attention for more than a moment.
When their salads came, we noticed with
astonishment that the man carefully lifted the onion rings
off his salad and gingerly placed them on his bread plate,
while his female companions ate theirs with enthusiasm.
Unbelievable, we thought.
Who is this unadventurous, cautious person?
For a moment, from the way they were reacting to
each other, we wondered: ménage à trois?
But this is a guy who doesn't eat his onions.
Forget it.

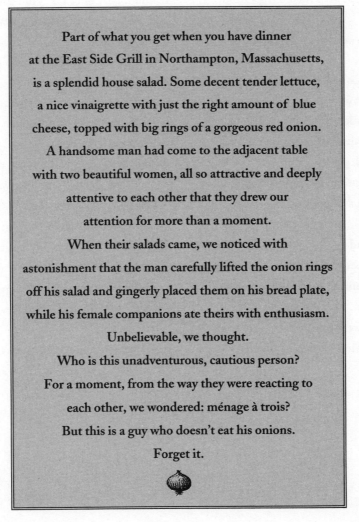

Orecchiette with Sausage, Sweet Onions & Tomatoes

ORECCHIETTE are little ear-shaped pasta, cupped just enough to grab hold of this fresh tomato sauce.

SERVES 2

2	tablespoons olive oil
2	garlic cloves, minced
1	small dried chile pepper, crumbled
1	pound fresh sausage (we like to use lamb), cut into 1-inch pieces
½	jumbo sweet onion, coarsely chopped
2	cups fresh tomato puree or 16 ounces canned
	Kosher salt and freshly ground black pepper
½	pound orecchiette pasta
1-2	tablespoons minced fresh thyme leaves and flowers
¼	cup chopped fresh basil leaves
⅓	cup freshly grated Parmesan cheese

Heat olive oil in a large nonaluminum skillet over medium heat until hot. Add garlic, chile and sausage and cook, stirring often, until sausage is well browned, 5 to 7 minutes.

Meanwhile, fill a large soup pot with salted water and bring to a boil.

Add onion to sausage mixture and cook until onion begins to become tender, about 10 minutes. Add tomato puree and salt and pepper to taste. Reduce heat to low and simmer.

Add orecchiette to boiling water and cook until tender but still firm to the bite, 15 to 18 minutes. Drain thoroughly. Add pasta to simmering sauce mixture. Stir in thyme and basil and cook, stirring, over low heat for 1 minute.

Ladle pasta into heated soup plates, sprinkle generously with Parmesan, and serve.

**Wine: Castello di Ama Colline di Ama
(Italy: Tuscany)**

Buckwheat Pasta with Cabbage, Onions & Sage

JAPANESE SOBA NOODLES are made from buckwheat, and their earthy flavor is enhanced by sautéed cabbage and onions. Soba noodles are readily available in health-food stores and Asian markets.

SERVES 4

5	tablespoons unsalted butter
2-4	tablespoons olive oil
4	cups shredded Savoy cabbage
6	sage leaves, minced, or ½ teaspoon dried
1	small dried chile pepper, crumbled
1	large white onion, thinly sliced
2	large garlic cloves, minced
¼	pound pancetta or smoked bacon, diced
3	tablespoons dry white wine
	Kosher salt and freshly ground white pepper
1	pound buckwheat noodles (soba)
½	cup freshly grated Parmesan cheese

Combine 2 tablespoons butter with 2 tablespoons olive oil in a large skillet and melt over medium heat. Add cabbage, sage and chile and stir to coat well. Cover and cook over low heat, stirring often and adding more olive oil if cabbage seems too dry, until cabbage is tender, about 20 minutes.

Meanwhile, melt remaining 3 tablespoons butter in a large heavy-bottomed saucepan over medium heat. Add onions and garlic and reduce heat to low. Cover and cook, stirring often, until onions are just at the point of caramelizing but aren't yet browned, 15 to 20 minutes. Add onions to cooked cabbage.

Meanwhile, bring a large pot of salted water to a boil.

In a small skillet, cook pancetta or bacon over medium heat until crisp. Add wine and cook for 1 minute. Add bacon mixture to cooked cabbage, stir well, and season generously with salt and pepper. Keep warm over very low heat.

Cook noodles in boiling water until tender but still firm to the bite, 4 to 5 minutes. Drain thoroughly.

Toss noodles with cabbage mixture. Add cheese and toss thoroughly. Serve in heated soup plates.

Wine: Giacomo Conterno Barbera
(Italy: Piedmont)

Little Shells with Caramelized Onion Sauce

THIS SIMPLE AND DELICIOUS DISH was suggested by caterer Dede Wilson of Amherst, Massachusetts, as we worked together one day in publicist Lisa Ekus's kitchen. You can make it just as it is, or add a bit of crisp smoked bacon or ham and some peas. We think that this sauce is best with a pasta that gives the sauce little "cups" in which to nestle.

SERVES 2

7   tablespoons unsalted butter

2   tablespoons olive oil

1   jumbo sweet onion, coarsely diced

2   tablespoons dry vermouth

1   tablespoon fresh thyme leaves

½   teaspoon kosher salt

½   teaspoon freshly ground black pepper

½   pound conchiglie or small shell pasta

¼   cup freshly grated Parmesan cheese

In a heavy-bottomed saucepan over very low heat, combine butter and oil. Add onion, cover, and cook, stirring often, until onion caramelizes, about 1 hour.

Stir vermouth, thyme, salt and pepper into onion mixture. Cover and cook for 5 minutes. Keep warm over very low heat.

Meanwhile, bring a large pot of salted water to a boil.

Cook shells until tender but still firm to the bite, about 12 to 15 minutes. Drain thoroughly.

Toss pasta with sauce. Serve in heated soup plates and sprinkle with Parmesan.

Wine: Volpe Pasini Sauvignon (Italy)

Barbara's Linguine with Red Onion-Tomato Sauce

THIS DELICIOUS PREPARATION came to us courtesy of Barbara Brown of Tucson, Arizona, a terrific cook. The red onions add texture to the otherwise smooth sauce.

SERVES 4 TO 6

3   tablespoons olive oil
2   large red onions, thinly sliced
3   large garlic cloves, minced
2   24-ounce cans crushed tomatoes
1   6-ounce can tomato paste
½   teaspoon dried red pepper flakes
     Kosher salt and freshly ground black pepper
2   pounds linguine
1   cup chopped fresh basil
1   cup freshly grated Romano cheese

Heat oil in a large nonaluminum skillet over low heat. Add onions and cook until softened, but not browned, about 20 minutes. Add garlic and cook, stirring from time to time, for 10 minutes. Add tomatoes, tomato paste, ½ paste can of water and red pepper flakes. Increase the heat and bring mixture to a simmer. Reduce the heat to low and simmer slowly for 20 minutes. Season with salt and pepper to taste.

Meanwhile, bring a large soup pot of salted water to a boil. Cook pasta until tender but still firm to the bite, about 10 minutes. Drain thoroughly.

Toss pasta with sauce, basil and grated Romano.

Wine: Caymus Vineyards Zinfandel
(California: Napa Valley)

FISH & SHELLFISH

Roasted Alaskan Salmon with Roasted Leek Sauce

QUICKLY SEARED SALMON FILLETS are slowly roasted over a bed of chopped leeks and lemongrass (available in Asian markets), a technique that results in an especially moist fish. You can substitute Atlantic salmon, but be sure to use the thickest salmon fillets available.

SERVES 2

¼	cup unbleached flour
2	Alaskan King salmon fillets (each about ½ pound), pin bones removed
2½	tablespoons olive oil
2	medium-sized leeks, trimmed, split, cleaned and finely chopped
2	teaspoons minced lemongrass bulb or 1½ teaspoons minced lemon zest Kosher salt and freshly ground white pepper
⅓	cup dry white wine
2	tablespoons fresh lemon juice
1	tablespoon unsalted butter
1	teaspoon minced fresh tarragon or fresh chives

Preheat oven to 250 degrees F.

Pour flour into a shallow soup plate. Dredge salmon fillets in flour and set aside.

In a large ovenproof skillet over high heat, heat 2 tablespoons olive oil until hot. Add salmon fillets and quickly sear on both sides. Set salmon aside on a plate.

Reduce heat to medium-low and add remaining ½ tablespoon oil to the skillet. When hot, add leeks and lemongrass or zest and sauté until very wilted, about 2 minutes. Remove skillet from heat.

Arrange salmon, skin side down, on leek bed and sprinkle with salt and white pepper. Place the skillet in the oven and roast until salmon is done, about 18 minutes. Gently part salmon flesh with a knife to check for doneness; we like to see a bit of rare flesh in the thickest part. Carefully transfer salmon fillets to heated plates. Add wine and lemon juice to the leeks in the skillet and cook over high heat, stirring, until liquids are reduced by ½, about 2 minutes. Remove the skillet from the heat, whisk in butter until melted and mixture has thickened. Stir in tarragon or chives and salt and pepper to taste. Nap fish with leek sauce.

Wine: Adelsheim Vineyard Pinot Noir Polk County (Oregon)

Ali Barker's Cusk Roasted on Leeks

WITH SHALLOT VINAIGRETTE

CUSK, A MEMBER OF THE COD FAMILY, is a marvelous fish found in deep waters off the New Hampshire and Massachusetts coasts. We had never tasted it until Chef Ali Barker first brought it to Cleveland, where it continues to be a very popular item on Piperade's menu. If you cannot obtain cusk, substitute cod, halibut or swordfish.

This recipe calls for steaming the leeks and placing the seared fish over them. Each serving is napped with a tasty vinaigrette of minced shallots, Dijon mustard and red-wine vinegar.

SERVES 6

Leeks

6   leeks, each about 1 inch in diameter, split lengthwise, cleaned and trimmed to include tender greens
     Salt and freshly ground black pepper
     3 tablespoons canola or other vegetable oil

Vinaigrette

¾   cup canola or other vegetable oil
3   small shallots, quartered
3-6   tablespoons hot water
⅓   cup red-wine vinegar
2   tablespoons Dijon mustard
     Kosher salt and freshly ground black pepper

Fish

6   tablespoons canola or other vegetable oil
6   tablespoons (¾ stick) unsalted butter
2¼   pounds cusk, cod, halibut or swordfish fillets, cut into 6 serving pieces
     Kosher salt and freshly ground black pepper
     Watercress for garnish

To make leeks: Carefully steam leeks until just tender, 4 to 5 minutes. Drain well and refresh with cold water; drain again and pat dry. Place in a roasting pan large enough to hold leeks in a single layer. Season with salt and pepper and sprinkle with oil.

To make vinaigrette: In a small nonaluminum saucepan, heat oil with shallots until they begin to sizzle. Remove from heat and let cool to room temperature, 10 to 15 minutes. In a blender, combine 3 tablespoons hot water, vinegar, mustard and salt and pepper to taste. Blend well. With the motor running, slowly add oil and shallot mixture. If mixture is too thick, add remaining 3 tablespoons water, a little bit at a time, until mixture reaches desired consistency. Adjust seasonings and set aside.

To cook fish: Preheat oven to 450 degrees F. In a large skillet, heat 2 tablespoons oil over medium-high heat. When oil is hot, add 2 tablespoons butter. When butter melts, add 2 pieces of fish and quickly brown on both sides. Place fish on top of leeks. Pour off butter mixture. Repeat process until all fish is browned. Place roasting pan in preheated oven and roast until fish is cooked through, 10 to 12 minutes, depending upon thickness

Remove from oven. Divide fish and leeks among 6 heated serving plates. Pour vinaigrette around the fish. Garnish each plate with a bunch of watercress.

Wine: Burgess Cellars Chardonnay "Triere Vineyard" (California: Napa Valley)

THE SHALLOT KING

I F THERE IS AN EXPERT on *Allium ascalonicum* in America, it surely must be Raymond Saufroy, a restaurateur turned farmer. In fact, he is responsible for that tasty little bulb being here at all. "Before 1954, shallots were never mentioned in the USA," he told us. "They never appeared in recipes."

After our conversation with Saufroy, we ran to our bookshelves to see if he was right. *Life* magazine's great *Picture Cook Book* of 1958, although it had some traditional French recipes, made no mention of shallots. Nor did Robert Carrier's *Great Dishes of the World* (1964) or Eve Brown's 1972 *Plaza Cookbook*. In the first edition (1961) of Craig Claiborne's *New York Times Cookbook* we found one recipe calling for them. In the 1966 edition, there was one reference in the index. In the 1979 edition, shallots were mentioned just five times.

In Pellaprat's *Modern French Culinary Art* (1966), only once do you see the word *echalotes*—in the list of the cook's raw materials. We jumped ahead in time to *Cooking with Lydie Marshall*, published in 1982. There is a single mention of shallots in the index. In an introductory note to beurre blanc, Marshall says, "I prefer scallions to shallots because they will melt into a pureelike consistency while the shallots, even minced, stay very hard."

Even now, no one seems to be paying much attention to the shallot, even though you can find this little bulb in almost any supermarket.

The ebullient Saufroy came to America from France after World War II. He had been a coal miner in his native country as a teenager, but he wasn't about to head off to West Virginia or Kentucky to the mines. Instead, he ended up a busboy at the Waldorf Astoria. That lead to a career as a restaurateur in New York, where Craig Claiborne took note of one of his shallot and herb sauces. "There were thousands of inquiries about shallots from that little article, about where they could get them," laughs Saufroy.

The answer, however, was "nowhere." By this time Raymond had married (coincidentally, his wife is named Ray), and there were babies on the way. They discussed their options and decided to go into the

(continued on page 214)

SHALLOTS

(continued from page 212)

shallot business, leaving the restaurant and buying a small farm in West Danville, Vermont.

Then came another major mention, this time in *Family Circle* magazine. It brought in 50,000 pieces of correspondence, orders mostly, sorely taxing the little town's post office and the bank, which had to deal with thousands of one-dollar checks—all the Saufroys charged for a starter kit of shallots. Le Jardin du Gourmet, the Saufroys' mail-order herb and shallot company, was born.

SHALLOTS ARE COSTLY at the supermarket because, even now, not many farmers grow them and bring them to market. We've seen them sold for as much as $12.50 a pound. But home gardeners can have an endless supply inexpensively. Shallots, whose scientific name derives from Askalon, in Israel, the historic home of the Philistines, where these alliums are first thought to have been cultivated, are not difficult to grow. It's best to start them from sets, says Saufroy. Plant one bulb; harvest a dozen. Save a couple for next year. The soil requirements of the shallot are modest; just give them a sandy, not particularly rich, patch and they will thrive.

The Saufroys have sold the business to their son-in-law, Paul, who is as busy as his father-in-law had ever been purveying shallots. And nowadays, Raymond Saufroy, the retired shallot king, putters around the house. "My wife has enough work for me to last until 2001. She even washes the rocks she puts in the rock garden."

Baked Bluefish with Onions & Tomatoes

THERE'S NOTHING SHY about the flavor of blue-fish, so we like to complement it with zesty sea-sonings. Baking it in a mixture of garlic, onions, shallots, tomatoes and herbs yields a tender and moist fish in a chunky sauce. Feel free to create your own herb combinations. You can substitute tarragon for fennel fronds and some lemon zest and regular thyme and basil for the lemon-flavored varieties.

SERVES 4 TO 6

1   tablespoon olive oil
4   large fennel fronds plus 1 heaping
    tablespoon minced fennel fronds
½   bunch flat-leaf parsley
4   branches thyme or lemon thyme (optional)
5   fresh basil leaves
¾   cup finely diced yellow onions
2   large bluefish fillets (each about 1¼ pounds)
2   plump garlic cloves, minced
1   large shallot, minced
2   large ripe tomatoes, peeled, seeded and
    finely diced

    Kosher salt and freshly ground black pepper
1   tablespoon extra-virgin olive oil

Preheat oven to 400 degrees F. Lightly coat a large, shallow baking dish with olive oil.

Scatter 4 fennel fronds, parsley, thyme, if using, and basil over the bottom of the baking dish. Sprinkle with ¼ cup onion. Arrange bluefish fillets, skin sides down, on top. Sprinkle with minced fennel, garlic and shallot. Scatter remaining ½ cup onions over fillets. Sprinkle tomatoes over onions. Season with salt and lots of pepper. Drizzle ½ tablespoon extra-virgin olive oil over each fillet. Bake until fish flakes easily when tested with a fork, but doesn't look dry, 17 to 18 minutes. Don't overcook; if whole fillets are less than 1 pound, test after 15 minutes. Divide cooked fish among heated plates and spoon some pan sauce over each.

**Wine: Trimbach Tokay-Pinot Gris Reserve
(France, Alsace) or
Ponzi Vineyards Pinot Gris (Oregon)**

Marinated Swordfish with Lemon-Chive Butter

RED ONIONS are especially flavorful in this lemon-and-thyme marinade. The grilled fish is topped with a tad of lemon-and-chive butter. Lemon balm can take over the garden, but it's great in marinades and it makes a terrific stuffing for baked fish or chicken. If you don't have an herb garden, you can substitute some minced fresh lemon zest for lemon balm and verbena.

SERVES 4

Marinade

⅓ cup Champagne vinegar or other white-wine vinegar

1 tablespoon fresh lemon juice

1 teaspoon Dijon mustard

⅓ cup extra-virgin olive oil

¼ cup vegetable oil

½ cup minced red onions

3 tablespoons minced lemon balm or verbena or zest of 1 lemon, minced

1 teaspoon minced fresh thyme leaves, preferably lemon thyme, or ½ teaspoon dried

2 tablespoons minced fresh chives

½ teaspoon freshly ground black pepper

2 pounds swordfish steaks, 1 inch thick, cut into 4 serving pieces

Herb Butter

¼ cup (½ stick) unsalted butter, softened

1 tablespoon minced fresh chives

1 teaspoon minced lemon balm or verbena or ½ teaspoon minced lemon zest

Kosher salt

To make marinade: In a glass or ceramic dish large enough to hold fish in a single layer, combine vinegar, lemon juice and mustard. Vigorously whisk in both oils to make a thick emulsion. Blend in onions, lemon balm or verbena or zest, thyme, chives and pepper. Thoroughly coat swordfish with marinade, cover with plastic and refrigerate for several hours. Bring to room temperature before proceeding.

Meanwhile, make herb butter: Blend softened butter with chives and lemon balm or verbena or zest. Place on a sheet of wax paper and roll into a log. Chill until needed, at least 2 hours.

Thoroughly clean the surface of a gas or charcoal grill with a metal brush; coat the rack evenly with vegetable oil. Preheat the grill until hot.

Remove fish from marinade, and sprinkle with salt. Place fish on the prepared grill, cover and cook for 5 minutes. Turn fish, cover and cook for 5 minutes more.

Place a slice of herb butter on each portion of fish and serve.

Wine: Girard Winery Chardonnay "Reserve" (California: Napa Valley)

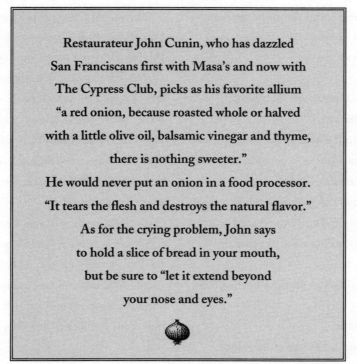

Restaurateur John Cunin, who has dazzled
San Franciscans first with Masa's and now with
The Cypress Club, picks as his favorite allium
"a red onion, because roasted whole or halved
with a little olive oil, balsamic vinegar and thyme,
there is nothing sweeter."
He would never put an onion in a food processor.
"It tears the flesh and destroys the natural flavor."
As for the crying problem, John says
to hold a slice of bread in your mouth,
but be sure to "let it extend beyond
your nose and eyes."

Brook Trout & Shallots in Riesling

W E ENJOY THE DELICATE FLAVORS of these trout braised in wine and finished with a simple cream sauce. The attractive lettuce wrappings serve as a protective case to hold a generous sprinkling of shallots against each fish during cooking. While this dish requires a modicum of patience in wrapping the trout, it's not difficult.

SERVES 4

20	large lettuce leaves (about 1¼ pounds), tough stems removed
⅔	cup finely minced shallots
4	brook trout (each about ¾ pound), cleaned with heads and tails intact
	Kosher salt and freshly ground white pepper
1	tablespoon unsalted butter, softened
2	cups Alsatian Riesling wine or other dry white wine
⅔	cup fish stock, chicken stock or bottled clam juice
1¼	cups heavy cream
2	tablespoons minced fresh fennel fronds, tarragon leaves or chervil leaves
1	tablespoon minced fresh parsley
	Pinch cayenne
	Fresh herbs and lemon wedges for garnish

Preheat oven to 450 degrees F.

Fill a large skillet with water and bring to a boil. Blanch 5 lettuce leaves at a time, about 5 seconds. Spread out 4 or 5 leaves on a large work surface, slightly overlapping as necessary, to make a wrapping large enough to enclose the body of a trout. Make 3 more "beds." Sprinkle each with 1 tablespoon shallots. Place 1 fish on each, head and tail exposed, sprinkle with some salt and white pepper, wrap each trout and set aside. Repeat the process until all 4 trout are wrapped.

Butter a shallow baking dish large enough to hold fish in a single layer. Scatter remaining shallots over the bottom; arrange fish packages on shallots. In a small nonaluminum saucepan over medium heat, combine wine and stock or clam juice and bring to a boil. Pour hot liquid over fish; cover baking dish with foil.

Bake until each fish feels firm when pressed with

your fingers and flesh is opaque, about 15 minutes (longer if fish are larger).

Remove fish and keep warm. Carefully drain liquid in the baking dish through a strainer into a heavy nonaluminum saucepan. Place saucepan over high heat and boil vigorously until mixture reduces to ¼ cup, about 5 minutes. Meanwhile, pour cream into another saucepan and cook over low heat until slightly thickened. Combine cream with reduced stock and whisk together over high heat until mixture thickens, about 1 minute. Stir in minced herbs and cayenne; season with salt and pepper.

Place each fish on a heated serving plate and garnish with fresh herbs and lemon. Serve sauce on the side.

Wine: Clos St. Landelin Riesling
(France: Alsace)

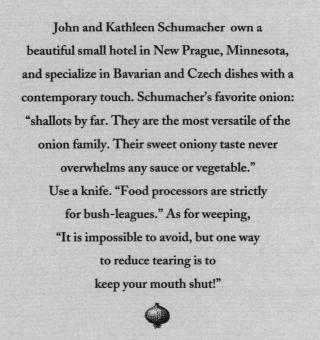

John and Kathleen Schumacher own a beautiful small hotel in New Prague, Minnesota, and specialize in Bavarian and Czech dishes with a contemporary touch. Schumacher's favorite onion: "shallots by far. They are the most versatile of the onion family. Their sweet oniony taste never overwhelms any sauce or vegetable." Use a knife. "Food processors are strictly for bush-leagues." As for weeping, "It is impossible to avoid, but one way to reduce tearing is to keep your mouth shut!"

Sautéed Steelhead Salmon or Trout

WITH SHALLOTS, GINGER & LIME

A SIMPLE SHALLOT SAUCE with ginger and lime adds just the right touch to this butterflied sautéed fish. A dash of soy, a few sesame seeds for texture and an accompanying vegetable dish of bok choy suggest the Orient. If you don't have access to steelhead salmon, use salmon-trout or ordinary trout.

SERVES 4

½   cup unbleached flour

½   teaspoon salt

½   teaspoon freshly ground white pepper

4   steelhead salmon, salmon-trout or trout (about ¾ pound each), split and boned, heads and tails removed

4   tablespoons olive oil

¼   cup (½ stick) unsalted butter

¼   cup minced shallots

2   teaspoons peeled minced fresh ginger

1   tablespoon sesame seeds

1   tablespoon fresh lime juice

1   tablespoon soy sauce
    Steamed and buttered bok choy as accompaniment

Combine flour, salt and pepper on a plate. Lightly dust fish with flour mixture and set aside.

Pour 2 tablespoons olive oil in a large skillet and heat over high heat until hot. Sauté fish for about 3 minutes a side. Keep cooked fish warm while sautéing remaining fish in remaining oil as needed.

Drain oil from pan, add butter, shallots, ginger and sesame seeds. Cook, stirring constantly, over medium heat for 2 minutes. Add lime juice and soy sauce and cook, stirring, for 1 minute.

Spoon sauce over fish and accompany with buttered bok choy.

Wine: Robert Talbott Vineyards Chardonnay
(California: Monterey County)

Smoked Fish Cakes with Red Onion-Corn Relish

THESE DELICATE smoked sablefish cakes were inspired by whitefish cakes at Pete and Mickey's, a charming bistro in Charlevoix, Michigan, owned by Harlan "Pete" Peterson and Mickey Bakst. Smoked sablefish, which is actually smoked black cod, is commonly available in Jewish-style delis. You can substitute smoked trout or whitefish.

SERVES 4 TO 6

1	pound Yukon Gold or red-skinned potatoes, peeled and cut into ½-inch dice
1¼	pounds smoked sablefish
4-5	tablespoons unsalted butter
2	tablespoons low-fat sour cream
⅓	cup minced sweet onion
3	scallions, trimmed to include 1 inch green, finely minced
1	cup fine dry bread crumbs
2	large eggs, lightly beaten
	Kosher salt and freshly ground white pepper
	Red Onion-Corn Relish (page 224)

Place potatoes in a large saucepan, cover with salted cold water and bring to a boil over high heat. Reduce heat to medium and cook until potatoes are tender, about 15 minutes.

While potatoes are cooking, skin fish, remove all bones and coarsely chop flesh.

Thoroughly drain cooked potatoes. Combine potatoes with 2 tablespoons butter in a large bowl. Using a potato masher, mash potatoes until smooth. Stir in sour cream, onion, scallions, ⅓ cup bread crumbs and fish. Add eggs and salt and white pepper to taste; mix until evenly blended. Sprinkle ⅓ cup bread crumbs over a small baking sheet. Form fish cakes that are 4 inches in circumference and about ⅔ inch thick (you can make smaller cakes, if you prefer) and place fish cakes on top of crumbs. Sprinkle tops of fish cakes with remaining ⅓ cup bread crumbs. Cover with plastic wrap and chill for at least 4 hours.

Melt remaining 2 to 3 tablespoons butter in a large nonstick skillet over medium heat until hot. Add fish cakes and fry until crisp and golden, about 3 minutes a side. Serve with Red Onion-Corn Relish.

Wine: Peter Michael Winery
"Mon Plaisir" Chardonnay
(California: Sonoma County, Alexander Valley)

Salmon, Mushrooms & Carrots

WITH SHALLOT-LIME BUTTER IN PARCHMENT

ROASTING FISH IN PARCHMENT seals in all of the natural juices, yielding an intensely flavored dish. Preparation can be done early in the day, with final baking just before serving, leaving no last-minute mess to clean up. While this dish does make an elegant main course, we usually serve it as the first course for a festive dinner. If served as a main course, distribute ingredients among 4 larger parchment rounds, but don't alter the cooking time.

SERVES 8 AS A FIRST COURSE;

4 AS A MAIN COURSE

8   9-inch circles of parchment paper
    Olive oil

7   tablespoons unsalted butter, softened

1   medium-sized sweet onion, cut into matchstick lengths

2   medium-sized carrots, cut into matchstick lengths

4   large mushrooms, caps cut into matchstick lengths

1   teaspoon minced fresh tarragon leaves, plus 16 fresh tarragon leaves
    Kosher salt and freshly ground white pepper

1   rounded tablespoon minced shallots

1   teaspoon julienned lime zest

¾   pound skinned salmon fillet, cut into ⅛-inch-thick slices

7   tablespoons dry white wine

1   tablespoon fresh lime juice

¼   cup fish stock or bottled clam juice

Fold parchment circles in half, crease and re-open. Brush lightly all over with olive oil; set aside. Melt 4 tablespoons butter in a nonstick sauté pan. Add onion and carrots, cover and cook over medium-low heat, stirring often, for 5 minutes. Stir in mushrooms, cover and cook for 3 minutes. Add minced tarragon and salt and white pepper to taste. Cover and cook for 4 minutes. Remove from the heat.

Divide mixture among the parchment circles, spooning vegetables into the center of the lower half of the circle, just to one side of the fold.

Blend together remaining 3 tablespoons butter, shallots and lime zest; set aside.

Place an equal number of salmon slices, overlapping slightly, on top of each mound of vegetables. Season salmon with salt and white pepper. Place

2 tarragon leaves on each portion of salmon, and then ⅛ of butter mixture.

Combine wine, lime juice and stock or clam juice. Taking 1 packet at a time, spoon 1½ tablespoons liquid over salmon and quickly crimp the edges tightly to seal. Place packages on 2 large baking sheets. *(Packets can be stored in the refrigerator for several hours, if you wish. Bring to room temperature before baking.)*

Preheat oven to 500 degrees F. Place the baking sheets in the oven. Bake for 3 minutes. Slit packets in front of the guests so each will enjoy the wonderful fragrance.

Wine: Babcock Vineyards "11 Oaks" Sauvignon Blanc (California: Santa Barbara)

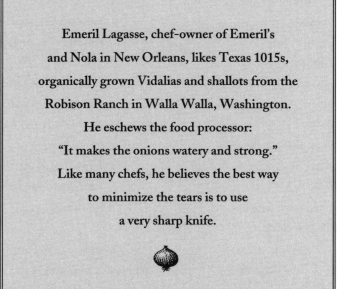

Emeril Lagasse, chef-owner of Emeril's and Nola in New Orleans, likes Texas 1015s, organically grown Vidalias and shallots from the Robison Ranch in Walla Walla, Washington. He eschews the food processor: "It makes the onions watery and strong." Like many chefs, he believes the best way to minimize the tears is to use a very sharp knife.

Grilled Tuna with Shallot-Herb Marinade

& RED ONION-CORN RELISH

ANY COMBINATION of tuna with onion is bound to be a good one. In winter, when we have to use our broiler instead of the grill, we marinate the tuna, then broil it under a layer of sliced white onions. Even out-of-season corn is a welcome sight when part of our favorite relish.

SERVES 6

Marinade & Fish

¼   cup plus 1 tablespoon red-wine vinegar
⅔   cup vegetable oil
⅓   cup minced shallots
2   plump garlic cloves, finely minced
2   tablespoons minced fresh tarragon leaves or 1 tablespoon dried
3   tablespoons minced fresh parsley
6   tuna steaks, cut 1 inch thick

Red Onion-Corn Relish

3   large ears fresh sweet corn
2   tablespoons red-wine vinegar
3   tablespoons extra-virgin olive oil
½   cup finely diced red onion

1   small red bell pepper, seeded and finely diced
1   tablespoon minced fresh cilantro
1   tablespoon minced fresh chives
2   teaspoons minced fresh thyme or lemon thyme leaves
1   teaspoon minced fresh lemon verbena or lemon balm, or 1 teaspoon minced lemon zest
1   small fresh hot chile pepper, seeded and minced (optional)
    Kosher salt and freshly ground white pepper

Shredded nasturtium and borage flowers and/or minced fresh herbs for garnish (optional)

To marinate fish: Pour vinegar into a small bowl. Vigorously whisk in ⅔ cup oil. Blend in shallots, garlic, tarragon and parsley. Place tuna steaks in a large glass or ceramic dish and pour marinade over them. Marinate for at least 4 hours in the refrigerator, turning several times.

Meanwhile, make relish: Remove corn husks and silk, rub ears with olive oil, wrap in foil and roast over a hot grill, turning often, until tender and browned, 5 to 7 minutes. Unwrap and let cool. Cut kernels off cobs with a sharp knife.

In a large bowl, whisk together vinegar and oil until a thick emulsion forms. Add roasted corn, onion, bell pepper, herbs and chile pepper, if using; mix gently. Season with salt and white pepper to taste. Cover and chill until ready to serve.

To cook fish: Thoroughly clean the surface of a gas or charcoal grill with a metal brush; coat the rack evenly with vegetable oil. Preheat the grill. When it is hot, remove tuna from marinade, season with salt and pepper, and grill on one side for 4 minutes. Baste with marinade, turn and grill the other side for 4 minutes.

To serve, spoon relish over part of the fish, allowing part of relish to spill onto the plate. Garnish with flowers and herbs, if using.

**Wine: Saint Gregory Chardonnay
(California: Mendocino)**

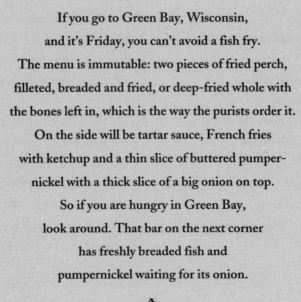

If you go to Green Bay, Wisconsin,
and it's Friday, you can't avoid a fish fry.
The menu is immutable: two pieces of fried perch,
filleted, breaded and fried, or deep-fried whole with
the bones left in, which is the way the purists order it.
On the side will be tartar sauce, French fries
with ketchup and a thin slice of buttered pumpernickel with a thick slice of a big onion on top.
So if you are hungry in Green Bay,
look around. That bar on the next corner
has freshly breaded fish and
pumpernickel waiting for its onion.

Salmon Loaf with Cucumber-Onion Sour Cream Sauce

THIS SALMON LOAF is delicious either hot or cold. And while you can always used canned salmon, the dish is infinitely better when you poach some fresh salmon instead. This makes a simple supper served hot in the winter, cold in summer, and it's good for a picnic served with Roasted Red Potato Salad with Red Onions, Herbs & Bacon (page 136).

SERVES 4

1 lemon, sliced
¼ cup dry white wine
1⅔ pounds fresh salmon fillet, skinned, or 32 ounces canned
1 cup low-fat evaporated milk
1¾ cups fine dry bread crumbs
⅓ cup minced white onions or shallots
2 tablespoons minced fresh dill
2 large eggs, beaten
    Kosher salt and freshly ground white pepper
2 tablespoons butter, melted
½ English cucumber, trimmed and unpeeled, cut into pieces
½ medium-sized sweet onion, such as Vidalia, Walla Walla or Spanish
1 cup low-fat sour cream

If using fresh salmon, place lemon, wine and salmon in a 3-quart nonaluminum saucepan. Cover with water and bring to a boil. Reduce heat and simmer slowly until fish is just at the point of flaking, but still slightly rare in the middle, 10 to 15 minutes, depending upon thickness of fillet. Drain quickly and chill. If using canned salmon, drain thoroughly and remove any skin and bones.

Preheat oven to 350 degrees F. Thoroughly grease a loaf pan.

In the bowl of an electric mixer, combine evaporated milk and 1½ cups bread crumbs. Let stand for 15 minutes. Add salmon fillet or canned salmon, onions or shallots and 1 tablespoon dill. Beat until mixture is well combined. Add eggs and salt and white pepper to taste; beat again. Spoon mixture into the prepared pan. Sprinkle top evenly with remaining

¼ cup bread crumbs. Drizzle with melted butter. Bake in the preheated oven for 50 minutes, or until firm to the touch and lightly browned.

Meanwhile, combine cucumber and onion in the bowl of a food processor fitted with the metal blade. Puree. Add sour cream and remaining 1 tablespoon dill, and process until well blended. Stir in salt and white pepper to taste. Scrape sauce into a serving dish and chill until salmon loaf is ready.

Unmold loaf before serving. Serve salmon loaf hot or cold, depending on your preference, in ½-to-¾-inch-thick slices with a dollop of sauce on top.

**Wine: Carmenet Vineyard French Columbard
"Old Vines," Cyril Chavez Vineyard
(California: Napa Valley)**

**Someone once called the onion
"the truffle of the poor."**

Heavenly Fish Stew

CIOPPINO, a soupy fish and shellfish stew, uses whatever fresh fish you have in a flavorful base of tomatoes, onions and garlic. While the list of ingredients is long, the steps are simple. Serve this with thick slices of good sourdough bread. We prefer to cook the shrimp in their shells to give more flavor to the sauce; guests peel the shells with their fingers as they eat—messy, yes, but part of cioppino, and fun.

SERVES 6 TO 8

¼ cup olive oil

2½ cups finely diced yellow onions

3 garlic cloves, minced

1 small dried red chile pepper, crushed

1 bunch scallions with tender greens, finely chopped

1 medium-large leek with tender green, trimmed, cleaned and finely sliced

1 green bell pepper, cut into medium dice

1 32-ounce can Italian plum tomatoes

2 teaspoons minced fresh thyme leaves or 1 teaspoon dried

1 tablespoon minced fresh basil leaves or 2 teaspoons dried

2 teaspoons minced fresh tarragon leaves or 1 teaspoon dried

1 tablespoon minced fresh fennel fronds or 1 teaspoon dried fennel seeds

1 bay leaf

1 6-ounce can tomato paste

3 cups dry red wine

3 cups fish stock or bottled clam juice

¼ teaspoon saffron threads

Kosher salt and freshly ground black pepper

18 mussels, scrubbed

3 pounds halibut or monkfish fillets, cut into serving portions

1 pound large raw shrimp, unshelled

18 littleneck clams, scrubbed

Minced fresh chives and lemon wedges for garnish

In a heavy nonaluminum soup pot or Dutch oven, heat olive oil over low heat. Add onions, garlic, chile pepper, scallions, leek and bell pepper and cook over low heat, stirring often, until onions wilt, 10 to 15 minutes.

Stir in tomatoes and herbs. Break tomatoes into pieces and cook until heated through. Stir in tomato paste and blend well. Add wine and stock or clam juice. Cook, uncovered, over low heat for 30 minutes.

Combine saffron with ½ cup hot tomato mixture

and stir until saffron dissolves. Return mixture to the pot and simmer for 5 minutes. Season with salt and pepper to taste. *(Sauce can be made to this point and reheated to boiling just before serving.)*

Debeard mussels just before cooking. Arrange fish in a single layer in hot tomato mixture; layer on shrimp, and then clams and mussels. Bring mixture to a boil over high heat. Cover, reduce heat to low and simmer until clams open, 12 to 15 minutes. Ladle into large soup plates, discarding bay leaf and any unopened clams and mussels. Sprinkle with chives and garnish with lemon wedges.

**Wine: Patz and Hall Chardonnay
(California: Napa Valley)**

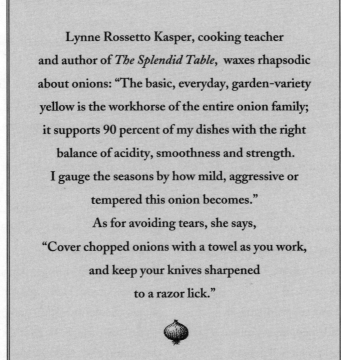

Lynne Rossetto Kasper, cooking teacher and author of *The Splendid Table*, waxes rhapsodic about onions: "The basic, everyday, garden-variety yellow is the workhorse of the entire onion family; it supports 90 percent of my dishes with the right balance of acidity, smoothness and strength. I gauge the seasons by how mild, aggressive or tempered this onion becomes." As for avoiding tears, she says, "Cover chopped onions with a towel as you work, and keep your knives sharpened to a razor lick."

Chinese Sweet & Sour Shrimp with Scallions

ONIONS PLAY an important role in any sweet and sour sauce. While this particular preparation lays no claim to authenticity, we find it wonderfully delicious and simple, offering the flavors familiar to devotees of this Chinese-American dish.

SERVES 2 TO 4

Marinade & Shrimp

1   egg white
3   tablespoons rice wine
2   tablespoons cornstarch
1   scallion, smashed with flat side of cleaver
1   thin slice fresh ginger, smashed with flat side of cleaver
1   pound large raw shrimp, peeled and deveined

Seasonings

¼   cup minced scallions, including tender green
¼   cup finely diced white onion
1   plump garlic clove, minced
2   teaspoons peeled minced fresh ginger
1   small dried red chile pepper, crumbled
½   cup medium-diced green bell pepper

Sauce

1   teaspoon cornstarch
¼   cup chicken stock
2   tablespoons red-wine vinegar
3   tablespoons ketchup
2   teaspoons sugar
1   tablespoon rice wine
1   teaspoon soy sauce
1   teaspoon Oriental sesame oil

4-5   tablespoons peanut oil, for frying
3   scallions, trimmed to include 1 inch green, chopped, for garnish

To marinate shrimp: Place egg white in a medium-sized bowl and beat lightly with rice wine and cornstarch. Stir in scallion and ginger. Add shrimp and toss well to coat. Marinate at room temperature for 1 hour.

To make seasonings: In a small bowl, combine scallions, onion, garlic, ginger, chile pepper and bell pepper. Set aside within easy reach of the stove.

To make sauce: In another bowl, whisk together cornstarch and stock. Whisk in vinegar; stir in ketchup, sugar, rice wine, soy sauce and sesame oil. Set aside with seasonings; place shrimp nearby.

To cook shrimp: Pour 3 tablespoons peanut oil in a wok and set over high heat until hot. Remove shrimp from marinade, add to the wok and toss, adding more oil only if needed, until shrimp turn pink, about 3 to 5 minutes. Remove shrimp to a warm platter.

To assemble: Add remaining 1 tablespoon peanut oil to the wok and heat. Quickly add seasoning mixture and toss over high heat until bell peppers begin to wilt, about 1 minute. Quickly whisk sauce mixture to blend; add to the wok. Toss over high heat until sauce is hot and thickened. Return shrimp to mixture, toss to coat well and heat through. Remove the wok from the heat.

Spoon mixture into a heated serving dish, and garnish with scallions.

Wine: Domaine Weinbach Gewürztraminer "Réserve Personelle" (France: Alsace)

Creole Shrimp & Pearl Onions

FOLKS IN NEW ORLEANS, where Creole cookery developed, have no hard and fast rules for making this shrimp dish. But the term "Creole" suggests a food preparation cooked in a thick sauce of tomatoes and onions, generally with lemon, green pepper and cayenne, often served on rice. We've included pearl onions for additional flavor and texture. This makes a good dish to serve to company; assemble it in the morning and add the shrimp and finish the cooking right before serving. If you must do the whole thing ahead, be careful not to ruin the shrimp by overcooking them when you reheat.

SERVES 6 TO 8

2 pounds large raw shrimp, peeled and deveined, with shells reserved

4 cups water

1 teaspoon black peppercorns

1 lemon, sliced

3 tablespoons vegetable oil

2 celery ribs, finely diced

1 medium-sized yellow onion, finely diced

3 plump garlic cloves, minced

1 large green bell pepper, cut into medium dice

¼ teaspoon cayenne

2 tablespoons unbleached flour

4 cups fresh tomato puree or 32 ounces canned

1 tablespoon fresh lemon juice

2 bay leaves

1 teaspoon minced fresh thyme leaves or ½ teaspoon dried
Kosher salt and freshly ground black pepper

1 pint pearl onions, blanched and peeled (pages 37-38)

4 cups hot long-grain white rice (about 1⅓ cups raw) for serving

1 bunch scallions, trimmed to include 1 inch green, minced

Place shrimp shells in a medium-sized saucepan and add water to cover, peppercorns and lemon. Bring to a boil. Reduce heat and simmer for 1 hour. Remove shells and simmer briskly until liquid reduces to 2 cups; set aside.

In a large nonaluminum sauté pan, heat oil over medium heat. Add celery and onion, reduce heat to low and stir until wilted, about 5 minutes. Add garlic, bell pepper and cayenne and cook, stirring often, until peppers wilt, 5 to 7 minutes more. Sprinkle vegetables with flour, increase heat to medium-high and stir until flour turns golden, 2 to 3 minutes. Stir in tomato puree, lemon juice and reserved shrimp stock. Add bay leaves, thyme and salt and pepper to taste. Increase heat and bring sauce almost to a boil. Reduce heat to low, cover and simmer for 50 minutes.

Stir in pearl onions, cover and simmer for 15 minutes.

Shortly before serving, increase heat to medium and bring to a brisk simmer. Stir in shrimp, cover and cook over low heat for 10 minutes. Remove bay leaves and serve over hot rice in heated soup plates. Garnish generously with minced scallions.

Wine: Murphy-Goode Winery Fumé Blanc (California: Sonoma County, Alexander Valley)

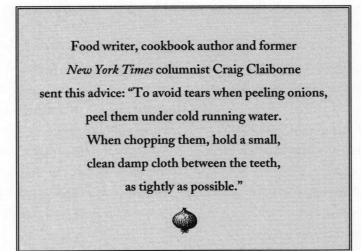

Food writer, cookbook author and former
New York Times columnist Craig Claiborne
sent this advice: "To avoid tears when peeling onions,
peel them under cold running water.
When chopping them, hold a small,
clean damp cloth between the teeth,
as tightly as possible."

Grilled Oysters & Corn with Scallion Vinaigrette

WE LOVE OYSTERS, but always find them to be impossible to shuck. If you put them on a hot grill, not only will the shells open by themselves, but the succulent oysters will take on a pleasing smoky flavor. A zesty scallion and tarragon vinaigrette is a good sauce for both oysters and corn. Italian Bread Salad with Red Onions, Tomatoes & Fresh Basil (page 140) makes a fine addition to this meal.

SERVES 2

Vinaigrette

⅓   cup minced scallions, including tender
     green parts

1   small dried red chile pepper, crumbled

3   tablespoons tarragon white-wine vinegar or
     Champagne vinegar

1   tablespoon fresh lemon juice

½   cup extra-virgin olive oil

¼   teaspoon kosher salt

¼   teaspoon freshly ground white pepper

2   dozen fresh oysters, scrubbed

4   ears fresh sweet corn, shucked

1   tablespoon olive oil
     Salt and freshly ground black pepper

To make vinaigrette: Several hours ahead, combine scallions, chile pepper, vinegar and lemon juice in a small bowl. Whisk in extra-virgin olive oil, salt and pepper. Let stand at room temperature until needed.

Check oysters to make certain that each is well scrubbed and tightly closed. Rub corn with olive oil and wrap each ear in a square of foil.

Thoroughly clean the surface of a gas or charcoal grill with a metal brush; coat the rack evenly with vegetable oil. Preheat the grill until hot. Arrange oysters and corn on the grill rack. Cover and grill for 4 minutes. Turn corn, cover again and grill until oysters open, 2 to 4 minutes.

Place corn and oysters on heated plates. Unwrap corn; gently remove the top of each oyster shell. Whisk vinaigrette and spoon some onto each oyster. Serve with remaining vinaigrette on the side.

**Wine: François Raveneau Chablis
"Montée Tonnerre" (France: Burgundy)**

Crawfish Boil

WITH ONIONS, CORN & ANDOUILLE SAUSAGE

UNLESS YOU LIVE in Louisiana or Texas, crawfish are hard, but not impossible, to obtain. We first learned about cooking crawfish from Nut Ledet, a crawfish farmer near Houma, Louisiana. Sausages and onions add depth of flavor to the crawfish and corn.

SERVES 2

12   cups (3 quarts) water
4   tablespoons kosher salt
1   bag Zatarain's Crab Boil or other crab boil
2   lemons, sliced
¼   cup plus 1 tablespoon cayenne
1   pound white onions, chopped
1½   pounds andouille sausage
4   pounds fresh crawfish
4   ears fresh sweet corn, shucked and cut in thirds
    Ice cubes

In a large nonaluminum stockpot, combine water, 3 tablespoons salt, crab boil, lemons and ¼ cup cayenne. Bring mixture to a rolling boil. Add onions and sausage and boil for 10 minutes. Add crawfish and corn, cover and boil for 6 minutes. Add remaining 1 tablespoon salt and remaining 1 tablespoon cayenne; boil 1 minute. Turn off heat. Add a large bowl of ice cubes and let the pot stand for 7 minutes before serving. (The ice helps the crawfish to absorb some of the flavors of the seasonings.)

Use a strainer or slotted spoon to remove crawfish, corn and sausage from the pot, discarding any crawfish that are not curled. Cut sausage into chunks. Serve crawfish mounded on large, heated dinner plates with sausage and corn on the side.

Wine: Domaine Mumm "Winery Lake" Sparkling Wine (Napa Valley) or beer

BEEF, PORK, VEAL & LAMB

BEEF

Three Meat & Onion Meat Loaf with Bourbon-Onion Chili Sauce . . . 238

Mom's Beef Brisket with Onion & Beer Sauce . . . 239

Provençal Beef Stew with Onions & Olives . . . 242

Piperade's Grilled Hanger Steak with Fried Leeks . . . 244

Scallion-Orange Beef . . . 246

Peppered Tenderloin with Sautéed Onions & Mushrooms . . . 248

Grilled Flank Steak with Red Jerk Sauce . . . 251

Barbecued Short Ribs . . . 253

PORK

Pork & Onion Pozole . . . 256

Paul's Hot Italian Sausage with Sweet Peppers & Onions . . . 257

Roasted Andouille Sausage with Onions, Pineapple & Beer . . . 258

Onion & Apple-Smothered Pork Chops . . . 259

Grilled Pork Loin in Roasted Onion Adobo . . . 260

Roasted Pork Loin & Shallots with Onions & Ginger . . . 262

Grilled Pork Chops with Green Jerk Sauce . . . 264

Grilled Herb & Onion-Marinated Pork Tenderloin . . . 266

Grilled Pork Tenderloin with Onions & Chipotle Fruit Sauce . . . 267

VEAL

LAMB

Three Meat & Onion Meat Loaf

WITH BOURBON-ONION CHILI SAUCE

W E LOVE COLD MEAT LOAF, so we always make a big one. While we prefer to make this with spicy sausage meat, you can substitute ground pork, more seasonings and a teaspoon of cayenne. If you don't have fresh herbs, prepare a mix of 3 tablespoons blended dried with ¼ cup minced fresh parsley.

SERVES 8 TO 10

2¼	pounds ground chuck
1½	pounds ground veal
1¼	pounds raw hot sausage, removed from casings
3	large eggs
⅔	cup minced yellow onion
2	scallions, finely minced
1	shallot, finely minced
2	plump garlic cloves, minced
1	tablespoon kosher salt
2	teaspoons freshly ground black pepper
⅔	cup fine dry bread crumbs
⅔	cup warm water
½	cup mixed minced fresh herbs: fennel, thyme, marjoram, oregano, rosemary and/or parsley
2	fresh sage leaves, minced, or ¼ teaspoon ground
2	bay leaves

Bourbon-Onion Chili Sauce (page 85) for serving

Place meats and eggs in a large bowl. With an electric mixer fitted with a paddle, or by hand, beat for 2 minutes. Add all ingredients except for bay leaves and sauce, and mix thoroughly.

Turn mixture into a roasting pan and firmly pack meat, forming it into a long loaf 4 to 6 inches wide and 4 to 5 inches high. Place bay leaves on top. Cover and chill for at least 2 hours. Remove from refrigerator 1 hour before roasting.

Preheat oven to 350 degrees F.

Bake meat loaf for 45 minutes. Increase oven temperature to 425 degrees and bake for 40 minutes more. Serve with chili sauce.

Wine: Ridge Vineyards Zinfandel "Geyserville" (California: Sonoma County)

Mom's Beef Brisket with Onion & Beer Sauce

THIS IS HOW Linda's mom, Gert LeVine, has made brisket for at least 50 years (with a few changes from us, of course). If you prefer, you can slice the onions instead of chopping them. Serve this dish with Potatoes & Onions Boulangère (page 354) or the Skillet Potato Cake with Shallots & Chives (page 352). Like most brisket preparations, this dish keeps quite nicely for several days in the refrigerator.

SERVES 10

1	whole, untrimmed brisket (9-12 pounds)
1	tablespoon kosher salt
1	tablespoon freshly ground black pepper
1	tablespoon garlic powder
2	teaspoons dried thyme
1½	pounds Spanish onions, cut into medium dice
2	celery ribs, cut into medium dice
1	12-ounce bottle Bennett's Chili Sauce or another spicy chili sauce
½	cup water
1	12-ounce bottle dark beer

At least 1 day ahead, bring brisket to room temperature. Preheat oven to 325 degrees F.

In a small bowl, combine salt, pepper, garlic powder and thyme. Vigorously rub dry seasonings all over brisket and place meat, fat side up, in a large roasting pan that has a tight-fitting cover. Distribute onions and celery evenly over top of meat. Pour chili sauce over vegetables and meat. Place pan in the preheated oven and roast, uncovered, for 45 minutes. Add water, cover and roast for 1½ hours. Add beer. Cover and roast until meat is very tender when tested with a fork, 45 minutes to 1½ hours longer.

When cooked, let meat cool. Remove it from the roasting pan and wrap thoroughly, first in plastic and then in foil. Pour liquid from the pan into a large bowl and cover. Chill meat and gravy overnight.

To carve: Trim all excess fat from top of brisket; discard. Carefully separate top piece from bottom with a sharp knife. With a sharp carving knife, beginning at the top, slice each piece on an slight angle, cutting across the grain. Arrange overlapping slices in an ovenproof casserole, with the ones from the top of brisket on the bottom of the casserole.

Preheat oven to 325 degrees.

Remove fat from surface of gravy and discard. Pour gravy over sliced meat. Cover the casserole tightly and bake until piping hot, 30 to 40 minutes.

Wine: De Loach Vineyards Zinfandel (California: Sonoma County)

MUCKMAN

RICHARD HASSELL has spent his professional life in the muck, learning so much about it that he holds a Ph.D. in the subject. We had called the Ohio Agricultural Research and Development Center at Wooster looking for their number-one onion man. We found Hassell at the center's Muck Crop Branch at Celeryville, a mile south of Willard, Ohio.

It is a startling mile to travel. Out of ordinary Ohio corn and soybean and alfalfa fields, you suddenly enter a huge amphitheater of coal black and emerald green. It is a glacial bowl, carved out 20,000 years ago. Undergirded by blue clay, the bowl held water, and became, over thousands of years, a rich bog, building up layer after layer of organic material, until in some places the black soil is 20 feet thick.

Although farmers call it muck, it is actually peat. Its organic content is between 50 and 60 percent by volume. In the last century, it was quarried and used as fuel. A carelessly thrown cigarette butt can set the soil on fire. More than once, workers have had to dig ditches and fill them with water to contain a blaze. For almost 100 years, this intensely rich area has been improved by the farmers, who have built a system of reservoirs, canals and inflatable dams to carry the water to where they want it, as well as underground drainage tiles to carry away all the water if there should be too much of it.

Altogether there are 3,000 acres here, where Ohio farmers raise lettuces, radishes, celery, dill, spinach, potatoes, turnip greens and onions. No one knows as much about this former bog as Richard Hassell.

Hassell is a Utah native, who, after undergraduate work at Brigham Young University, earned a master's degree at Cornell. He headed back to the West and worked in horticultural research at Texas Tech. But when an opportunity was offered him by Ohio State, he came. Since 1981, he has been assigned to the Muck Crop Branch of the university, which awarded him a Ph.D. in 1993. Hassell knows his onions, since both green and storage onions are grown in quantity in this enclave.

His main mission is learning which varieties work best for the specific day-lengths, climates, water conditions, insect pests, plant diseases and soils that occur in Ohio and the Midwest. Scores of varieties are tested for every one that finds a place in the market.

Hassell has dealt with a number of problems that trouble onion farmers. When an onion develops a double or triple center, it might be fine for smothering a steak, but not so good for onion rings, and the ring business buys a lot of onions. Hassell's research shows that stress creates the multiple centers. "Too close together, or excess water, drought or heat—any of these could cause it," he tells us.

WHY DO ONLY SOME ONIONS in a field bolt, or grow a seed stalk and a flower, instead of investing their energy in the bulb? The seed companies want every onion in the field to bolt and create seeds. But the farmer wants no bolting at all. Hassell has shown that the storage temperatures for the onion seed has something to do with whether they bolt readily, and that sometimes crowding can make an onion grow seeds instead of an edible bulb.

He is also interested in helping the farmer maximize the yield per acre. How many pounds of onion seed should be used to get optimum results? How densely can they be planted? When onions are crowded in a field, they are smaller. If they have space to grow, they get bigger. But if they have too much space, the onions may be bigger but there will be fewer of them, and the yield per acre will go down. Hassell is in quest of the happy medium.

He likes running his tests in the muck; it grows crops in a hurry. It is black and hot, which means he can start things earlier, and the reservoir and elaborate tile drainage in the fields let him control the water. His horticultural trials over the years in the mid-Ohio muck have helped a lot of America's farmers.

"Oh, if I could say just one thing more," said Hassell. "Handle onions with care. Don't throw the bags around."

Muckman. Doctor of Philosophy. Friend of the onions.

Provençal Beef Stew with Onions & Olives

ORANGE PEEL and niçoise olives season this stew of beef marinated in a mixture of red wine and shallots.

SERVES 6 TO 8

Marinade & Beef

1   cup dry red wine
½   cup minced shallots
1   garlic clove, minced
1   bay leaf
3   pounds top sirloin butt, cut into
    2-inch cubes

Stew

1   cup unbleached flour
5-6 tablespoons olive oil
1   cup finely diced yellow onions
3   plump garlic cloves, thinly sliced
3   strips bacon, preferably smoked, diced and
    blanched
4   carrots, scrubbed and cut into
    1-inch lengths
1   32-ounce can crushed tomatoes
1   rounded tablespoon herbes de Provence
12 boiling onions, peeled

1   bottle (750 ml) Syrah or Côtes du Rhône
    wine
    Zest of 1 orange, julienned
    Kosher salt and freshly ground black pepper
1   cup niçoise olives, pitted

Thickener (optional)

3   tablespoons unbleached flour
3   tablespoons unsalted butter, softened

Chopped fresh parsley for garnish

To marinate beef: Combine wine, shallots, garlic and bay leaf in a large glass or ceramic bowl. Add beef and turn to coat with marinade. Cover with plastic wrap and refrigerate 6 hours or overnight.

To make stew: Preheat oven to 325 degrees F. Place flour in a plastic bag. Remove beef from marinade and reserve marinade. Working in batches, toss beef with flour to coat thoroughly. Heat 3 tablespoons olive oil in a cast-iron Dutch oven or casserole over medium-high heat. Add beef in batches and brown well on all sides, adding more oil as needed. (Remove browned beef to a bowl as you go.)

Add 2 to 3 tablespoons oil to the pot and add

diced onions and garlic. Sauté, stirring, until onions are limp, 5 to 7 minutes. Add bacon and stir to release some fat, about 2 minutes. Pour in reserved marinade and stir over high heat to loosen any browned particles that adhere to the pot. Add beef, carrots, tomatoes, herbes de Provence, boiling onions, wine, zest and salt and pepper to taste. Stir over high heat until liquids begin to bubble.

Cover with a tight-fitting lid and place in the preheated oven for 2 hours. Stir in olives and check for doneness; beef should be nearly tender at this point. Continue cooking for 15 minutes more, until beef is fork-tender.

When beef is tender, transfer the pot from the oven to the stovetop. Set over medium heat and skim off fat.

To make thickener: If sauce needs thickening, make a paste of flour and butter. Slowly stir in paste, a little at a time, and cook until thickened. Sprinkle with fresh parsley.

Wine: Domaine de Trévallon
Côteaux d'Aix en Provence
(France: Les Côteaux des Baux)

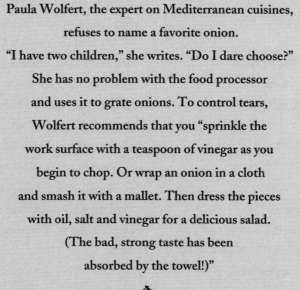

Paula Wolfert, the expert on Mediterranean cuisines, refuses to name a favorite onion.
"I have two children," she writes. "Do I dare choose?"
She has no problem with the food processor and uses it to grate onions. To control tears, Wolfert recommends that you "sprinkle the work surface with a teaspoon of vinegar as you begin to chop. Or wrap an onion in a cloth and smash it with a mallet. Then dress the pieces with oil, salt and vinegar for a delicious salad. (The bad, strong taste has been absorbed by the towel!)"

Piperade's Grilled Hanger Steak with Fried Leeks

MOST STEAK SANDWICHES are made from thinly sliced sirloin, but this one is thicker and made from a more flavorful cut, served open face and topped with crisply fried leeks. Thick slices of toast soak up the juices from the onion marinade. You can use skirt or flank steak, or if you can get it, hanger steak. Known in France as the *onglet*, the butcher's tenderloin, the hanger is the cut that the butcher usually saves for himself, since it's so richly flavored. We thank Ali Barker, owner/chef of Piperade restaurant in Cleveland, Ohio, for sharing this recipe with us.

SERVES 4

Steak & Marinade

1 large yellow onion, thinly sliced

2 plump garlic cloves, minced

½ cup soy sauce

½ cup dry sherry

¼ cup rice wine

Juice of 2 lemons

5 drops Tabasco sauce

4 beef hanger steaks (8-12 ounces each)

2 tablespoons canola or other vegetable oil

Freshly ground black pepper

Leeks

2 leeks, white parts only, split lengthwise and cleaned

2 cups canola oil for frying

4 thick slices good bread, toasted, for serving

To marinate steak: In a glass baking dish, mix together onion, garlic, soy sauce, sherry, rice wine, lemon juice and Tabasco. Pound steaks until ⅔ inch thick. Rub meat with oil and season well with pepper. Add steaks to marinade. Let stand for 1 hour.

Meanwhile, prepare leeks: Cut leeks into 2-inch lengths. Finely julienne each length. Soak julienned leeks in cold water for at least 30 minutes.

To cook steaks: Thoroughly clean the surface of a gas or charcoal grill with a metal brush; coat the rack evenly with vegetable oil. Preheat the grill until hot.

Remove steaks from marinade; discard marinade. Grill steaks for 3 minutes on one side. Turn and grill for 2 minutes on second side for medium-rare; set aside to rest on a carving platter while you finish leeks.

To finish leeks: Pour oil into a wok and quickly heat to 225 degrees F, or until hot enough to brown a cube of bread tossed into it. Meanwhile, drain leeks and pat completely dry. Deep-fry leeks in 3 batches just until lightly browned, 2 to 4 minutes. Drain well on paper towels; season with salt and pepper.

To assemble: Place toast on heated serving plates. Slice hanger steaks on an angle and distribute over toast. Scatter fried leeks over meat and serve.

Wine: Conn Valley Vineyards
Cabernet Sauvignon (California: Napa Valley)

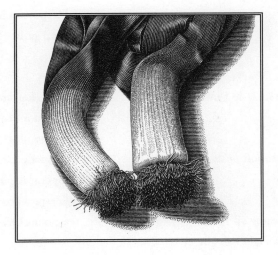

Scallion-Orange Beef

WHILE WE LOVE orange-peel beef, it was hard to find a restaurant in our area that made it the way we liked. Then, after an inspirational visit from the talented writer and teacher Nina Simonds, we began to experiment ourselves. This is the pleasing result. (Dried orange and tangerine peels are available in Asian markets.)

SERVES 4

Beef & Marinade

12   scallions, trimmed to include 1 inch of green

1½   pounds flank steak

2   egg whites, beaten into soft peaks

2   tablespoons soy sauce

2   tablespoons rice wine

1   teaspoon Oriental sesame oil

1   tablespoon peeled minced fresh ginger

2   scallions, minced

1   garlic clove, minced

Seasonings

12   pieces dried orange or tangerine peel, softened in boiling water

4   small dried chile peppers

2   small, fresh serrano chile peppers, red or green, about 1½ inches long, thinly sliced

1   tablespoon minced scallion

1   plump garlic clove, minced

Sauce

½   cup chicken stock

3   tablespoons soy sauce

2   tablespoons rice wine

1   tablespoon Chinese black vinegar

1   teaspoon sugar

1   tablespoon cornstarch

2   teaspoons Oriental sesame oil

2   cups peanut oil for frying

Scallions, julienned, for garnish

Roll-cut scallions: cut each one with a sharp knife into ½-inch pieces by making a slice on a sharp angle, turning scallion ¼ turn, cutting on an angle and repeating until scallion is completely cut; set aside in a small dish.

To marinate beef: Cut flank steak across the grain and at a slight angle into ¼-inch-thick strips. (This is easily done when steak is partially frozen.) Place in a large bowl. Toss beef strips with egg whites and mix well. Add remaining marinade ingredients to beef and mix. Set aside for at least 30 minutes.

To make seasonings: Cut softened peel into ½-inch-wide strips. In a small bowl, combine peel, dried and fresh chile peppers, minced scallion and garlic; set aside.

To make sauce: In another bowl, combine stock, soy sauce, rice wine, vinegar, sugar and cornstarch. Whisk well to dissolve cornstarch. Stir in sesame oil; set aside.

To cook beef: Pour peanut oil into the wok and heat over high heat until hot enough to brown a cube of bread tossed into it. Add ⅓ of the beef and fry until it loses its color, 1 to 2 minutes. Remove beef with a skimmer or slotted spoon and set aside in a bowl. Repeat until all beef is browned. Pour off all but 2 tablespoons of oil.

To assemble: Return the wok to high heat. Add seasoning mixture and stir-fry rapidly for 30 seconds. Add roll-cut scallions and toss for 30 seconds. Add sauce mixture and stir until hot and thickened. Drain beef of pan juices, discard juices and add beef to the wok; toss until beef is heated through, about 1 minute.

Sprinkle with lots of julienned scallions and serve.

**Wine: Shafer Vineyards Merlot
(California: Napa Valley)**

Peppered Tenderloin

WITH SAUTÉED ONIONS & MUSHROOMS

E DON'T OFTEN MAKE beef tenderloin, but when we do, we prefer it with this pepper marinade. Nothing is better with the dish than sautéed onions and mushrooms.

SERVES 8

Beef & Marinade

2   tablespoons tomato paste
¼   cup Chinese black vinegar
¼   cup rice wine
2   tablespoons red-wine vinegar
¾   cup mushroom soy sauce (available in Asian markets) or regular soy sauce
¼   cup cracked black peppercorns
1   beef tenderloin (4-4½ pounds), trimmed and tied

Mushrooms

6   tablespoons (¾ stick) unsalted butter
1½ pounds mixed portobello and shiitake mushrooms caps, thinly sliced (2 pounds with stems)
2   teaspoons soy sauce
1   large Spanish onion, medium diced

1   plump garlic clove, minced
2   teaspoons hot Hungarian paprika
    Kosher salt and freshly ground black pepper
¼   cup minced fresh flat-leaf parsley

To marinate beef: In a glass or ceramic dish just large enough to hold beef, whisk together tomato paste and black vinegar until smooth. Whisk in rice wine, red-wine vinegar, soy sauce and peppercorns; blend well. Add tenderloin and roll in marinade until well coated. Spoon marinade over the top. Cover and let stand, turning from time to time, for at least 1 hour and up to 3 hours in the refrigerator. Bring to room temperature before continuing.

Place oven rack in the middle of the oven. Preheat oven to 475 degrees F. Place tenderloin in a shallow roasting pan. Spoon about ⅓ cup marinade over it. Roast for 32 minutes for medium-rare.

Remove tenderloin from the oven, place on a carving board, and let rest in a warm place for 10 minutes before carving. Reserve pan drippings.

To make mushrooms: While tenderloin is roasting, melt 5 tablespoons butter in a large skillet over medium heat. Add sliced mushrooms and soy sauce and toss well. Cover skillet and cook for 5 minutes. Remove cover, add remaining 1 tablespoon butter, onion, garlic and paprika. Sauté over high heat, stirring constantly, until onions are very tender and golden, 5 to 8 minutes. Stir in drippings from the roasting pan; season with salt and pepper to taste and parsley. Carve tenderloin and arrange several slices on heated serving plates. Garnish each with some of the sautéed onions and mushrooms.

Wine: Cain Cellars "Cain Five" (California: Napa Valley)

Hiroshi Tsuji, the chef-owner of Shuhei, a Japanese restaurant in Cleveland, Ohio, uses a lot of onions in his cooking. His favorite kind: Spanish onions. Does he have a way to manage tears? "Yes," he says, "I get someone else to chop them."

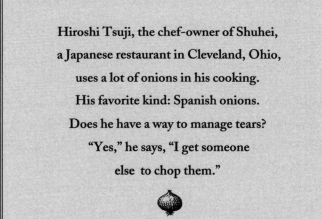

Bern, Baby, Bern

WE WORK IN TELEVISION, and that means we don't travel in November during the rating periods. So, until we retire, we must make peace with the idea that we will never get to attend the *Zibele-märit*, the great Bern, Switzerland, onion festival.

The Swiss National Tourist Office in New York was appalled that we were not going to be in Bern on the last Monday of November. "Retire early," they urged, "and come to Bern."

We couldn't, so they sent us the next-best thing, a batch of photographs of the doings at the most recent onion market. Nothing we had seen in Vidalia country prepared us for the sight of a phalanx of young people dressed as onions, their roots and leaves trailing behind them, parading through the streets of Bern.

The event has its roots at the start of the fifteenth century, when Bern burned. Even before the embers had cooled, farmers from the surrounding countryside poured into the town to help. As a gesture of thanks, the town gave them the right to sell their produce in the city. From these modest beginnings, a major fall market was born. For decades, it was a two-week extravaganza.

Contemporary farmers don't have time for festivals that run for two weeks, so now the celebration lasts for only a day. But the farmers make the most of it, setting up hundreds of stalls in the plaza between the Parliament buildings and the train station. It's a carnival: Bands of costumed jesters visit every restaurant and café, confetti falls into everything, drums and trumpets are heard throughout the town. While all kinds of things are sold, nothing overshadows the 100 tons of plaited strings of onions that will enhance the soups and stews of the citizens of Bern during the coming cold Swiss winter.

The event didn't start out as an onion festival. The farmers of the region produce a variety of crops, mostly potatoes. But over the years, it was the onion that grew to be the star of the festival. After all, a man dancing in the street cuts a much finer figure dressed as an onion than if he were wearing the dull raiment of a dusty brown potato. It was natural selection—the frolicsome eclipsing the sleepy and the dull.

If there is a more spectacular celebration of onions in the cosmos, let us know. And if it's not during ratings, we'll be there.

Grilled Flank Steak with Red Jerk Sauce

WHOEVER BROUGHT Jamaican jerk sauces to the U.S. deserves high praise. We enjoy the onions, peppers and spices that fall in the category of "jerk." If you don't make the sauce too fiery, you can taste all the flavors. Serve with lamb and chicken.

MAKES 2 CUPS SAUCE; SERVES 4 TO 6

1   medium-sized Spanish onion, quartered
6   scallions, trimmed to include 2 inches of green, cut into thirds
4   garlic cloves, peeled
1   ½-x-1-inch piece fresh ginger, peeled
1   fresh Scotch bonnet or red chile pepper, seeded and minced
2   teaspoons ground allspice
1   teaspoon dried thyme
1   teaspoon dried oregano
1   teaspoon freshly grated nutmeg
1   teaspoon ground cinnamon
½   teaspoon cayenne
2   teaspoons kosher salt
1   teaspoon freshly ground black pepper
    Juice of 2 lemons
¼   cup fresh orange juice
¼   cup cider vinegar
2   flank steaks (1¼ pounds each)

In the bowl of a food processor fitted with the metal blade, combine onion, scallions, garlic, ginger, chile pepper, allspice, thyme, oregano, nutmeg, cinnamon, cayenne, salt, pepper, citrus juices and vinegar. Pulse until onions are pureed.

Arrange flank steaks in a glass baking dish and coat well with sauce. Let marinate in the refrigerator for 2 to 4 hours, turning several times. (Any remaining sauce should be refrigerated in a tightly closed container.) Bring to room temperature before continuing.

Thoroughly clean the surface of a gas or charcoal grill with a metal brush; coat the rack evenly with vegetable oil. Preheat the grill until hot.

Remove steaks from marinade. Place on grill and cook for 5 minutes. Turn and grill for 3 minutes on second side for medium-rare. Let steaks rest on a carving board for at least 5 minutes before carving.

To carve, cut on a slight angle across the grain into thin slices. Nap with the collected juices and serve.

Wine: Louis Jadot Beaujolais-Villages (France: Beaujolais)

GARLIC

Barbecued Short Ribs

THE THICK BARBECUE SAUCE for these short ribs is outstanding, its tomato and onion taste darkened by overtones of molasses and spice and rounded out by beer and Canadian whisky. We are very fond of short ribs and prepare them in a variety of ways. To get meat that is not too fatty, ask your butcher for flanken (ungraded beef short ribs cut from the plate). Have the meat cut into pieces and figure that 5 pounds will serve about 4 people.

SERVES 4

Marinade & Beef

¾ cup dark beer
¾ cup ketchup
⅓ cup cider vinegar
3 tablespoons Worcestershire sauce
Juice of 1 lime
1 cup finely minced yellow onion
1 plump garlic clove, minced
2 teaspoons peeled minced fresh ginger
2 teaspoons coarsely ground black pepper
2 fresh marjoram stems
1 bay leaf
5 pounds flanken (beef short ribs cut from the plate), cut crosswise into 2-inch pieces, or other short ribs

Barbecue Sauce

1 tablespoon vegetable oil
1¼ cups finely minced white onion
2 plump garlic cloves, minced
2 teaspoons minced lemongrass bulb or 1 teaspoon minced lemon zest
2 cups ketchup
1 cup dark beer
⅓ cup cider vinegar
¼ cup Canadian Club whisky
¼ cup dark molasses, unsulphured preferred
2 tablespoons soy sauce
2 tablespoons Worcestershire sauce
2 teaspoons Chinese chili sauce
Juice of 1 lime
½ cup firmly packed dark brown sugar
1 teaspoon cayenne
1 teaspoon ground cumin
1 teaspoon freshly ground white pepper
1 bay leaf
3 inches lemongrass stem or ½ lemon
Salt

To marinate beef: In a small nonaluminum saucepan, combine beer, ketchup, vinegar, Worcestershire sauce, lime juice, onion, garlic, ginger, pep-

253

per, marjoram and bay leaf. Bring to a boil over medium heat; set aside to cool.

Combine marinade with short ribs in a glass baking dish just large enough to hold short ribs in a single layer. Marinate in the refrigerator for at least 3 hours, or overnight. Bring to room temperature before continuing

Meanwhile, make barbecue sauce: Heat oil in a 3-quart nonaluminum saucepan over medium heat until hot. Add onion, garlic and minced lemongrass or lemon zest and cook, stirring often, until onion is translucent but not browned, about 5 minutes. Add all remaining sauce ingredients and bring to a boil. Reduce heat to low and simmer for 30 minutes. Remove and discard bay leaf and lemongrass stem or lemon.

To cook beef: Thoroughly clean the surface of a gas or charcoal grill with a metal brush; coat the rack evenly with vegetable oil. Preheat the grill until hot.

While grill is heating, tear off 4 large (12-x-12-inch) squares of heavy-duty foil. Divide beef, bone sides down, between 2 sheets. Pour about ¼ cup marinade over beef in each package; wrap each package neatly. Wrap each in a second sheet. Place packages, bone sides down, on the heated grill. Cover and cook until beef is very tender, about 1 hour.

Shortly before meat is done, reheat barbecue sauce over low heat.

Carefully open packages of beef and place ribs, bone sides up, directly on the grill rack. Cover and grill for 1 to 2 minutes to glaze.

To serve, slather ribs with barbecue sauce. Serve with additional sauce on the side.

Wine: Domaine Gramenon Côtes du Rhône (France: Rhône)

Fit to be Dried

HENRY A. JONES, botanist and onion guru, credits a hunger for onions among our soldiers and sailors in World War II for the development of the nation's multibillion-dollar dehydrated food industry. Hundreds of thousands of our servicemen and servicewomen had to be fed three times a day. The prospect of lugging fresh food to inaccessible battlefields was a logistical nightmare, and ultimately led to the development of the enormous dehydration industry. It made sense. Take the water out of a ton of onions, and you have only a couple of hundred pounds of dry onion flakes to ship. By the end of the war, members of the armed forces everywhere were eating rations like creamed chipped beef (made from dehydrated beef) flavored with dehydrated onions.

In later years, as chief scientist at California's Dessert Seed Company, Jones developed a number of onion varieties especially for the dehydration industry. These onions are low in water content; their oniony power is therefore more concentrated, with pungency enough to last when dried. They have names like Primero, Creoso, Dehyso and Dehydrator No. 2 through Dehydrator No. 14—varieties maturing from early in the season to late, ensuring a supply of fresh onions to the industry throughout the year. Most onions used for dehydration and other processing are still grown in California, where it is estimated that over two-thirds of the onion acreage is given to those special-purpose cultivars.

And when you buy Knorr, Lipton or McCormick dried onion soups, dried onion dips or onion flakes, you are a beneficiary of that wartime breakthrough.

Asked to name their favorite onions, authors Jane and Michael Stern,

chroniclers of Americana and keen students of

what we eat, chose Lipton's Onion Soup Mix.

"It makes such good meat loaf and California Dip."

Pork & Onion Pozole

POZOLE IS A MEXICAN stew-like soup (or a soup-like stew) made with pork and dried white field corn that has been treated with slaked lime. Usually sold under the name pozole, it has a fresher corn flavor and a firmer texture than canned hominy, which may be substituted. We created this recipe after an inspirational meal at the restaurant Rancho Casados in Espanola, New Mexico, where JoAnn Casados produces traditional Hispanic dishes. (See Special Products, page 374 for ordering pozole.) Serve this dish with warm corn bread for a satisfying cold-weather supper.

SERVES 6 TO 8

2	tablespoons vegetable oil
2	pounds boneless pork loin, cut into 1-inch cubes
2	garlic cloves, minced
1½	cups minced Spanish onions
2-3	tablespoons medium-hot chile powder or other chili powder
1	pound presoaked dried hominy (pozole) or 4 cups canned hominy, drained and rinsed
12	cups (3 quarts) chicken stock
2	cups canned crushed tomatoes or cooked and pureed fresh tomatoes
2	tablespoons minced fresh parsley
2	tablespoons minced fresh chives
1	tablespoon minced fresh oregano leaves or 2 teaspoons dried
	Kosher salt and freshly ground black pepper
2	tablespoons minced fresh cilantro for garnish

Heat oil over medium heat in a large nonaluminum Dutch oven or casserole. Add pork and brown on all sides, 6 to 8 minutes. Add garlic, onions and chile powder and cook over low heat until onions are translucent, about 10 minutes.

Add hominy, 6 cups chicken stock, tomatoes, oregano, parsley, chives and salt and pepper to taste. Bring to a brisk simmer. Cover and cook over very low heat, stirring from time to time and adding more stock as needed, for 4 hours.

Uncover and add several cups of stock. Continue to simmer slowly, adding stock as needed (about 3 cups), until hominy is tender and the mixture is thick but soupy, up to 2 hours longer.

To serve, spoon pozole into heated soup plates and sprinkle with cilantro.

Wine: Talley Vineyard Pinot Noir (California: Arroyo Grande)

Paul's Hot Italian Sausage with Sweet Peppers & Onions

NOTHING COULD BE SIMPLER than this rustic version of the classic Italian combination of sausages, peppers and onions from our friend, Cleveland chef Paul Minnillo. When he can find them, Paul uses sweet Hungarian peppers; otherwise, he uses red bells. He chooses the sweetest onions available as a contrast to the hot sausage.

SERVES 2 TO 4

2   pounds hot Italian sausage, in casings

2-4   tablespoons olive oil

4   medium-sized sweet onions, such as Vidalias, Walla Wallas or Texas 1015s, coarsely diced

2   large red bell peppers or 6 Hungarian sweet peppers, julienned

Kosher salt and freshly ground black pepper

Cut sausage into 12 equal pieces. Lightly coat a large skillet with 2 to 3 tablespoons olive oil and set over medium-high heat. Add sausage and sauté until browned but only partially cooked through, about 5 minutes. Remove sausage from skillet and set aside.

If needed, add more oil and set over medium-high heat. Stir in onions and peppers and sauté until onions are golden, about 10 minutes. Return sausage to skillet, cover, and cook over low heat for 15 minutes, or until sausage is fully cooked. Season with salt and pepper to taste. Serve on heated plates.

Wine: Girard Winery Ol' Blue Jay Zinfandel (California: Napa Valley)

Roasted Andouille Sausage

WITH ONIONS, PINEAPPLE & BEER

PAUL PRUDHOMME INTRODUCED the world to the pleasures of andouille sausage. Once nearly impossible to find outside Louisiana, it's now available in most metropolitan areas. The onions and pineapple make a great counterpoint to the hot, spicy sausage in this dish. Add a little beer and you have a hearty Sunday supper—any night of the week.

SERVES 4

1   large (1-pound) white onion, finely chopped in food processor

1   cup crushed pineapple, thoroughly drained of juice

2   pounds andouille sausage

½   cup dark beer

Preheat oven to 425 degrees F.

Combine onions and pineapple in a nonaluminum 11-x-8-inch shallow baking dish. Gently score sausages every 3 inches; add to the dish, spooning some of the onion mixture over them. Baste with ½ cup beer.

Place the baking dish in the oven and roast, basting frequently with onion mixture and adding more beer if the contents of the dish appear to be drying out, about 45 minutes, until tops of sausages are covered with nicely browned onions and pineapple. Serve on heated plates with a generous portion of pineapple-onion mixture.

Wine: Tualatin Vineyards Gewürztraminer (Oregon)

Onion & Apple-Smothered Pork Chops

ONIONS AND APPLES are a happy combination with any pork dish. Serve this with Hungarian Sautéed Cabbage, Onions & Noodles (page 369) or the Chive & Shallot Mashed Potatoes (page 349).

SERVES 4

⅓	cup unbleached flour
4	center-cut loin pork chops, cut 1½ inches thick
3	tablespoons vegetable oil
1	pound yellow onions, thinly sliced
1	plump garlic clove, minced
2	tart cooking apples
2	teaspoons sugar
¼	cup Calvados or applejack
2	teaspoons herbes de Provence
⅛	teaspoon cayenne
	Kosher salt and freshly ground black pepper
½	cup apple cider
1-1½	cups chicken stock

Preheat oven to 325 degrees F.

Place flour in a soup plate. Carefully coat chops in flour; set aside on a rack.

Pour oil into a large cast-iron skillet that has a tight-fitting lid and heat oil over medium-high heat. Add pork chops and brown on both sides, 1 to 2 minutes. Remove chops to a plate. Pour in more oil as needed, add onions and garlic and cook over low heat to soften, stirring from time to time, about 5 minutes.

Meanwhile, peel, core and grate apples. Add apples to softened onions; sprinkle with sugar. Cook over high heat, stirring constantly. Add Calvados or applejack, reduce heat to medium, and stir, scooping up any browned bits on the bottom. Remove the skillet from the heat.

Push onion mixture to one side, return chops to the skillet and cover with onion-apple mixture. Sprinkle with herbes de Provence, cayenne and salt and pepper to taste. Add cider and 1 cup stock. Cover and braise in hot oven, basting chops several times and adding more stock if sauce gets too thick, about 1 hour and 10 minutes. Serve chops on heated plates, napped generously with onion-apple sauce.

Wine: Williams-Seylem Pinot Noir "Olivet Lane" (California: Sonoma County)

Grilled Pork Loin in Roasted Onion Adobo

HOT AND SMOKY PEPPERS, a blend of herbs, a jab of garlic and a blast of orange combine to make a tasty seasoning for pork loin. This spicy Mexican adobo sauce is excellent with spareribs, thick pork chops or skirt steak.

Boneless pork loin will cook fairly rapidly on the grill. We prefer ours at 145 to 150 degrees F, or medium, so that it will be juicy and have the faintest blush of pink. Recent studies indicate that if pork has been frozen for 72 hours, there is no threat of trichinosis when the meat is not well done. Two dried ancho chiles and 2 canned chipotles in adobo may be substituted for the combination of dried chile peppers.

SERVES 6 TO 8

1   dried mulato chile pepper, seeds and stem discarded
2   dried chipotle chile peppers, seeds and stems discarded
1   dried pasilla chile pepper, seeds and stem discarded
3   plump garlic cloves, peeled
1   large white onion, baked (see page 45)
4   plum tomatoes, blackened on all sides over a grill
¼   cup medium-hot chile powder or other chili powder
1   tablespoon ground cumin
1   teaspoon dried oregano
    Grated zest of 1 large orange
½-⅔   cup fresh orange juice
4½   pounds boneless pork loin, exterior membrane removed
    Kosher salt and freshly ground black pepper

Place all dried chiles in a small saucepan, add water to cover and bring to a boil. Reduce heat and simmer until softened, about 25 minutes. Drain, reserving the hot cooking liquid.

Combine garlic, onion, tomatoes and softened chiles in the bowl of a food processor fitted with the metal blade. Add 3 tablespoons of the chile cooking liquid and puree. Push pulp through a food mill into a mixing bowl or stir sauce through a large-mesh strainer to remove any solids. Stir in chile powder, cumin, oregano, orange zest and ½ cup orange juice. Blend with a whisk until adobo is the consistency of very thick tomato sauce; thin with additional orange juice, if necessary.

Place pork loin in a glass or ceramic baking dish and coat evenly with adobo. Marinate for 6 to 9 hours in the refrigerator. (Save excess adobo for another dish.) Bring to room temperature before continuing.

Thoroughly clean the surface of a gas or charcoal grill with a metal brush; coat the rack evenly with vegetable oil. Preheat the grill until very hot.

Season pork loin with salt and pepper. Place on the grill, cover and grill for 12 minutes. Baste with a little orange juice, turn, cover and grill for 12 minutes. Check center of pork with an instant-read thermometer before removing from the grill; pork should be between 135 and 140 degrees.

Let roast rest in a warm place for 10 minutes. (Remember that meat continues cooking during this resting period.) Slice and serve with the natural juices.

Wine: Monte Volpe Barbera
(California: Mendocino Country)

The skins of two red onions or yellow storage onions are sufficient to dye one dozen eggs.

Roasted Pork Loin & Shallots with Onions & Ginger

MARINATED IN A spicy soy sauce mixture, the pork is roasted on lightly gingered onions, which then become the base for a simple, tasty pan sauce.

SERVES 6 TO 8

Marinade & Pork

6-8 scallions, trimmed to include 2 inches of green, halved crosswise

3-4 plump shallots, peeled

1 large chunk (1½ inches) fresh ginger, peeled

2 plump garlic cloves, peeled

1 dried chile pepper, crumbled

2 teaspoons dry mustard

2 tablespoons soy sauce

1 tablespoon olive oil

4½ pounds boneless pork loin, exterior membrane removed

Shallots

2 cups chopped yellow onions

1 tablespoon sugar

2 teaspoons grated fresh ginger

1 teaspoon kosher salt

1 teaspoon freshly ground black pepper

12-16 shallots, peeled

2-3 tablespoons olive oil

1 cup chicken stock

1 teaspoon arrowroot

½ cup dry white wine

1 tablespoon minced fresh parsley

2-3 tablespoons minced fresh cilantro leaves

To make marinade & pork: In the bowl of a food processor fitted with the metal blade, combine scallions, shallots, ginger, garlic, chile pepper, mustard, soy sauce and olive oil. Pulse until well chopped; puree into a paste. Coat pork loin with paste, wrap in plastic and marinate in the refrigerator for at least 4 hours, or up to 8 hours. Bring to room temperature before cooking.

To make shallots: Preheat oven to 350 degrees F. Lightly oil a roasting pan. Combine onions, sugar and grated ginger in the pan and toss to blend well. Place coated pork loin on onion mixture and sprinkle with salt and pepper. Rub shallots with olive oil and place around pork.

To cook pork: Roast pork until an instant-read thermometer inserted into center reaches 135 to 140 degrees, about 1 hour and 10 minutes. Place pork roast on a carving platter and keep warm, letting it rest for 10 minutes. (During this time, the internal temperature will reach 145 to 150 degrees and pork will be medium and juicy.)

Meanwhile, place roasting pan on the stovetop over medium heat. Add chicken stock and bring to a boil, stirring and scraping up all browned bits that adhere to the pan. When mixture boils, quickly whisk together arrowroot and wine. Add to pan sauce and stir until sauce thickens, 2 to 4 minutes. Blend in parsley and cilantro, and add lots of freshly ground black pepper. Serve sauce over sliced pork.

Wine: Patz and Hall Chardonnay (California: Napa Valley)

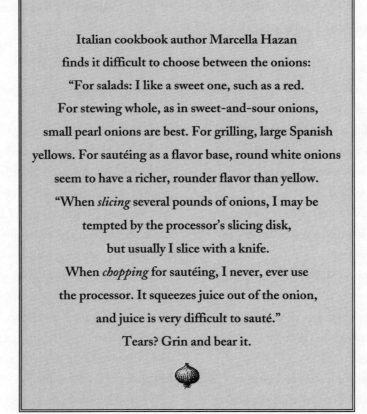

Italian cookbook author Marcella Hazan
finds it difficult to choose between the onions:
"For salads: I like a sweet one, such as a red.
For stewing whole, as in sweet-and-sour onions,
small pearl onions are best. For grilling, large Spanish
yellows. For sautéing as a flavor base, round white onions
seem to have a richer, rounder flavor than yellow.
"When *slicing* several pounds of onions, I may be
tempted by the processor's slicing disk,
but usually I slice with a knife.
When *chopping* for sautéing, I never, ever use
the processor. It squeezes juice out of the onion,
and juice is very difficult to sauté."
Tears? Grin and bear it.

Grilled Pork Chops with Green Jerk Sauce

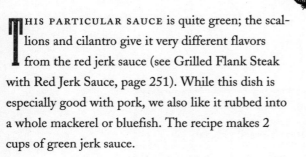

THIS PARTICULAR SAUCE is quite green; the scallions and cilantro give it very different flavors from the red jerk sauce (see Grilled Flank Steak with Red Jerk Sauce, page 251). While this dish is especially good with pork, we also like it rubbed into a whole mackerel or bluefish. The recipe makes 2 cups of green jerk sauce.

SERVES 6

Green Jerk Sauce

2 bunches scallions with 2 inches of green, trimmed and cut crosswise into thirds

¼ cup minced fresh cilantro leaves

3 garlic cloves, peeled

1 1-inch-long piece fresh ginger, peeled

1 fresh Scotch bonnet or red chile pepper, seeded and minced

1½ teaspoons ground allspice (freshly ground, if possible)

1 teaspoon dried thyme

½ teaspoon freshly grated nutmeg

1 teaspoon kosher salt

1 teaspoon freshly ground black pepper

1 teaspoon tamarind concentrate (available in Indian markets), or substitute juice of 1 lemon

Juice of 2 limes

¼ cup fresh orange juice

¼ cup cider vinegar

2 tablespoons vegetable oil

1 teaspoon Tabasco sauce (optional)

6 loin pork chops, cut 1½ inches thick

2 cups apple or cherry wood chips, soaked, for grilling

To make jerk sauce: In the bowl of a food processor fitted with the metal blade, combine scallions, cilantro, garlic, ginger, chile pepper, allspice, thyme, nutmeg, salt, pepper, tamarind or lemon juice, citrus juices and vinegar and pulse until pureed. Add oil and Tabasco, if using; blend well. Arrange pork chops in a layer in the bottom of a glass baking dish and coat well on both sides with sauce. Marinate in the refrigerator for 2 to 4 hours, turning several times. (Remaining jerk sauce should be stored in an airtight container in the refrigerator.) Bring to room temperature before cooking.

Thoroughly clean the surface of a gas or charcoal grill with a metal brush; coat the rack evenly with vegetable oil. Preheat the grill until hot. Drain wood chips and add to fire. Place chops on the grill, cover and grill for 7 minutes. Turn chops, cover and grill until an instant-read thermometer inserted into the centers registers 145 to 150 degrees F, about 7 minutes. Divide chops among heated plates and serve.

Wine: Qupé Los Olivos Cuvée (California: Santa Barbara County)

People can always find a reason for getting together. Grace Allison, who writes for *Farm and Dairy*, a publication for the farm community in central Ohio, discovered that in 1818, a group of farmers had formed "The Onion Society of Canfield." The little group's constitution defined its mission: "The object of this association is to feast on the delicious vegetable, the onion . . . and [its] grand helpmate, pork." Pork and onions. Think about it. What could be better together? What better excuse could you find for staging a party? Some of the earliest members of the onion society were teetotalers. But Allison says they got over that. By 1833, the society ceased to function, she wrote, "either from the lack of onions, or an overindulgence of the menu." Still, as late as the 1880s, there were old men in Canfield who fondly remembered their onion orgies at the tables of the community's most prosperous farmers.

Grilled Herb & Onion-Marinated Pork Tenderloin

THESE PORK TENDERLOINS, marinated in herbs, lime juice and onions, make a simple and delicious dinner, especially in summer after a day outdoors. Just put the marinade together in the morning and add the tenderloins a few hours before serving. You could serve it with the Kugel (Baked Noodles) with Chèvre, Scallions & Chives (page 200) or a big couscous salad.

SERVES 8

1   cup finely diced white onion
2   shallots, minced
2   plump garlic cloves, minced
¼   cup minced fresh flat-leaf parsley
1   tablespoon minced fresh oregano leaves or
    1½ teaspoons dried
1   tablespoon minced fresh basil leaves or
    1½ teaspoons dried
1   tablespoon fresh thyme leaves or
    1½ teaspoons dried
2   teaspoons minced fresh rosemary leaves or
    1 teaspoon dried
1   small dried red chile pepper, crumbled
2   tablespoons red-wine vinegar
1   tablespoon fresh lime juice
2   teaspoons freshly ground black pepper

¼   cup olive oil
4   pork tenderloins, each about 1 pound
    Kosher salt
3   tablespoons minced fresh chives for garnish

Combine onion, shallots, garlic, herbs, chile pepper, vinegar, lime juice, black pepper and oil in a small bowl; mix well. Place tenderloins in a glass dish and coat with marinade. Let marinate 2 to 4 hours in the refrigerator. Bring to room temperature before cooking.

Thoroughly clean the surface of a gas or charcoal grill with a metal brush; coat the rack evenly with vegetable oil. Preheat the grill until hot.

Place tenderloins on the hot grill, cover and grill for 7 minutes. Turn, cover and grill until an instant-read thermometer inserted into centers of tenderloins registers 145 to 150 degrees F, about 6 minutes more for medium.

Remove tenderloins from heat and let rest for 5 minutes in a warm place. Sprinkle pork with salt to taste. Slice on an angle and fan out slices on a heated serving plate. Sprinkle with chives and serve.

Wine: Gundlach-Bundschu Winery Zinfandel
(California: Sonoma County)

Grilled Pork Tenderloin

WITH ONIONS & CHIPOTLE FRUIT SAUCE

A CHILE RUB gives these tenderloins their spicy taste, but the sauce is the best part. It is smoky from the chipotles, oniony and fruity—a thick, complex sauce that is at once hot, sweet and tart, with an added dash of cinnamon. This sauce is one we enjoy eating with a spoon. Roasted and well-buttered corn would be a good accompaniment to this dish. Canned chipotle chiles in adobo sauce are commonly available wherever Mexican ingredients are sold. Chipotles, by the way, are smoked jalapeño chiles.

SERVES 4

Spice Rub

1 teaspoon dried thyme
2 teaspoons medium-hot chile powder or other chili powder
2 teaspoons ground cumin
1 teaspoon freshly ground white pepper
2 pork tenderloins, each about 1 pound
1 tablespoon vegetable oil

Sauce

½ large white onion, coarsely chopped
2 garlic cloves, peeled
2 canned chipotle chile peppers in adobo sauce
½ cup cranberry juice
½ cup fresh orange juice
    Juice of 1 lime
1 tablespoon cider vinegar
3 tablespoons port wine
2 tablespoons sugar
1-2 teaspoons chile powder or other chili powder
1 teaspoon ground cumin
⅛ teaspoon ground cinnamon

Chopped scallions and minced fresh cilantro for garnish

To make spice rub: In a small bowl, blend together thyme, chile powder, cumin and white pepper. Rub tenderloins with oil, then rub with seasoning mixture. Let tenderloins rest on a platter at room temperature for 1 hour.

To make sauce: Combine onion, garlic and chipotles in the bowl of a food processor fitted with the metal blade. Pulse until onion is pureed. Add fruit juices, vinegar, port wine, sugar, chile powder, cumin and cinnamon and blend thoroughly.

Pour mixture into a small nonaluminum saucepan and bring to a boil. Reduce heat to low, partially cover and simmer for 1 hour.

To cook pork: Thoroughly clean the surface of a gas or charcoal grill with a metal brush; coat the rack evenly with vegetable oil. Preheat the grill until hot.

Place tenderloins on the grill, cover and cook for 6 minutes. Turn meat and grill until an instant-read thermometer inserted into centers registers 145 to 150 degrees F, about 6 minutes more for medium.

Remove tenderloins from the heat and let rest for 5 minutes in a warm place. Slice on an angle. Fan the slices out on a heated serving plate over a generous puddle of sauce. Sprinkle with scallions and cilantro.

**Wine: Duckhorn Vineyards Merlot
(California: Napa Valley)**

Veal Stew with Olives & Onions

THIS STEW of braised veal, livened with onions, goes well with mashed potatoes or polenta.

SERVES 6 TO 8

1   cup unbleached flour

½   teaspoon kosher salt

½   teaspoon freshly ground white pepper

¼   teaspoon cayenne

1   teaspoon dried thyme

3   pounds veal stew meat, fat and gristle removed, cut into 1½-2-inch cubes

¼   cup (½ stick) unsalted butter

2   tablespoons vegetable oil

½   pound mushrooms, cut into ¼-inch slices

6   baby Vidalias or other sweet onions, tough green parts discarded, cut into ½-inch-thick lengths or 1 cup medium-diced white onions plus 6 diced scallions

2   carrots, cut into 1-inch lengths

⅔   cup dry white wine

2   cups chicken stock

¾   cup sliced stuffed Spanish olives

1   tablespoon minced fresh thyme leaves or 2 teaspoons dried

1   tablespoon minced fresh flat-leaf parsley

Preheat oven to 350 degrees F.

In a plastic bag, combine flour, salt, white pepper, cayenne and dried thyme; blend well. Working in batches, thoroughly dredge veal in flour mixture. Set remaining seasoned flour aside.

Combine butter and oil in a Dutch oven or non-aluminum casserole and set over high heat. Quickly brown veal in 3 batches, on all sides, adjusting heat to prevent flour from burning; transfer to a large bowl. Add more oil if necessary.

When all veal is browned, add mushrooms, onions and carrots to the pot. Sprinkle with 1 tablespoon of reserved flour and stir over medium heat for 3 minutes. Add wine and stir vegetables briskly, scraping all browned bits that adhere to the skillet.

Pour veal and collected juices back into the pot. Stir in chicken stock and olives. Cook over low heat until mixture is heated through. Stir in thyme, parsley and salt and white pepper to taste.

Cover the pot and braise until veal is tender, about 1½ hours. Serve on heated plates.

Wine: Domaine de la Gautière
(France: Provence, Buis-Les-Baronnies) or
Frog's Leap Winery Cabernet Sauvignon
(California: Napa Valley)

Roasted Veal Brisket

WITH POTATO-ONION STUFFING & ONION GRAVY

LINDA'S GRANDMA WELLER used to make wonderful veal breast with this stuffing, which is based on a traditional Jewish potato kugel. The veal briskets called for here have little fat and no gristle; they are much nicer than veal breasts. They are available wherever veal is sold; ask your butcher to create pockets in the veal by cutting into the middle of the meat across one short side and down almost to the other end. If you are horrified at the thought of using chicken fat, use butter—but it's not the same.

SERVES 8

1 tablespoon olive oil

3 pounds Spanish onions, thinly sliced

2 teaspoons sweet Hungarian paprika

1½ teaspoons garlic powder

2½ teaspoons kosher salt

2 teaspoons freshly ground black pepper

2 veal briskets (each about 2½ pounds), each with a pocket cut into 1 short side

7 large russet potatoes, peeled

1 large white onion

2 large eggs, beaten

¼ cup unbleached flour

1 tablespoon chicken fat or butter, melted

1¼ cups chicken stock

2 tablespoons tomato paste

1 tablespoon minced fresh chives

Preheat oven to 350 degrees F.

Coat a large roasting pan with olive oil. Scatter ½ of the sliced onions evenly over the bottom.

In a small bowl, combine paprika, garlic powder, 1½ teaspoons salt and 1 teaspoon pepper; blend well. Rub seasoning mixture all over each brisket. Place seasoned briskets, fat sides up, on top of onions; set aside.

Finely grate potatoes and white onion into a colander; squeeze out as much of the water as possible. Transfer to a large bowl, add eggs, flour, chicken fat or butter, remaining 1 teaspoon salt and 1 teaspoon pepper and blend well.

Divide filling between brisket pockets and close with skewers. Scatter remaining sliced onions over briskets; pour chicken stock into the bottom of the pan. Tightly cover the roasting pan with foil or a lid. Roast for 1¼ hours.

Carefully turn briskets, cover, and roast until fork-tender, about 1¼ hours more.

Remove briskets to a carving board, and let stand for 10 minutes. Place the roasting pan on the stovetop and stir in tomato paste. Cook over medium heat, stirring constantly, until sauce is blended. Skim off any fat and pour gravy into a heated serving bowl.

Cut briskets, across the grain, into thick slices. Serve with sauce and garnish with chives.

Wine: Viader Napa Valley Red Table Wine (California: Napa Valley)

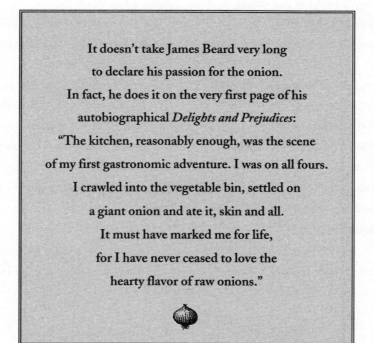

It doesn't take James Beard very long
to declare his passion for the onion.
In fact, he does it on the very first page of his
autobiographical *Delights and Prejudices*:
"The kitchen, reasonably enough, was the scene
of my first gastronomic adventure. I was on all fours.
I crawled into the vegetable bin, settled on
a giant onion and ate it, skin and all.
It must have marked me for life,
for I have never ceased to love the
hearty flavor of raw onions."

Zack's Calf's Liver with Caramelized Onions & Bacon

AT ZACK BRUELL's Cleveland restaurant, Z Contemporary Cuisine, this calf's liver is one of the most popular items on the menu. If you prefer, you can grill the liver instead of pan-frying it, allowing about 30 seconds per side.

SERVES 2 TO 4

½   pound bacon, preferably smoked, cut into ¼-inch dice

1   Spanish onion, coarsely diced

1   pound calf's liver, deveined and cut into ¼-inch-thick slices

1   tablespoon olive oil
    Kosher salt and freshly ground black pepper

2-4   teaspoons balsamic vinegar

In a medium skillet, cook bacon over medium-low heat until crisp, 10 to 15 minutes. Drain; place in a bowl. Add onion to bacon fat in the skillet and cook over low heat, stirring frequently, until caramelized, about 20 minutes.

Add onion to bacon; set aside and keep warm.

Set a large cast-iron skillet over high heat until hot. Brush liver with some olive oil; sprinkle with salt and pepper to taste. Coat the skillet with remaining oil. Quickly sauté liver over high heat until medium-rare, about 1 minute per side.

Arrange liver slices on heated plates. Spoon onion and bacon mixture over the top. Add a few grindings of pepper, and pour 1 teaspoon vinegar over each serving.

Wine: Le Vieux Donjon Châteauneuf-du-Pape (France: Rhône)

SPANISH ONION

Orchids & Onions

THE GATEWAY PRESS, a weekly newspaper serving the Cleveland suburbs around Streetsboro, runs a column in which readers award people orchids for their good deeds. Readers are also allowed to lash out in print at anyone who might have made them mad. The objects of their wrath receive *onions*. How can this be? The one truly ubiquitous vegetable, eaten by everyone, disliked by practically no one, used as a symbol for disgust?

"A courtroom full of slimy, worm-infested onions to all the shyster lawyers who live off the misery of their clients . . ."

"A lawbook full of slimy, moldy, stinky onions to the shyster lawyer I paid a consultation fee to recently."

"Quidnuncsic onions right back to you, sweetheart! You really made my day, knowing how much I annoyed you."

"Fiscally irresponsible onions to the mayor of Aurora . . ."

"Instant onions to the person who watches us scrape off our instant lottery tickets in the privacy of our own cars."

"Slippery onions to the idiots who have cars with higher IQs than they do."

"Smelly, smelly, ripe ramps and onions to the . . . lane hoppers."

"Sliced, tear-jerking onions to all the 'witchy' (I am being nice) waitresses who complain about their small tips. If you spent as much energy working with your hands as you do your mouths, you'd be rich."

For some reason, the people who manage the schools come in for a lot of onion abuse:

"A big, rotten, stinky onion . . . to the school board."

"A classroom full of onions to the school board."

"One hundred school terms full of onions to the . . . school board."

The cops get a "prowl car full of onions." The basketball coach gets a "basketball full of onions."

"A farmhouse full of rotting onions . . . to people who dump their unwanted pets."

"Onions to whoever is stealing The Plain Dealer *from my mailbox."*

"Onions to the slimeball who stole my groceries from Sparkle Market."

If a few onions are bad, how much worse a lot of onions would be:

"Onions, onions and some more onions to the Garrettsville Library for allowing teenagers to use the magazine area as a make-out area."

"Onions—a whole township of onions—to Hiram Township for not taking care of Hankee Road."

"A big bushel of onions to the planner for thinking of wanting grade level buildings . . ."

"Tons of onions to local gas stations . . . who gouge the Sea World visitors and us along with them."

"A truckload of rotten, diesel-soaked onions to the inconsiderate slobs who drive their semis down our street every morning and wake me up."

Sometimes the onions are very expensive:

"A 16-million-dollar onion to Aurora."

Once in a while an onion giver has second thoughts:

"OK. I will give myself an onion for remarks I made after the game."

Clearly, the onion gets a bad rap, portrayed as corrosive, nasty, bitter, malodorous and insulting. We hope this book will persuade people to think positively of onions and find some other vegetable to give to people who transgress. Maybe rapini? Or okra?

Oniony Osso Buco

THIS IS ONE OF OUR FAVORITE wintertime dishes, and another one that goes well with mashed potatoes or polenta. It's topped with a fresh garnish of gremolata, a mixture of finely minced garlic, parsley and lemon zest.

SERVES 6

Osso Buco

6 tablespoons olive oil

1 cup finely chopped fresh white onion bulbs (creaming onions) or 1 medium-sized white onion plus 6 scallions, trimmed to include green parts, chopped

1 cup minced Spanish onion

⅔ cup finely chopped celery

1 cup finely chopped carrots

1 tablespoon minced garlic

½ cup unbleached flour

6 veal shanks, cut 3 inches thick

1 cup dry white wine

1 28-ounce can crushed Italian tomatoes

1 cup chicken stock

2 bay leaves

½ cup chopped fresh flat-leaf parsley

1 tablespoon chopped fresh basil leaves or 2 teaspoons dried

1 teaspoon fresh thyme leaves or ½ teaspoon dried

1 teaspoon minced fresh oregano leaves or ½ teaspoon dried

Kosher salt and freshly ground black pepper

Gremolata

⅓ cup minced fresh flat-leaf parsley

1 tablespoon minced garlic

Minced zest of 2 lemons

To make osso buco: In a Dutch oven or nonaluminum casserole, heat 3 tablespoons olive oil over low heat. Add both onions, celery, carrots and garlic and toss to coat with oil. Cover with a tight-fitting lid and cook over very low heat for 10 minutes. Turn heat off, but keep vegetables covered.

Place oven rack at the lowest position. Preheat oven to 350 degrees F.

Pour flour into a shallow soup plate and thoroughly coat veal shanks. Heat remaining 3 tablespoons olive oil in a large cast-iron skillet over medium-high heat until hot. Add veal shanks and carefully brown on all sides.

Arrange shanks in a single layer over vegetables in the Dutch oven. Pour off any accumulated fats in the cast-iron skillet, add wine, and bring to a boil over high heat. Boil, scraping the skillet well until all browned particles are loosened, until wine is reduced by ½. Add tomatoes, stock and all herbs and bring to a boil. Taste and season with salt and pepper.

Pour sauce over veal shanks. Tightly cover and bake until meat is very tender, about 1¼ hours.

Carefully transfer shanks to a shallow, ovenproof dish (we use a ceramic paella pan). Discard bay leaves. Puree cooked vegetables and sauce through a food mill or in a food processor. Pour sauce over and around shanks. (*The dish can be prepared to this point several hours prior to serving.*)

To finish, place oven rack in the top third of the oven. Preheat oven to 450 degrees. Roast shanks in the oven until heated through, 10 to 15 minutes.

Meanwhile, make gremolata: Stir together parsley, garlic and lemon zest.

Place 1 shank on each heated dinner plate. Spoon sauce over and around the shank and sprinkle with some gremolata.

Wine: Sean Thackery "Orion" Syrah (California: Napa Valley)

Pounded Veal Chops with Scallion Salad Topping

MENTION JOHNNY'S BAR to a business traveler to Cleveland and chances are you will hear raves. We've watched it grow from a neighborhood beer joint to the city's hottest restaurant. This recipe for a lightly crusted veal chop, contributed by owner Joe Santosuosso, has been our favorite item on the menu for nearly 10 years.

SERVES 2

2   long-bone rib veal chops (French cut),
     about 1½ inches thick
1   teaspoon minced garlic
     Kosher salt and freshly ground black pepper
½   cup unbleached flour
1   large egg
1   teaspoon water
½   cup fine dry bread crumbs
4   tablespoons extra-virgin olive oil
1   teaspoon sugar
1   garlic clove, crushed
1   teaspoon minced shallots
2   tablespoons balsamic vinegar
2   tablespoons minced fresh basil
1   bunch arugula, washed, stemmed and dried
6   scallions, coarsely chopped
1   ripe tomato, peeled, seeded and diced

Preheat oven to 425 degrees F.

Pound each veal chop until ½ inch thick. Rub each side with minced garlic and season with salt and pepper.

Pour flour onto a large plate; beat egg with the water in a soup plate; pour bread crumbs onto another plate. Dredge each chop first in flour, then in egg, and finally in bread crumbs. Press crumbs firmly onto coated chops and let chops rest on a rack.

In a medium bowl, whisk together 2 tablespoons olive oil, sugar, crushed garlic, shallots, vinegar and basil; set vinaigrette aside.

In an ovenproof skillet large enough to hold both chops, heat remaining 2 tablespoons oil over medium-high heat until hot. Add chops and sauté until golden, about 1½ minutes on each side.

Place the skillet in the oven and bake until the chops feel firm when pressed with a finger, 5 to 6 minutes.

Remove chops from the oven and blot on paper towels to remove any excess oil; place on heated plates. Add arugula, scallions and tomato to reserved vinaigrette, season with salt and pepper to taste, and toss. Divide salad between the plates and serve.

Wine: Laurel Glen Cabernet Sauvignon Sonoma Mountain (California: Sonoma County)

Veal Chops with Caramelized Onions

& SHIITAKE MUSHROOMS

CARAMELIZED ONIONS are combined with shiitake mushrooms and sun-dried tomatoes to make an elegant braising sauce for veal chops. We thank our friend Russell Trusso, anesthesiologist, successful fashion designer, jewelry maker and cook, for sharing his recipe.

SERVES 4

4   long-bone rib veal chops (French cut), 1½ inches thick
    Freshly ground black pepper

1   jumbo sweet onion, such as Vidalia, Walla Walla or Maui, coarsely chopped
    About 2 cups water

3   tablespoons olive oil

¾   pound fresh shiitake mushrooms, stems discarded and caps sliced

6   oil-packed sun-dried tomatoes

1   plump garlic clove, minced

¼   cup Madeira wine
    Kosher salt

2   tablespoons minced fresh flat-leaf parsley

Season each veal chop with black pepper and set aside.

In a large cast-iron skillet over high heat, combine onion and ¼ cup water. Cook, stirring briskly until water completely evaporates, about 1 to 3 minutes. Stir 15 seconds longer. Add another ¼ cup water and repeat entire process. Continue adding and evaporating water until onions are caramelized to a deep brown color, 15 to 20 minutes. (Do not burn.) Transfer onions to a medium bowl.

Add oil, mushrooms, sun-dried tomatoes and garlic to the skillet. Cover and cook over low heat, stirring often, for 5 minutes. Transfer mixture to onions.

Adding a bit more oil to the skillet, if needed, set the skillet over high heat until very hot. Sear chops until browned, about 2½ minutes on each side.

Reduce heat to medium, add Madeira and onion mixture. Cook for 6 minutes. Turn chops and cook just until firm, about 6 minutes for medium. Season with salt and chopped fresh parsley and serve.

Wine: Girard Winery Cabernet Sauvignon "Reserve" (California: Napa Valley)

Son-of-a-Bitch Stew

WHEN WE FIRST HEARD references to son-of-a-bitch stew (sometimes called son-of-a-gun stew), it was in the context of using wild onions of one type or another in a grab-bag kind of ranch-hand supper. We found the following recipe for the dish in *Tastes and Tales from Texas* by Peg Hein, published in 1984. Hein credits the recipe to Edwin "Goose" Ramey of Dimmitt, Texas, who was 94 in 1984. Strangely, however, there is no mention of onions in the recipe, but we expect "Goose" Ramey would tell us, if he could, that as many wild onions as you can find should go into the stew.

"Buster" Arnim, a Texas expatriate who, with his wife, Julie, runs the House on the Hill Bed and Breakfast in Ellsworth, Michigan, told us, "Of course, there has to be onions in son-of-a-bitch stew. You need the strongest onions possible to counteract all of that other stuff!"

1 calf tongue

½ calf liver

1 oxtail soup bone

½ calf heart

Butcher steak

Marrow gut

Calf brains

Sweetbreads

Hunk of kidney fat the size of a croquet ball

Boil tongue 30 min, then scrape good. (Delete if you don't like it.) Boil liver 30 to 40 min. (Leave out if you don't like liver.) Boil oxtail until meat is done and remove from bones.
Cut everything into 1-inch chunks and put in large kettle. Cover with water. Simmer 3 to 4 hours.
Add brains, sweetbreads, salt and pepper and simmer 30 to 45 more minutes.

Ground Lamb & Onion Kabobs with Minted Yogurt

ZESTILY SPICED ground lamb is shaped like a sausage, grilled and then served with a dollop of minted yogurt mixed with cucumber and red onion. They are wonderful with the Oniony Curried Potatoes, Cauliflower & Green Beans (page 357).

SERVES 4

1	heaping tablespoon cumin seeds
2	pounds lean ground lamb
½	cup fine dry bread crumbs
1	large egg
3	tablespoons water
2	tablespoons olive oil
¼	cup minced fresh mint leaves
¼	cup minced white onion
¼	cup minced shallots
2	tablespoons minced fresh parsley
1	small hot red chile pepper, seeded and minced
2	teaspoons kosher salt
1	teaspoon freshly ground black pepper
⅔	cup plain yogurt
¼	cup grated cucumber
2	tablespoons grated red onion

Place cumin seeds in a small, dry skillet and toast over high heat, stirring constantly, until browned, 1 to 2 minutes. Remove from the heat and let cool. Grind to a fine powder in a coffee grinder or in a mortar with a pestle; set aside.

In a large bowl, combine lamb, bread crumbs, egg, water, oil, 2 tablespoons mint, onion, shallots, parsley, chile pepper and 2 teaspoons ground cumin and salt and pepper. Beat with an electric mixer or by hand until mixture is fluffy. Form into 8 fat, sausage-like tubes, about 1 inch in diameter and 4 inches long. Cover and chill until needed.

Combine remaining 2 tablespoons mint and 1 teaspoon ground cumin with yogurt, cucumber and red onion; blend well. Cover and chill.

Preheat the broiler until hot. Broil kabobs about 4 inches from the heat for 5 minutes. Turn and broil until kabobs are nicely pink in the middle, another 5 minutes. Serve with yogurt sauce.

Wine: Lytton Springs Winery Zinfandel Valle Vista Vineyard (California: Sonoma County)

Shepherd's Pie with Onion-Mashed Potato Topping

SHEPHERD'S PIE IS USUALLY MADE with lamb leftovers. Our version, made with fresh ground lamb and veal, is flavored with a variety of spices and herbs and capped by an exceptionally creamy layer of whipped potatoes. It makes a fantastic party dish. Although the recipe is long, it is very simple and can be prepared a day ahead. Cover tightly and refrigerate, and bring it to room temperature before baking.

SERVES 8 TO 10

Filling

2   tablespoons olive oil
2   large yellow onions, minced
2   plump garlic cloves, minced
2   pounds ground lamb
1   pound ground veal
1   hot red chile pepper, minced
    Zest of 1 orange, minced
1   tablespoon hot curry powder
2   celery ribs, diced
1   green bell pepper, diced
2   tablespoons unbleached flour
1   cup chopped peeled fresh tomatoes or
    1 cup drained canned
½   cup dry red wine

½   cup beef stock
¼   cup fresh orange juice
2   tablespoons tomato paste
3   tablespoons minced fresh chives
2   tablespoons minced fresh marjoram leaves
    or 1 tablespoon dried
1   tablespoon minced fresh thyme leaves or
    1½ teaspoons dried
    Kosher salt and freshly ground pepper
¾   cup fresh or frozen peas
¾   cup fresh or frozen corn kernels

Potato Topping

2   tablespoons olive oil
1   pound white onions, finely chopped
    (2¼ cups)
3   pounds white potatoes, peeled, cooked and
    mashed
2   cups milk
½   cup (1 stick) butter
3   large eggs
1   cup grated Swiss or Gruyère cheese
    (¼ pound)
4   scallions, minced
½   teaspoon freshly grated nutmeg
    Kosher salt and freshly ground black pepper

To make filling: Thoroughly butter or oil a 4-to-6-quart ovenproof casserole.

In a large nonaluminum skillet over medium heat, combine oil, onions and garlic. Cover with a tight-fitting lid, reduce heat to very low and cook until onions are somewhat tender, 3 to 5 minutes. Transfer onions to a dish.

Add both ground meats, chile pepper, orange zest and curry powder to oil remaining in skillet. Cook over medium heat until browned, about 5 minutes. Add celery and bell pepper and cook until wilted, 2 to 3 minutes. Return onions to meat mixture. Sprinkle flour over mixture and toss well. Quickly add tomatoes, wine, stock, orange juice, tomato paste, herbs and salt and pepper to taste. Bring to a boil. Cover, reduce heat to low and simmer for 20 minutes, stirring from time to time.

Spoon mixture into the prepared casserole. Blend in peas and corn; taste and adjust seasonings. Preheat oven to 400 degrees F.

To make potato topping: Heat olive oil in a large skillet over low heat. Add onions, cover and cook for 5 minutes. Uncover, increase heat to medium, and cook, stirring frequently, until golden, 5 to 10 minutes; set aside.

Place potatoes, milk and butter in a bowl. With an electric mixer, beat until potatoes are light and fluffy. Beat in cooked onions, eggs, cheese, scallions, nutmeg and salt and pepper to taste. Carefully spoon potato topping on top of meat filling and spread evenly.

Bake casserole in the oven for 40 minutes. Turn on the broiler and cook until potatoes are lightly browned on top, 2 to 3 minutes.

Wine: August Clape Cornas (France: Rhône)

ALLIUM LAWYER

ALLIUM CEPA, our common onion, does not exist in the wild. In fact, if you turn it loose, it will not thrive and dies. But it must have had a undomesticated ancestor. Most investigators now believe that *A. cepa* somehow came into existence as a result of early cultivation of a wild onion from central Asia, *A. vavilovii*, named after a Soviet scientist. If scientists could find some naturally occurring stands of that species, they could gather its germ plasm, inventory its genetic content and confirm their hypothesis by comparing it to the genes of *A. cepa*. But more importantly, they could introduce its strengths into breeding lines and improve commercial onions.

In the summer of 1989, in two all-terrain vehicles, scientists launched an expedition into the craggy mountains and desert highlands of Turkmenia, a part of central Asia often thought to be the source of the onion.

There were six people in the party: a scientist from Tashkent who knew the territory; Poland's leading specialist in onion culture; an interpreter and three Americans. Chosen by the Department of Agriculture to spend an arduous three weeks in the barren mountains were Dr. Philipp W. Simon, an onion and carrot man from the University of Wisconsin, Dr. Leonard Pike, the Texas A&M scientist who created the 1015Y sweet onion, and John Swenson, attorney-at-law.

The involvement of an Illinois lawyer in such an assignment had its genesis in an elm blight that killed his shade trees over 20 years before. John Swenson's backyard had long been a refuge from the summer sun, but suddenly that summer, the shade was gone. Swenson cut up the dead elms and surveyed the sunny expanse. It would take an eon to have new trees, but he could have a garden right away.

IN A SEED CATALOG, he saw rocambole, an old-fashioned top-seeding garlic. Swenson ordered some, and he liked how it grew and how it tasted. That led him to the Seed Savers' Exchange, an organization dedicated to preserving original and historic plant lines. He was intrigued with Seed Savers' work, but especially with what they knew about garlics and shallots. Suddenly, Swenson found himself hooked on alliums. In fact, he gave up law to raise and sell shallots and garlic and to study the science of plants. By the time of the central Asian expedition, he was widely recognized as one of the world's leading authorities on alliums.

If you had *A. vavilovii* from the wild, Swenson explained, you could open up many opportunities for breeding. Swenson had tasted it and remembers it as being "extremely pungent—not for salads." He believes that the plant's genetic material might strengthen the onions we grow today, possibly resulting in a much sturdier plant, resistant to heat, cold and disease.

For three weeks, the scientists methodically explored the rugged hills and the upland meadows of Turkmenia. The dusty trek took them over open range, along cattle trails and through pastoral villages, places where their quarry is known to have grown.

Shepherds they met along the way told the scientists that *A. vavilovii* had been gathered and sold in the local markets as recently as the early 1960s. "But now, owing to grazing," said Swenson, "it was gone, nowhere to be found—in that region at least, extinct. We had heard that there might be some few stands of *A. vavilovii* in Iran, but there was no way we could check it out. And there is some in a botanical garden, but the act of sequestering a wild plant in a place to which it is not native changes it.

"There's an important message here," he continued. "We are losing the wild gene pool. What we saw in Turkmenia is a microcosm of what's happening in the rain forests—the loss of irreplaceable genetic material.

"If a plant becomes extinct, you don't know what you've lost. It might be of great value—in nutrition, in agriculture, in medicine. What we learned on this expedition helps sound the alarm."

You get the feeling that the allium lawyer wishes he could bring a lawsuit to stop the degradation.

Lamb Vindaloo with Slow-Fried Onions

VINDALOO, a hot and spicy lamb stew, has its roots in Goa, on the southwest coast of India. Onions play an important role in both the marinade and the final dish. Tamarind pulp, from the pod of a tamarind tree, has a dark, sour flavor that is important in the thick, oniony sauce, but if it's unavailable, substitute ⅓ cup lemon juice and reduce the boiling water to 1 cup, adding more lemon juice later as called for in the recipe. In India, the mustard plants yield black seeds, not the yellow ones common in the west. Both of these are commonly available in Indian markets.

SERVES 6

1   teaspoon black mustard seeds
3   small dried red chile peppers (5, if you like things very hot), crushed
2   teaspoons cumin seeds
5   plump garlic cloves, peeled
1   medium-sized yellow onion, quartered
1   chunk (about 1½ inches long) fresh ginger, peeled
2   teaspoons cayenne
½   teaspoon ground cloves
1   teaspoon ground cardamom
1   teaspoon ground cinnamon

1   teaspoon fenugreek
3   tablespoons red-wine vinegar
⅔   cup plus 1 tablespoon vegetable oil
3   pounds boneless leg of lamb, fat removed, cut into 1-inch cubes
1   rounded teaspoon tamarind concentrate
1½ cups boiling water
1½ pounds yellow onions, thinly sliced
2   teaspoons ground turmeric
1   teaspoon ground coriander
    Juice of 1 lemon
2   teaspoons kosher salt
½   teaspoon freshly ground white pepper

Combine mustard seeds, chile peppers and cumin seeds in a small, dry skillet and stir over medium heat until cumin seeds and chiles darken and mustard seeds turn gray, about 3 minutes. Remove from the heat and let cool. Grind to a powder in a coffee grinder or in a mortar with a pestle.

Place spice mixture in the bowl of a food processor fitted with the metal blade, and add garlic, quartered onion, ginger, cayenne, cloves, cardamom, cinnamon, fenugreek, vinegar and 1 tablespoon oil. Puree thoroughly; pour into a large ceramic or glass mixing bowl. Add lamb and toss until well coated.

Cover the bowl tightly and marinate in the refrigerator for 24 hours.

Dissolve tamarind concentrate in boiling water and set aside. In a large, heavy sauté pan, heat ⅓ cup oil over medium heat. Add sliced onions and stir constantly until onions are a dark caramel color, 20 to 25 minutes. (Carefully increase heat after onions begin to darken, but keep stirring.) Add turmeric and coriander and stir for 1 minute. Transfer onions to a large bowl.

Add 3 tablespoons oil to skillet and increase heat to high. Working in batches, sear lamb until browned on all sides, adding more oil as needed. Reserve marinade. Add seared lamb to reserved onions.

When all lamb is seared, return meat and onions to the pan. Increase the heat, add remaining marinade, tamarind water, lemon juice, salt and pepper. When mixture begins to bubble, cover, reduce the heat to low and cook for 30 minutes.

Remove cover, stir, and simmer until lamb is tender, about 15 minutes more.

Wine: Saintsbury "Garnet" Pinot Noir (California: Carneros)

Doxie's Roasted Leg of Lamb on an Onion Bed

EVERY WEEK, the Ambeliotis family gathers in Warren, Ohio, for a traditional Greek Sunday meal that includes a luscious leg of lamb. The cooking is long, resulting in a moist, well-done roast with a rich, full-flavored gravy. We ask the butcher to remove the cumbersome pelvic bone to make carving easier.

SERVES 8

1   tablespoon vegetable oil
2   pounds yellow onions, thinly sliced
1   leg of lamb (8-9 pounds), pelvic bone removed
3   garlic cloves, thinly sliced
1-2 tablespoons olive oil
    Salt and freshly ground black pepper
1   tablespoon minced fresh rosemary leaves or 1½ teaspoons dried
    Juice of 1 lemon
3   large ripe tomatoes, thinly sliced
1   bottle (750 ml) dry red wine
⅓   cup minced fresh parsley for gravy

Thoroughly oil a large roasting pan. Arrange onions in an even layer to make a bed for lamb.

With a sharp knife, make about 20 deep slits on both sides of lamb. Insert garlic slices into each. Rub the lamb with olive oil. Place lamb, fat side up, in the roasting pan. Season generously with salt and pepper. Sprinkle rosemary over meat; sprinkle with lemon juice. Cover top of lamb with overlapping slices of tomatoes. Let stand for 2 to 4 hours refrigerated; bring to room temperature before proceeding.

Preheat oven to 350 degrees F. Pour 2 cups wine in the bottom of the roasting pan. Place the pan in the oven and roast for 3 hours, basting lamb every 30 minutes with pan drippings and adding wine as needed. If leg is smaller, reduce cooking time accordingly, allowing about 20 minutes per pound.

Remove lamb to a carving board and let meat stand for 15 minutes before carving.

Remove tomatoes from top of lamb and add to drippings in the roasting pan. Place the roasting pan over high heat, add at least ¼ cup wine and stir until particles loosen from the bottom of the pan and gravy is slightly reduced, about 4 minutes. Remove the pan from the heat and season sauce with salt and pepper to taste; stir in parsley.

Slice meat parallel to bone and serve on heated plates with sauce.

Wine: Spottswoode Cabernet Sauvignon (California: Napa Valley)

YELLOW ONIONS

Braised Lamb Shanks

WITH ONIONS, CARROTS & WHITE BEANS

WE LOVE BRAISED LAMB SHANKS and especially enjoy them served with beans or lentils. Since without onions, lamb shanks would be boring, this preparation calls for two types. Be sure to have some good bread on hand for mopping up the sauce.

SERVES 2

¼	cup unbleached flour
2	large lamb shanks (about 1 pound each)
2-3	tablespoons olive oil
¾	cup finely diced yellow onion
2	plump garlic cloves, diced
2	rounded tablespoons tomato paste
2	cups dry red wine
4	white boiling onions, peeled
2	large carrots, cut into ½-inch slices
½	teaspoon kosher salt
½	teaspoon freshly ground black pepper
2	teaspoons fresh thyme leaves or 1 teaspoon dried
2	teaspoons minced fresh rosemary leaves or 1 teaspoon dried
1	teaspoon minced fresh sage leaves or ½ teaspoon dried
¼	cup minced fresh parsley
1	cup cooked Great Northern white beans (¾ cup raw)
	Additional fresh herbs for garnish

Preheat oven to 325 degrees F.

Place flour on a plate and dredge shanks to coat evenly. Pour 2 tablespoons oil into a large cast-iron or other ovenproof skillet and heat over medium-high heat. Quickly sear shanks, browning on all sides, 3 to 4 minutes. Remove shanks from the skillet.

Add 1 tablespoon more oil, if needed, and add onion and garlic. Stir over medium heat to wilt onion, about 3 minutes. Stir in tomato paste. Slowly add wine, scraping the skillet to loosen any browned particles that adhere to the bottom. Bring sauce to a boil. Return shanks to the skillet and add boiling onions and carrots. Sprinkle with salt, pepper and herbs. Spoon some sauce over shanks and cover the skillet with a tight-fitting lid.

Place the skillet in the oven and braise shanks until very tender, about 2½ hours. Carefully remove the skillet from the oven and place on the stovetop.

Remove the lid, lift shanks out of sauce and place on a heated platter. Add cooked beans to sauce and cook over high heat until beans are heated through, about 2 minutes.

Spoon sauce and vegetables onto 2 heated serving plates. Arrange 1 shank in the middle of each plate. Sprinkle with more salt and pepper. Garnish with fresh herbs.

Wine: Von Strasser Cabernet Sauvignon Diamond Mountain (California: Napa Valley)

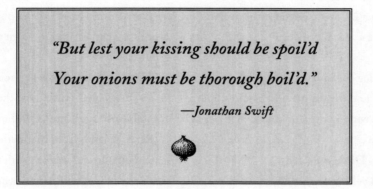

"But lest your kissing should be spoil'd
Your onions must be thorough boil'd."

—*Jonathan Swift*

Grilled Butterflied Leg of Lamb

IN ONION-HERB MARINADE

BECAUSE OF THE VARYING thickness of this cut, it will range from well-done to rare, so every guest will be pleased. We thank Betsy Cohen for this recipe.

SERVES 6 TO 8

1	butterflied leg of lamb (6-7 pounds)
	Kosher salt and freshly ground black pepper
1	cup dry red wine
¼	cup olive oil
2	tablespoons Dijon mustard
1	cup minced yellow onions
2	tablespoons fennel seeds
2	tablespoons minced garlic
2	tablespoons ground cumin
1	teaspoon fresh thyme leaves or
	½ teaspoon dried
1	bay leaf, crumbled
2	tablespoons butter

Season lamb with salt and pepper. Place in a glass or ceramic baking dish large enough to hold it flat. In a large mixing bowl, mix together wine, oil and mustard. Add onions, fennel, garlic, cumin, thyme, bay leaf and 1 teaspoon freshly ground black pepper; whisk well. Pour marinade over meat and turn to coat both sides. Cover the dish with plastic and refrigerate, turning from time to time, for 5 hours or overnight. Bring lamb to room temperature before grilling.

Thoroughly clean the surface of a gas or charcoal grill with a metal brush; coat the rack evenly with vegetable oil. Preheat the grill until hot.

Remove lamb from marinade; scrape onions back into marinade and season lamb with salt. Transfer marinade to a nonaluminum saucepan, add butter and set over low heat. Bring sauce to a boil. Reduce heat and simmer for 5 minutes.

Meanwhile, place lamb on the grill, cover and cook for 10 minutes.

Turn lamb and grill for 10 minutes more for rare. An instant-read thermometer inserted into the center of the thickest part of lamb should read 120 degrees F.

Transfer lamb to a shallow dish. Pour heated marinade mixture over lamb, and let stand in a warm place for 10 minutes. Slice and serve with sauce.

Wine: Pahlmeyer Caldwell Vineyard Red Table Wine (California: Napa Valley)

SINGING ONION SONGS

FROM TIME TO TIME, people have lifted their voices in song in tribute to foods. We think fondly of "Yes, We Have No Bananas," a durable popular classic. Or of "Green Corn, Green Corn, Come Along Charlie," a Leadbelly song that college folkies used to play in the old days.

Since the onion is the world's number-one vegetable, we thought we would find a lot of references to it in music. But we couldn't think of any. As we pondered, we finally remembered a Richard Dyer-Bennett song in which a retired Irish soldier says, "Content with shallots, I'll live on half pay."

Michael Feinstein, a popular singer, reminded us that there is an onion mention in a song by Rodgers and Hart, although you have to go to the third verse to find it: "Isn't it romantic, on a moonlit night she'll make me onion soup."

But that was it. Hardly enough for a chapter in an onion book. But little by little, we found other songs with onions in the titles:

- *"Green Onions," by Booker T and the MGs*
- *"Onions and Love Affairs," by Ann J. Morton*
- *"Onions," written and recorded by John Lee Hooker*
- *"Onion Song," written by the team of Ashford and Simpson and recorded by Marvin Gaye and Tammy Terrell*
- *"Onion Skin," by Farnan*
- *"Onion Roll," by Herb Ellis and the Tijuana Brass*
- *"Glass Onion," a Beatles song recorded on* **The White Album**

We will be grateful to any reader who knows of an onion song we missed and who is willing to let us know about it. Write to us in care of our publisher.

Grilled Lamb Tenderloin & Bulgur Salad

WITH RED ONIONS

ADDING LAMB to this oniony bulgur salad turns it into a main dish for summer. You'll taste a suggestion of the Middle East in the spices. Lamb tenderloins, available through specialty meat purveyors, are small and especially delicious when marinated and grilled. (If you cannot obtain tenderloins, marinate some lamb rib chops instead.) We often serve this on weekends for lunch or as dinner on a very hot evening.

SERVES 6

Tenderloins

½   cup olive oil

¼   cup vegetable oil

1   garlic clove, minced

1   shallot, minced

1   bay leaf

2   teaspoons chopped fresh mint

¼   teaspoon ground allspice

½   teaspoon ground cumin

¼   teaspoon cayenne

6   lamb tenderloins, exterior membrane removed and excess fat discarded

Salad

1   cup medium-sized bulgur (available in natural food stores)

4   cups boiling water

½   cup diced red onions

1   medium-sized cucumber, unpeeled, seeded and diced

⅓   cup thinly sliced scallions

⅓   cup diced radish

⅓   cup chopped fresh parsley

⅓   cup chopped fresh spearmint or pineapple mint

¼   cup olive oil

    Juice of 2-3 lemons

    Kosher salt and freshly ground pepper

1   medium-sized ripe yellow tomato, diced

1   medium-sized ripe red tomato, diced

3   ounces feta cheese, crumbled (optional)

    Large kale leaves, mint leaves and chopped tomatoes for garnish (optional)

To marinate tenderloins: Combine both oils, garlic, shallot, bay leaf, mint, allspice, cumin and cayenne in a mixing bowl; whisk well. Arrange lamb tenderloins in a shallow glass baking dish and add marinade; turn lamb to coat well. Cover the dish with plastic wrap and refrigerate, turning tenderloins from time to time, for at least 6 hours or overnight.

To make salad: Combine bulgur and boiling water in a bowl and set aside to soak for 1 hour. Drain bulgur; place in a large mixing bowl. Add red onions, cucumber, scallions, radish, parsley and mint and blend well. Add oil, juice of 2 lemons and salt and pepper to taste. Let stand for at least 1 hour.

Just before serving, add yellow and red tomatoes and feta, if using. Taste and adjust seasonings, adding more lemon juice, if you wish.

To cook tenderloins: Coat a clean grill rack with vegetable oil. Preheat the rack until hot. Remove tenderloins from marinade and season with salt and pepper to taste. When the grill is hot, cook tenderloins for 1 to 2 minutes on each side, or until medium-rare, basting with marinade. Let rest off the heat for 5 minutes.

To assemble: Arrange kale leaves, if using, in the center of 6 large serving plates. Spoon generous portions of salad on each, then slice tenderloins on an angle and scatter over salad. Garnish with mint leaves and chopped tomatoes.

Wine: Laurel Glen "Terra Rosa" Cabernet Sauvignon (California)

POULTRY & FEATHERED GAME

Chicken Breasts with Shallots & Sun-Dried Tomatoes

WE'VE BEEN MAKING this dish for years. A flavorful mixture of minced shallots, sun-dried tomatoes and fresh goat cheese is inserted under the skin of the chicken. It can be prepared early in the day and baked (bring it to room temperature first) just in time for dinner. Start the meal with Little Shells with Caramelized Onion Sauce (page 206), and accompany the chicken with a vegetable and simple salad.

SERVES 4

4   large oil-packed sun-dried tomatoes, drained

1   large shallot, halved

1   tablespoon chopped fresh chives

4   fresh basil leaves or ¼ teaspoon dried

2   teaspoons fresh oregano leaves or
    1 teaspoon dried

1   tablespoon freshly ground black pepper

4   tablespoons olive oil

6   ounces fresh chèvre (goat cheese)

2   whole chicken breasts ,with skin on, split
    Kosher salt
    Juice of 1 lemon
    Fresh basil and oregano leaves for garnish

Preheat oven to 400 degrees F. Oil a shallow baking dish large enough to hold the chicken breasts without touching.

In the bowl of a food processor fitted with the metal blade, combine tomatoes, shallot, chives, basil, oregano, pepper and 2 tablespoons olive oil. Pulse until finely chopped. Add chèvre and pulse until well combined. Scrape mixture from the bowl and form into a log. Divide into 4 equal parts; flatten each portion so that it can be easily inserted under skin on chicken breast.

Gently loosen skin of chicken breast with your fingers and put cheese mixture between skin and flesh. Pat down skin over cheese mixture.

Place breasts in the baking dish, rub each with some of remaining 2 tablespoons olive oil; sprinkle with salt and pepper to taste.

Bake, basting with remaining olive oil and lemon juice, until skin is nicely browned, about 1 hour. Garnish with fresh herbs.

**Wine: Spottswoode Sauvignon Blanc
(California: Napa Valley)**

White Chili & White Onions

WITH GREAT NORTHERN BEANS & CHICKEN

THIS PEPPY DISH is perfect to make when the cold weather of autumn first hits, since you can still find a wide variety of fresh chiles in the stores and the large-bulbed green onions have begun to appear. That's not to say, of course, that you can't make it any season, with other chiles and different onions. By the way, you can use the food processor for the onions and celery; just be careful not to liquefy them.

SERVES 6 TO 8

- 3 tablespoons olive oil
- 1 pound large-bulbed green onions, including tender green part, finely chopped (or 1 large white onion and 6 scallions, trimmed to include 1 inch of green)
- 3 celery ribs, finely chopped
- 3 banana Anaheim or Hungarian peppers, seeded and cut into thin rings
- 3 fresh cayenne or other hot red chile peppers, seeded and cut into thin rings
- 2 yellow bell peppers, seeded and cut into medium dice
- 1 orange bell pepper, seeded and cut into medium dice

- 3 plump garlic cloves, minced
- 1 tablespoon ground cumin
- 2 teaspoons freshly ground black pepper
- 2 teaspoons freshly ground white pepper
- 1 tablespoon medium-hot chile powder or other chili powder
- 2 tablespoons unbleached flour
- 4 cups (1 quart) chicken stock
- 3 pounds boneless, skinless chicken breasts, cut into ¾-inch cubes
- 3 cups cooked Great Northern beans
- 2 tablespoons minced fresh cilantro
- 1 tablespoon fresh thyme leaves or minced chives

  Kosher salt

  Sour cream, grated sharp Cheddar cheese and chopped scallions for garnishes

In a wide, heavy-bottomed 6-quart pot, heat olive oil over medium heat. Add onions, celery and all peppers and cook, stirring, until wilted, about 5 minutes. Add garlic, cumin, black and white pepper and chile powder; reduce heat to low, and cook, stirring often, for 5 minutes. Sprinkle flour over mixture, increase heat to medium and stir to cook flour, 2 to 3 minutes. Stir in stock, chicken and beans. Increase heat and stir often until liquids come to a simmer. Reduce heat to low, partially cover and cook for 30 minutes. Season with cilantro, thyme or chives and salt to taste. Ladle into heated bowls and garnish with dollops of sour cream, cheese and scallions.

Wine: Buehler Vineyards White Zinfandel (California: Napa Valley)

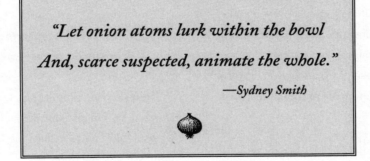

"Let onion atoms lurk within the bowl
And, scarce suspected, animate the whole."
—*Sydney Smith*

Roasted Chicken with Leeks, Onions & Herbs

WHEN YOU WANT to prepare a special dinner, this is the recipe. Two chickens are stuffed with herbs and roasted on a bed of leeks and onions. The breast meat is served first, napped with a simple and delicious leek-and-onion pan sauce. Then the leg and thigh meat is removed from the bone and tossed with a salad for the following course. If you make this in the summer, substitute branches of fresh herbs for the dried ones in the chicken cavities. Potatoes & Onions Boulangère (page 354) and steamed spinach make perfect accompaniments to the sliced breast and sauce.

SERVES 4

Vinaigrette

1   tablespoon fresh lemon juice
2   tablespoons Champagne vinegar or white-wine vinegar
    Kosher salt and freshly ground black pepper
⅓   cup extra-virgin olive oil
2   tablespoons minced fresh mint leaves

3   plump leeks, white and tender green parts, trimmed, cleaned and julienned
1   medium-sized white onion, thinly sliced
1   tablespoon herbes de Provence

2-3 tablespoons olive oil
     Kosher salt and freshly ground black pepper
2   frying chickens (3-3½ pounds each)
2   lemons, halved
1   bunch fresh flat-leaf parsley
1   teaspoon dried rosemary
1½   cups chicken stock
     Fresh Herbs, for garnish
2   cups tender lettuce leaves, torn for salad

To make vinaigrette: In a small bowl, combine lemon juice, vinegar and salt and pepper. Slowly whisk in olive oil to make a thick emulsion. Add mint, stir and set aside.

Preheat oven to 475 degrees F.

In a bowl, combine leeks, white onion and herbes de Provence. Thoroughly coat a 12-inch cast-iron skillet with 1 tablespoon olive oil.

Rub some salt and pepper inside each chicken. Stuff a small bunch of leek-onion mixture in each. Distribute remaining leeks and onions over the bottom of the skillet.

Rub each chicken with some olive oil; season with salt and pepper. Place chickens on the onion bed, with head end of one next to tail end of the other.

Squeeze juice of ½ lemon over each bird; place an

unsqueezed lemon half inside the cavity of each bird. Divide parsley between the 2 chicken cavities. Sprinkle the top of each chicken with some dried rosemary.

Place the skillet in the middle of the oven and roast for 20 minutes. Squeeze juice of ½ lemon over each bird and roast for 15 minutes.

Pour ½ cup stock into a bowl. Baste chicken with stock and roast, basting several more times, for 25 minutes. When done, juices should run clear when thigh is pierced with a fork.

Place chickens on a carving board and let stand in a warm place for 5 to 10 minutes.

Meanwhile, place the skillet on the stovetop and add remaining ¾ cup chicken stock. Turn heat to high and scrape up all browned bits that adhere to the bottom. Adjust seasonings. Pour liquid into a heatproof cup and spoon off the fat that collects at the top. (You will have just enough for 4 servings.)

Carefully carve chicken breast off the bone and place on heated serving plates. Spoon some of the gravy over the breast, garnish with fresh herbs and serve as a first course.

When you are finished with the first course, cut meat off legs and thighs, toss in a mixing bowl with vinaigrette. Add lettuces and toss. Divide among 4 plates and serve as a second course.

**Wine: Panther Creek Pinot Noir (Oregon)
with first course,
Sanford Winery Pinot Noir
(California: Santa Barbara) with second**

Roasted Chicken Dijon with Shallots & Onions

THIS HERB-INFUSED ROASTED CHICKEN has a crisp mustard coating and a deep-flavored caramelized leek-and-Dijon-mustard gravy. We created this dish when we received our first order from Kingsfield Farms in Blue Mounds, Wisconsin.

SERVES 2

4	tablespoons olive oil
2	medium leeks, including tender green parts, trimmed, split, cleaned and finely chopped
	Juice of 1 lemon (lemon halves reserved)
1½	tablespoons dry mustard
1	frying chicken (3½-4 pounds)
	Salt and freshly ground black pepper
3	branches fresh thyme or 1 teaspoon dried
1	branch fresh tarragon or ½ teaspoon dried
2	thin Italian bottle onions or 1 small red onion, quartered
4-6	shallots
8	gray shallots, tops and bottoms removed (optional)
1	cup chicken stock
2	tablespoons Dijon mustard
1	tablespoon minced fresh tarragon leaves

Preheat oven to 475 degrees F. Coat a large cast-iron or other ovenproof skillet with 1 tablespoon olive oil. Arrange chopped leeks in a mound in the center of the skillet; set aside.

In a small bowl, combine lemon juice, 1 tablespoon olive oil and dry mustard; whisk well. Coat chicken with this mixture, rubbing some between skin and breast meat as well. Season cavity with salt and pepper, and stuff with lemon halves and herbs.

Place chicken in the skillet on bed of leeks. Drizzle with some of the remaining 2 tablespoons olive oil; season with salt and pepper. Rub onions and peeled shallots with some of remaining oil and scatter around chicken.

Place the skillet in the preheated oven and roast for 15 minutes. Turn onions and shallots; add gray shallots, if using. Reduce oven temperature to 425 degrees and roast for 15 minutes.

Continue roasting, basting chicken with ¾ cup of chicken stock, until juices run clear when thigh is pierced with a fork, about 30 minutes more.

Remove skillet from the oven. Transfer chicken, shallots and onions to a carving board and keep warm.

Place skillet over medium heat on the stovetop.

Add the remaining ¼ cup stock and cook, scraping the pan well. Add accumulated juices from the carving board, whisk in Dijon mustard, and bring to a brisk boil, 1 to 2 minutes. Cook until sauce is thick. Add tarragon; adjust seasonings. Pour into a gravy boat.

Cut chicken into quarters and serve with shallots, onions and sauce.

Wine: Havens Cellars Merlot
(California: Napa Valley)

Odessa Piper, owner of Madison's
great restaurant L'Étoile, can step out of her
restaurant right into the Dane County Farmers' Market
on the statehouse grounds, where she buys her favorite
allium: "Kingsfield Gardens French gray shallot.
We caramelize them lightly and deglaze them
with a light fruit vinegar or sherry."
Her tool of choice is "a knife, always.
We've not come up with a way to avoid tears,
but we've noticed that, as one becomes acclimated,
the tears become fewer. I've also tried singing
through the tears to distract myself."

Chicken Fricassee in Shallot & Red-Wine Vinegar Sauce

THIS TRADITIONAL COUNTRY French dish features chicken and shallots braised in a thick, tangy red-wine vinegar sauce. Twice a year we bottle two cases of luscious red-wine vinegar from an old keg we keep near our furnace in winter and move to the garage in summer. If you don't have a keg of your own, be sure to buy a good-quality vinegar. If you want a stronger sauce, use white onions instead of shallots.

SERVES 8

2   chickens (each 3 pounds), each cut into
    8 pieces
½   cup unbleached flour
3   tablespoons olive oil
2   tablespoons vegetable oil
½   cup finely diced shallots
2   garlic cloves, minced
¼   cup minced celery
½   cup red-wine vinegar
¾   cup dry red wine
1   cup chicken stock
½   teaspoon dried sage
½   teaspoon dried rosemary
½   teaspoon dried thyme
    Kosher salt and freshly ground black pepper

2   tablespoons minced fresh chives
1   tablespoon minced fresh parsley

Dredge chicken pieces in flour to coat well.

Combine both oils in a large nonaluminum skillet over medium-high heat until hot. Working in batches of 6 to 8 pieces, carefully brown chicken on all sides. Remove chicken from the skillet and set aside. Add shallots, garlic and celery to the warm skillet. Reduce heat to medium and stir for 1 minute. Add vinegar and wine and stir over medium heat to loosen any particles that adhere to the bottom of the skillet. Return chicken to the skillet, cover, and simmer for 5 minutes.

Sprinkle chicken with dried herbs and salt and pepper to taste. Cover and simmer over low heat until chicken is tender, stirring from time to time, about 50 minutes.

Remove chicken from the skillet and keep warm. If sauce is too thin, increase heat and boil liquid briskly for a few minutes to reduce.

Spoon sauce over chicken and sprinkle with chives and parsley.

Wine: Judd's Hill Cabernet Sauvignon
(California: Napa Valley)

GIANT GARLIC

White Onion & Parsley-Smothered Chicken

THIS CHICKEN RETAINS its crisp coating although it is covered by thick, oniony gravy. The recipe has roots in a splendid Craig Claiborne recipe from *The New York Times*. For best results, use clarified butter to minimize burning during the long cooking.

To make clarified butter: Pour melted butter into a bowl; chill. Discard the milky liquid before using; the solid yellow part that remains is clarified butter.

SERVES 2 TO 4

4	tablespoons unbleached flour
	Kosher salt and freshly ground black pepper
1	frying chicken (3½-4 pounds), split down the back, backbone removed
3	tablespoons clarified butter
1	cup finely diced white onions
2	cups chicken stock
3	tablespoons minced fresh parsley
1	teaspoon fresh thyme leaves or ½ teaspoon dried
1	tablespoon minced fresh chives

Combine 2 tablespoons flour with salt and pepper; thoroughly rub mixture into both sides of chicken.

Place butter in a large cast-iron skillet over medium heat. Add chicken, skin side down, and set a large plate on top of chicken. Place a 5-pound weight, such as a brick, on the plate. Reduce heat to low and cook chicken until nicely browned, about 25 minutes. Turn chicken, replace the plate and weight, and cook other side until underside is browned, about 20 minutes. Remove chicken to a warm plate.

Whisk remaining 2 tablespoons flour into the skillet and cook, stirring over medium heat, until flour darkens slightly and cooks into fats, about 4 minutes. Quickly stir in onions; slowly add chicken stock and whisk well until sauce is thickened. Season to taste.

Return chicken, skin side up, to the skillet. Cover with the plate and weight, and cook over low heat until chicken is tender, about 30 minutes.

Remove chicken to a carving board and cut into quarters. Stir thyme and chives into gravy. Serve chicken generously napped with gravy and more freshly ground pepper.

Wine: Matanzas Creek Winery Chardonnay (California: Sonoma County)

Coq au Vin

THIS RECIPE for a succulent stew with a red-wine gravy is based on a traditional French way of preparing chicken and onions.

SERVES 6 TO 8

½ cup unbleached flour

3 whole chicken breasts, split

3 chicken legs and thighs, separated

¼ pound (3 thick slices) bacon, preferably smoked, diced

2-4 tablespoons (¼-½ stick) butter

1-2 tablespoons olive oil

1 pint pearl or 12 boiling onions, peeled (pages 37-38)

4 plump carrots, scraped and cut into 1-inch chunks

2 leeks, white parts only, trimmed, cleaned and sliced

2 plump garlic cloves, minced

⅓ cup applejack or cider

2 teaspoons fresh thyme leaves or 1 teaspoon dried

1 bay leaf

Kosher salt and freshly ground black pepper

1 bottle (750 ml) dry red wine

2 tablespoons softened butter blended with 2 tablespoons unbleached flour

Pour flour on a large plate. Dredge chicken parts in flour; set aside.

Fry bacon in a 5-quart cast-iron Dutch oven or casserole. When it begins to crisp, remove with a slotted spoon and set aside. Add 2 tablespoons butter and 1 tablespoon olive oil to bacon fat and heat over medium heat until hot. Brown chicken, about 4 pieces at a time, without crowding. Adjust heat to avoid burning flour, and add more butter if needed. Transfer browned chicken to a warm platter.

When chicken is browned, add more butter and oil to the pan, if necessary. Stir in onions, carrots, leeks and garlic and sauté until lightly browned, 4 to 6 minutes. Add applejack or cider and stir to loosen browned particles from the bottom of the pot. Reduce heat to medium, return chicken pieces to the pot and add thyme, bay leaf, salt and pepper to taste, bacon and wine. Cover the pot and cook over low heat until chicken is tender, 1 to 1½ hours. Remove and discard bay leaf.

Carefully remove chicken from the pot to a heated platter. Place the pot over medium heat and stir in bits of softened-butter-flour mixture until sauce is properly thickened. Adjust seasonings and serve.

Wine: Domaine du Cayron Gigondas (France: Rhône)

Roasted Chicken with Scallion-Quinoa Stuffing

& ROASTED SHALLOT SAUCE

QUINOA, a delicious grain native to the Andes, has become popular in recent years because of its high nutritional value and versatility. Slightly larger than couscous, its delicate nutty flavor and texture make it a fine grain for stuffing. In this recipe, it is combined with bell peppers, onions and scallions. Pureed caramelized shallots make a dark gravy that is especially thick and flavorful.

To cook quinoa: In a small saucepan, combine ½ cup rinsed raw quinoa with 1 cup water and bring to a boil over medium-high heat. Reduce heat to low, cover briefly and simmer until water is absorbed, 10 to 15 minutes. Fluff with a fork.

SERVES 2 TO 4

Stuffing

1½	tablespoons unsalted butter
⅓	cup medium-diced yellow onion
⅓	cup medium-diced red bell pepper
5	scallions, trimmed to include 1 inch of green, julienned
1	teaspoon fresh thyme leaves or lemon thyme or ½ teaspoon dried
½	teaspoon kosher salt
½	teaspoon freshly ground black pepper
⅛	teaspoon cayenne
1	cup cooked quinoa (about ½ cup raw)

Chicken

1	frying chicken (3½ pounds), excess fat discarded
	Kosher salt and freshly ground black pepper
1-2	tablespoons olive oil
6	large shallots
1	cup chicken stock
¼	teaspoon freshly ground white pepper

To make stuffing: In a medium-sized nonstick skillet, melt butter over medium heat. Add onion and bell pepper and sauté until onion wilts, 3 to 5 minutes. Add scallions, thyme, salt, black pepper and cayenne and cook, stirring often, until scallions wilt, about 2 minutes. Remove from heat. Add quinoa and blend thoroughly.

To make chicken: Preheat oven to 375 degrees F. Season cavity of chicken with salt and pepper; stuff with quinoa mixture. Skewer cavity closed. Lightly truss chicken by placing the middle of the string under tail, crossing over body, looping around drumsticks, around sides, and between first and second joint of wing, which you have bent back to make a "catch" for the string. Tie the string on underside.

Rub chicken with some olive oil and season with salt and pepper. Put chicken in a roasting pan. Lightly oil shallots and scatter them around bird. Roast chicken for 1 hour, basting several times with ½ cup chicken stock during the last 30 minutes.

Increase oven temperature to 400 degrees and roast until juices run clear when thigh is pierced with a fork, about 20 minutes more. Remove chicken from the oven and let stand for 10 minutes.

Meanwhile, make the gravy: Pour roasted shallots and pan drippings into a food processor fitted with the metal blade; puree. Pour puree back into the roasting pan and add remaining ½ cup chicken stock. Cook over high heat, scraping up all browned bits, until liquid comes to a boil. Reduce heat to medium and simmer briskly until sauce is thick, 3 to 5 minutes. Skim off any surface fat; season sauce with salt and white pepper.

Carefully cut bird in half; remove backbone. Cut into quarters, if desired. Place chicken on heated serving plates, garnish with some stuffing, then nap generously with shallot gravy.

Wine: Nalle Winery Zinfandel (California: Sonoma County)

Butterflied Chicken with Roasted Onion Tapenade

A PASTE OF ROASTED ONION, black olives and sun-dried tomatoes keeps the chicken moist during cooking and imparts a lusty flavor.

SERVES 4

½ cup Zack's Roasted Onion Tapenade (page 45)

2 tablespoons minced fresh parsley, plus more for garnish

1 tablespoon minced fresh oregano leaves or 1½ teaspoons dried

1 chicken (3½-4 pounds), split down the back, backbone removed

1-2 tablespoons olive oil
Kosher salt and freshly ground black pepper
Minced fresh chives for garnish

In a small bowl, blend together tapenade, parsley and oregano. Press chicken flat. Season underside with some olive oil and salt and pepper. Place chicken, skin side up, on a rack in a roasting pan. Carefully loosen skin with your fingers. Generously spread tapenade mixture under skin, all the way down thighs. Rub surface of skin with remaining olive oil; sprinkle with salt and lots of pepper. Let chicken stand at room temperature for 30 minutes.

Meanwhile, preheat oven to 500 degrees F. Roast chicken for 15 minutes. Reduce oven temperature to 375 degrees and roast until tender, about 25 minutes. To test, gently insert the point of a knife into thigh; when juices run golden yellow, chicken is done.

Cut chicken into quarters, sprinkle with minced parsley and chives and serve.

Wine: Beaux Frères Pinot Noir (Oregon)

Chicken Paprikas with Texas Sweets

THE SWEET ONION SAUCE of this chicken and paprika stew is laced with hot Hungarian paprika, sweet onions and tomatoes. The recipe came from a talented Hungarian photographer, who, after taking pictures of Linda's children, happily accepted an invitation to dine. His "thank you" came in the form of his mother's recipe for paprikas.

SERVES 6 TO 8

4-5	tablespoons vegetable oil
1½	frying chickens (about 5 pounds total), cut into 12 pieces
1¾	pounds Texas Sweet or other sweet onions, coarsely chopped
1	tablespoon hot Hungarian paprika
2	tablespoons dry white wine
½	teaspoon cayenne
1	large green bell pepper, cut into medium dice
1½	tablespoons tomato paste
⅔	cup chicken stock
	Kosher salt and freshly ground black pepper
1	cup sour cream

Buttered cooked egg noodles or mashed potatoes for serving

Pour 3 tablespoons vegetable oil into a large, deep nonaluminum sauté pan or casserole. Set over medium-high heat until hot. Working in batches, brown chicken pieces on both sides; set aside on a large platter.

Adding more oil to the pan if necessary, add onions and sauté over medium-low heat, stirring often, until fairly tender, about 8 minutes.

Add paprika and wine and stir constantly for 3 minutes. Return chicken pieces to the pan and sprinkle with cayenne. Add bell pepper, tomato paste, chicken stock and salt and pepper to taste. Gently stir several times. Reduce heat to low, cover and cook, stirring several times, until chicken is tender, 45 to 60 minutes.

Skim off any fat on surface. Gently blend sour cream into chicken mixture and heat until hot. Serve with noodles or potatoes.

Wine: Domaine Lucien Albrecht Riesling (France: Alsace)

Herb-Baked Chicken Breasts

WITH RED ONIONS & POTATOES

THIS BAKED CASSEROLE of herb-infused chicken breasts over sliced potatoes with wedges of onions is a cinch to make.

SERVES 4

3 tablespoons olive oil

2 garlic cloves, minced

1 tablespoon minced fresh rosemary leaves or 1½ teaspoons dried

¼ cup minced fresh flat-leaf parsley

1 dried red chile pepper, crumbled

4 large (1½ pounds) Yukon Gold or red-skinned potatoes, peeled

2 whole chicken breasts, with skin, split
Kosher salt and freshly ground black pepper

1 large (1-pound) red onion, cut into thin wedges

3 tablespoons balsamic vinegar

Preheat oven to 375 degrees F.

Pour 1 tablespoon olive oil into an ovenproof casserole or pan that will hold chicken breasts in a single layer without crowding. (We use a 10-inch cast-iron skillet.) Thoroughly coat sides and bottom of casserole with oil.

In a small dish, combine garlic, rosemary, parsley and chile pepper; set aside.

Cut potatoes lengthwise into thick slices; arrange over the bottom of the casserole. Season undersides of chicken breasts with salt and pepper. Carefully loosen skin and push some of herb mixture underneath, between skin and flesh of each breast. Place 4 breast halves, skin side up, over potatoes. Scatter in onion wedges, tucking them around and between chicken pieces. Sprinkle chicken with vinegar. Season generously with salt and pepper. Drizzle on remaining 2 tablespoons olive oil.

Bake chicken in the oven, basting often, until chicken is browned and cooked through and potatoes are done, about 1 hour and 10 minutes.

**Wine: Optima Chardonnay
(California: Sonoma County)**

Mediterranean Chicken

BRAISED IN A CHUNKY red-wine sauce of tomatoes, garlic and onions, this chicken stew is brightened with basil, oregano, olives and lemon zest.

SERVES 4 TO 6

⅓   cup unbleached flour
½   teaspoon kosher salt
½   teaspoon freshly ground black pepper
2   whole chicken breasts, split
2   chicken legs and thighs, separated
2   tablespoons butter
3   tablespoons olive oil
¾   cup dry red wine
1   cup finely diced yellow onions
2   plump garlic cloves, minced
3   tablespoons minced fresh flat-leaf parsley
3   cups chopped, peeled and seeded tomatoes
⅔   cup oil-cured black olives, pitted
2   teaspoons minced fresh oregano leaves or 1 teaspoon dried
2   tablespoons chopped fresh basil leaves or 1 tablespoon dried
2   teaspoons thyme leaves or 1 teaspoon dried
     Zest of 1 lemon, minced

On a large plate, combine flour, salt and pepper; dredge chicken, coating evenly on both sides.

In a large, nonaluminum skillet, melt butter with 1 tablespoon olive oil over medium-high heat. Working in batches, add chicken to skillet, skin sides down, and brown until golden, being careful to reduce heat as needed to prevent burning, 5 to 7 minutes. Turn and brown other side for about 5 minutes, removing finished pieces to a large platter. When all chicken pieces are browned, pour out fat from the skillet and return the skillet to high heat. Add wine and whisk, stirring to loosen all particles that adhere to the pan. Remove from heat and set the skillet aside.

In a large, deep sauté pan with a tight-fitting lid, heat remaining 2 tablespoons olive oil over medium heat. Reduce heat slightly, add onions and sauté, stirring constantly, until they begin to soften, about 15 minutes. Add garlic and parsley and cook, stirring often, until onion is golden, about 5 more minutes. Add reserved wine sauce, tomatoes, olives, herbs and lemon zest. Stir over medium heat until liquids bubble, about 4 to 6 minutes. Add chicken pieces, cover and cook over low heat until chicken is tender, about 45 minutes. Nap generously with sauce and serve.

Wine: Réserve St. Martin Rosé de Syrah
Vin de Pays d'Oc (France: Languedoc)

Ethiopian Chicken & Onion Stew

N AHU GIRMA, an Ethiopian transplant to Cleveland, gave us the recipe for this celebrated Ethiopian dish, a spicy chicken stew with a red onion and butter sauce that's garnished with hard-cooked eggs. Although Nahu uses 2 cups of butter when she makes this stew, we reduced that amount to 1 cup, and it still results in a very creamy, soft, complex sauce. While *berbere*, the traditional Ethiopian spice mixture used in this dish, can be purchased, we simulate it with a variety of spices here. (You can order *berbere* from Tu-Tu Market, 3811-A South George Mason Drive, Falls Church, Virginia 22041; (703) 998-5322).

SERVES 6

3   whole chicken breasts, skin removed and
    split
1   lime, quartered
8   cups water
1   tablespoon ground allspice
2   teaspoons minced fresh ginger
1   teaspoon freshly ground black pepper
1   plump garlic clove, minced
1   tablespoon plus 1 teaspoon cayenne
1   teaspoon ground cardamom
¼   teaspoon ground cloves

2   pounds (2 jumbo) red onions, finely
    chopped
1   cup (2 sticks) unsalted butter
1- 1½   cups chicken stock
    Kosher salt
4-6   hard-cooked eggs, peeled and sliced
    Cooked rice and plain yogurt for serving

Place split chicken breasts in a large bowl; add lime and water. Let stand while you prepare sauce.

Combine allspice, ginger, pepper and garlic in a mortar and mash to a paste with a pestle or grind in a food processor fitted with the metal blade. Add cayenne, cardamom and cloves and mix again; set aside.

Heat a large, deep sauté pan or casserole over medium heat. Without using any fat, add onions and stir constantly until some moisture has been released. Cook, stirring often, until onions are soft and some-what golden, 30 to 40 minutes. If the skillet gets too dry, add 1 to 2 tablespoons butter. This process is slow, but eventually, onions will take on a golden color.

Add remaining butter and spice paste and stir constantly until butter melts. Keep stirring over medium heat to release flavor of seasonings, 2 to 3 minutes. Stir in ½ cup chicken stock and cook for 3 minutes.

Remove chicken pieces from water, shake them dry, and push them into onion mixture. Cover and cook over medium-low heat for 7 minutes. Remove cover, stir in another ½ cup chicken stock and cook, uncovered, until chicken is tender, about 35 minutes. Add more stock if sauce gets too dry. (It should be creamy-saucy, not thin and runny.)

Sprinkle sauce with salt and more pepper to taste. Carefully stir in eggs, without breaking them up too much or tearing chicken off bone. Carefully spoon chicken, sauce and some egg onto heated plates.

Wine: Cline Cellars Côtes d'Oakley
(California: Contre Costa)

Phyllis's Chicken

IN THIS UNUSUAL baked chicken dish, the bird is marinated in a thick paste of chicken, garlic, ginger and turmeric. Although the paste is removed before cooking, the baked chicken will turn a beautiful golden yellow, with a mellow gingered-onion flavor. It's a recipe from the Sephardic Jewish community in Calcutta, India, where our friend Mervyn Sopher, and his sister, Phyllis Arakie, grew up.

SERVES 2 TO 4

1	large or 2 medium-sized yellow onions, quartered
2	plump garlic cloves, peeled
1	chunk (½ inch long) fresh ginger, peeled
2	teaspoons hot Hungarian paprika
1	teaspoon ground turmeric
1	teaspoon kosher salt
¼	teaspoon freshly ground black pepper
2	tablespoons vegetable oil
1	chicken (3½-4 pounds), cut into 8 pieces

In the bowl of a food processor fitted with the metal blade, combine onions, garlic, ginger, paprika, turmeric, salt, pepper and oil. Pulse until finely ground.

Rub paste into all sides of chicken pieces. Place coated chicken, skin sides up, on a large platter; let stand for 2 to 4 hours in the refrigerator.

Preheat oven to 325 degrees F. Generously oil a shallow baking dish large enough to hold chicken pieces in a single layer.

Wipe off and discard most of the paste from chicken. Arrange chicken pieces, skin sides up, in the baking dish. Bake chicken for 30 minutes. Increase oven temperature to 375 degrees, baste chicken with pan juices, and bake until chicken is nicely browned, 45 to 60 minutes more.

**Wine: Sky Vineyards Zinfandel
(California: Napa Valley, Mt. Veeder)**

ALL-AMERICAN ONIONS

IN THEIR SPLENDID BOOK *The Taste of America,* food historians John and Karen Hess call attention to *American Cookery* by Amelia Simmons, the first cookbook written and published in this country by someone who was actually born here. The Hesses describe the book, which was published in Hartford, Connecticut, in 1796, as a "competent but routine presentation of English cookery," but they take special note of Amelia Simmons' interest in onions, quoting from her book:

> *The Medeira white is best in market, esteemed softer flavored, and not so fiery, but the high red, round hard onions are the best; if you consult cheapness, the largest are the best; if you consult taste and softness, the very smallest are the most delicate, and used at the first tables. Onions grow in the richest, highest cultivated ground, and better and better year after year, on the same ground.*

The Hesses also refer to Simmons's recipe for turkey, which she roasts on a spit and tells us to "serve . . . up with boiled onions and cramberry [*sic*] sauce, mangoes, pickles or celery."

THAT RECIPE STILL SOUNDS PRETTY GOOD after nearly 200 years. Simmons's turkey probably had some character: It hadn't been neutered, it hadn't been injected with hormones, it hadn't been fed bland, chemically processed food on an assembly line, and it hadn't been frozen with its gizzard tucked inside in a plastic bag. Most likely, it was a tough bird that had eaten whatever it could find and had done its share of squabbling and scrapping with fellow turkeys.

Come to think of it, Simmons's Thanksgiving dinner, onions and all, probably tasted better than ours.

Roasted Turkey Breast with Orange-Shallot Sauce

GOSH, THIS SMELLS GOOD while it's roasting! We prepare this herb- and citrus-infused turkey breast on onions and shallots, basting it with orange juice. If you like turkey sandwiches, this simple preparation is especially for you. The leftovers make super sandwiches, especially on homemade bread.

SERVES 8

4	large shallots, halved, plus 8 large whole shallots
4	celery leaves
2	plump garlic cloves
1	tablespoon chopped fresh chives
2	teaspoons fresh thyme leaves or 1 teaspoon dried
½	teaspoon dried sage
	Zest of 1 orange, removed in strips
	Zest of ½ lemon, removed in strips
2	tablespoons unsalted butter
1½	cups finely diced yellow onions
1	turkey breast (7-9-pounds)
	Kosher salt and freshly ground black pepper
2	tablespoons olive oil
1	teaspoon hot Hungarian paprika
⅔	cup fresh orange juice

Preheat oven to 325 degrees F.

In the bowl of a food processor fitted with the metal blade, combine 4 halved shallots, celery leaves, garlic, chives, thyme, sage, citrus zests and butter. Pulse until mixture is pureed; reserve.

Mound diced onions in the center of a roasting pan. Season underside of turkey breast with salt and pepper; place breast, skin side up, on onion bed. Gently stuff pureed mixture under skin of turkey breast, distributing it as evenly as possible. Rub skin with some olive oil and season generously with salt and pepper. Sprinkle with paprika.

Coat 8 whole shallots with remaining oil; scatter in the roasting pan. Cover the roasting pan and place in the oven. Roast turkey for 20 minutes per pound (2⅓ to 3 hours total time), basting every 30 minutes with orange juice. Remove the cover for the last 30 minutes of roasting. When the internal temperature registers 160 degrees on an instant-read thermometer, remove turkey to a carving board. Let stand for 15 minutes.

Meanwhile, using a slotted spoon, transfer shallots and cooked onions to the bowl of a food processor fitted with the metal blade. Puree. Add 2 cups pan juices, discarding the rest, and blend well. Return puree to the roasting pan, place over high heat, and whisk to loosen any browned particles that adhere to the bottom. Cook briskly to thicken, 2 to 3 minutes. Season with salt and pepper to taste.

Slice turkey breast and serve with orange-shallot sauce.

Wine: Clos Mont Olivet Châteauneuf-du-Pape
(France: Rhône)

ONION POWER

THROUGHOUT HISTORY, onions have been credited with healing abilities surpassing those of aspirin or antibiotics.

- Chinese herbalists say that a slice of onion will soothe an insect sting, relieve the rash of a nettle and calm the hives caused by food allergies.
- British students of herbal medicine believed some onions could kill intestinal worms.
- Hawaiian farmers sometimes mixed chopped onions and garlic in the food for the poultry to keep down similar worms in turkeys and chickens.
- Appalachians believed that onion could be used to repel a serpent and prevent snakebite. If a snake does bite you, an onion can heal the wound.
- The Greeks held onions to be an erotic stimulant. (We imagine it was efficacious only when both parties ate them.)
- Bad teeth? Onions will strengthen them.
- Impotent? Try red pepper, beer, onions and whiskey. Enough of the whiskey and you won't care.
- About two ounces of a mixture of raw garlic and onion juice taken internally daily will help to restore hearing.
- Mix hot chamomile tea with onion juice to lighten the hair.
- For chest congestion, take a syrup of honey and onion juice.
- For sinus trouble, inhale freshly cut onions until the nasal passages unclog.
- For coughs, apply roasted onions to the chest.

Roasted Turkey

WITH SAUSAGE, ROASTED SHALLOT & SAGE STUFFING

THE STUFFING'S THE THING HERE: a light, fluffy mixture of challah (Jewish egg bread) and corn flakes with chopped roasted shallots, roasted sausage and sage. To calculate roasting time, multiply 11 minutes times the weight of the unstuffed bird. Check with an instant-read thermometer inserted into the turkey breast. It should read 160 degrees when the bird is ready. To bake any extra stuffing, pack it into a buttered casserole and bake for 1 hour at 350 degrees.

Stuffing

1	cup (2 sticks) unsalted butter
12	large shallots, unpeeled
2	tablespoons minced fresh sage leaves or 1 tablespoon dried
2	cups corn flakes
1	large challah (about 2 pounds), sliced and torn into chunks
4	large eggs, beaten
1	cup finely diced yellow onions
¾	cup finely chopped celery
2	tablespoons minced garlic
½	cup minced fresh parsley

1	tablespoon minced fresh thyme leaves or 1½ teaspoons dried
1	tablespoon hot Hungarian paprika
¼	cup dry white wine
1	pound smoked sausage or mild Italian sausage links, sautéed and thinly sliced

Turkey

1	turkey (18-24 pounds)
	Olive oil
	Kosher salt and freshly ground black pepper
	Garlic powder
1	large Spanish onion, unpeeled, quartered
2	carrots, scrubbed
2½	cups chicken stock

To make stuffing: Preheat oven to 325 degrees F. Melt ½ cup (1 stick) butter in a small ovenproof baking dish. Add shallots and sage and stir to coat well. Cover the dish with foil and bake for 1 hour. Remove the dish from the oven and let cool.

Remove shallots, peel and coarsely chop. Return shallots to the baking dish and combine with sage butter; set aside.

Meanwhile, place corn flakes and challah in a large bowl and cover with about 8 cups cold water or more, if needed. Set aside to soak for at least 1 hour.

Drain soaked mixture and squeeze out as much water as possible. Blend eggs into bread mixture with your hands and set aside.

Melt remaining ½ cup (1 stick) butter in a large nonaluminum skillet over medium heat. Add onions, celery and garlic and cook, stirring often, for 5 minutes. (Do not let onions brown.) Add parsley, thyme, paprika and wine and stir for 2 to 3 minutes. Reduce heat to low, stir in reserved shallot-sage butter mixture and cook until heated through. Pour over bread mixture in the bowl and blend thoroughly.

Return stuffing to the skillet and stir over very low heat until most of the liquid evaporates, about 4 minutes. Remove from heat and let cool to lukewarm. Mix sausage slices into stuffing.

To roast turkey: Preheat oven to 450 degrees F.

Wash turkey and pat dry. Season cavity with olive oil and salt and pepper. Loosely fill with stuffing; close with skewers. Rub exterior of turkey with more olive oil; sprinkle with salt, pepper and garlic powder.

Place turkey in a shallow roasting pan; scatter onion quarters and carrots around turkey. Roast, uncovered, for 45 minutes.

Reduce heat to 400 degrees. Baste turkey with ½ cup chicken stock. Rotate the pan and loosely cover turkey with some foil if it is getting too brown. Baste turkey at least 3 times more at 20-minute intervals, rotating the pan at least once more, until turkey breast registers 160 degrees on an instant-read thermometer.

Remove turkey to a carving board; let stand for 20 minutes before carving. Turkey will continue to cook as it stands.

Remove surface layer of fat from pan drippings; discard onion and carrots. Place the roasting pan over high heat, add remaining ½ cup chicken stock and cook, stirring, until all the crisp particles have been loosened. Slice turkey and arrange on a heated serving platter. Spoon stuffing into a heated bowl and pour pan gravy into a sauceboat and serve.

**Wine: Château Montelena Zinfandel
(California: Napa Valley) or
Hugel Gewürztraminer Jubilee
(France: Alsace)**

Grilled Turkey Tenderloins

WITH BACON, RED ONIONS & APPLE CIDER VINAIGRETTE

TURKEY TENDERLOINS, two fingerlike pieces on the underside of the turkey breast, are skinless and absolutely free of visible fat. Marinated and grilled, they are delicious additions to salad suppers. When Odessa Piper, owner of L'Étoile restaurant in Madison, Wisconsin, sent us this recipe for her tangy bacon and red onion vinaigrette, we knew we had a perfect match for the turkey tenderloin. (You can also use leftover cooked turkey breast or chicken.) While L'Étoile uses applewood-smoked bacon, we have found this dish to be delicious with any good-quality bacon.

SERVES 6 TO 8

Juice of 1 lemon
½ cup vegetable oil
⅓ cup finely chopped shallots
1 teaspoon minced lemon verbena or lemon balm leaves or 1 teaspoon minced lemon zest
1 teaspoon fresh thyme leaves or ½ teaspoon dried
6 turkey tenderloins, each 10-12 ounces
4 cups apple cider

½ pound bacon, preferably smoked, cut into ¼-inch dice
2 tablespoons unsalted butter
1 medium red onion, thinly sliced
  Kosher salt and freshly ground black pepper
⅔ cup cider vinegar
6-8 cups mixed salad greens

In a small bowl, combine lemon juice with oil and shallots and whisk thoroughly. Add lemon verbena or balm or zest and thyme. Arrange turkey tenderloins in a single layer in a glass dish; pour on lemon juice mixture and coat well. Marinate at room temperature for 1 hour or for up to 2 hours in the refrigerator. Bring to room temperature before continuing.

In a medium saucepan, bring cider to a boil. Reduce heat to medium-low and simmer briskly until reduced to 1 cup.

Meanwhile, fry bacon until crisp, about 5 minutes. Remove bacon from the pan with a slotted spoon and set aside; reserve ½ cup bacon fat.

Thoroughly clean the surface of a gas or charcoal grill with a metal brush; coat the rack evenly with vegetable oil. Preheat the grill until hot.

TORPEDO ONION

Meanwhile, in a large nonaluminum sauté pan over medium heat, heat bacon fat and butter. Add onions and cook until tender, about 10 minutes. Stir in bacon and season with salt and pepper to taste. Whisk in reduced cider and vinegar. Increase heat to high and whisk vigorously until mixture begins to boil. Keep warm while you grill turkey tenderloins.

Remove turkey tenderloins from marinade and grill for 3 to 4 minutes on each side, depending upon thickness of tenderloin. (Do not overcook.) Remove from grill and let stand in a warm place while you divide salad greens among 6 serving plates.

Slice tenderloins on a slight angle and arrange attractively on each plate over salad. Pour a generous amount of hot cider vinaigrette over each serving. Season with more salt and pepper and serve.

Wine: Robert Sinskey Vineyards "Aries" Pinot Noir (California: Napa Valley)

Pheasant Braised with Red Onions, Shallots & Apples

APPLES AND ONIONS are classic accompaniments to pheasant. In this dish, they become a braising base for the bird. A suggestion of tarragon, a splash of applejack and a dash of cream all come together to create a delicious pan sauce for the delicately flavored pheasant. While pheasant isn't commonly found in the supermarket, it is often available through specialty markets. If you are lucky, you'll have a game farm in your area.

SERVES 2

1   pheasant (2½-3 pounds)
     Salt and freshly ground black pepper
2   tablespoons vegetable oil
¼   cup (½ stick) butter
1½   cups finely diced red onions
3   tart cooking apples, peeled, cored and thinly sliced
¼   cup minced shallots
1   tablespoon minced fresh tarragon leaves or 1½ teaspoons dried
½   cup chicken stock
¼   cup applejack or Calvados
¾   cup heavy cream
     Freshly grated nutmeg

Preheat oven to 475 degrees F.

Rub pheasant inside and out with salt and pepper. Heat vegetable oil in a Dutch oven or casserole over high heat. When hot, quickly sear pheasant for 1 to 2 minutes on each side, until browned. Transfer pheasant to a plate; set aside. Pour off oil in the pan and melt butter over medium heat. Add onions, apples and shallots and cook, stirring often, for 5 minutes. Add tarragon and salt and pepper to taste. Place pheasant on top of apple mixture; baste with chicken stock. Cover and roast in the oven until pheasant is tender, about 45 minutes. Transfer pheasant to a carving board in a warm place.

Place Dutch oven over high heat and add applejack or Calvados. Light a long wooden match and, carefully averting your face, ignite pan liquids. Shake the pan until the flames subside. Stir in cream and cook, stirring, until slightly thickened. Add a few grinds of nutmeg and adjust seasonings.

Cut bird into quarters; remove backbone. Carefully separate breast meat from bones. Divide onion and apple mixture between 2 heated dinner plates. Top with breast meat and add a leg-thigh portion. Nap pheasant with sauce and serve.

Wine: Williams Seylems Pinot Noir Rochioli Vineyard (Sonoma County)

Crisp-Roasted Duck with Leek & Orange Stuffing

WITH THEIR DARK, CRISP SKIN and moist succulent meat, these ducks need no sauce. They are
good with sautéed mushrooms.

SERVES 4 TO 6

¼   cup (½ stick) unsalted butter
2   cups finely chopped leeks, white and tender
     green parts
⅓   cup finely diced shallots
1   celery rib, finely diced
2   garlic cloves, minced
1   medium-sized navel orange, peeled, pith
     and membranes removed, chopped
⅔   cup chopped toasted pecans
1   tablespoon minced fresh parsley
2   teaspoons minced fresh tarragon leaves or
     1 teaspoon dried
1   teaspoon freshly ground black pepper
1   teaspoon kosher salt
2   duck livers (optional)
2   cups cooked wild rice
2   tablespoons vegetable oil

2   ducks, about 5 pounds each, preferably
     frozen
1   cup fresh orange juice

Melt butter in a large skillet over medium heat.
Add leeks, shallots and celery, reduce heat slightly
and cook until leeks wilt, 6 to 8 minutes. Add garlic
and stir over medium heat for 5 minutes. Stir in orange, pecans, parsley, tarragon, pepper and salt; set
aside.

Heat oil in a small skillet. Add duck livers, if using, and sauté over high heat until pink inside, about
2 minutes per side. Remove with a slotted spoon,
cool to room temperature and coarsely chop. Preheat
oven to 450 degrees F.

Combine leek mixture with wild rice and duck
liver. Let mixture cool to room temperature.

Rub cavities of ducks with salt and pepper. Divide
stuffing between ducks; close the cavities with skewers.

Arrange ducks, bottom sides up, on racks in roasting pans. Prick skin all over with a skewer. Roast in
the oven for 30 minutes.

Drain or siphon off all fat from the pan. Turn ducks, breast sides up, and baste with some orange juice. Roast for 30 minutes.

Drain or siphon off any accumulated fat. Reduce oven temperature to 375 degrees. Baste ducks with more orange juice, and roast until crisp, about 30 minutes more. Let birds stand for 10 minutes.

Cut ducks into halves or quarters and serve on heated plates, with stuffing on the side.

Wine: Calera Wine Company Pinot Noir Mount Harlan "Mills" (California: San Benito)

> *"If leekes you like but do their smell disleek*
> *Eate onyons and you shalle not smelle the leeke.*
> *If you of onyons would the scent expelle,*
> *Eate garlicke, that shalle drowne*
> *the onyon's smelle."*
> —*Anonymous*

SIDE DISHES

Beer-Battered Sweet Onion Rings

THIS BATTER gets shiny and crisp in frying. If it is a tad too thin, it may slip off here and there—but that's nothing serious. After you've made these once, you'll get the hang of it.

SERVES 4

1   cup plus 2 tablespoons unbleached flour
1   teaspoon kosher salt
½   teaspoon freshly ground black pepper
½   teaspoon freshly ground white pepper
⅛   teaspoon cayenne
1   cup beer
1   large (at least 1-pound) Vidalia, Walla Walla, Maui or other sweet onion
4-8   cups vegetable oil for deep-frying

Combine flour, salt, black and white peppers and cayenne in a large mixing bowl. Add beer, all at once, and whisk until smooth. Set aside for 30 minutes.

Cut onion into slices at least ½ inch thick. Separate into rings.

Pour oil into a deep-fat fryer or wok to a depth of 2 to 3 inches and heat to 375 degrees F. Preheat the oven to warm (250 degrees F).

Stir batter. It should be somewhat thicker than pancake batter, so that onions will get a nice coating. If it is too thick, thin by gradually adding a bit more beer. Working in batches of 3 or 4, dip onion rings into batter.

Add battered onion rings, 3 to 4 at a time, to oil. Fry, without crowding, until golden brown, about 3 minutes, turning if necessary. Drain well on paper towels and keep warm in the oven. Repeat until all onion rings are fried. Sprinkle with salt and serve.

RING MASTER

"HOW DO YOU THINK IT LOOKS?" asked the stern vice president of Bass Brothers Produce, a large wholesaler in Akron, Ohio. "One of our customers goes into a night club, and there is the president of our company playing in the band!"

"I don't care how it looks," answered the president. "I love music, and I'll play it any time I can."

When we talked with Jerry Bass, big-band drummer and onion-ring king, he had long since retired from the produce-distribution business. But in retirement he still played music, sitting in with bands whenever he could and enjoying his first love.

But it was Bass's second love, his work with food, that occupied most of his life.

"We sold frozen French fries to restaurants. A big Cleveland steak house was among our customers, and one day the boss was grumbling about the labor cost of making the onion rings that they used to garnish their steaks. He had me cut up some onions, bread them and take them to the restaurant. I'll never forget sitting at the bar while the cook was frying the first batch. He brought them out, and they were great. When he asked me how much they would cost, he was shocked at the answer. They were labor-intensive for us, too. He said he'd just continue to make them in his own kitchen."

But Bass got a second chance. "One day I went by this famous place in Akron," he said. "They made great burgers. And great fries. I offered to make some onion rings and the owner said OK. We made 20-pound batches for this little drive-in. They were a lot of work and expensive, but people liked them. And the business just grew. Next thing you know, we were bringing in California onions, making raw breaded onion rings and sending them back to California."

For years, Bass Brothers had no serious competition. A Chicago processor had gone to market with some precooked onion rings that could be heated in the oven. Another competitor chopped the onions and mixed them with breading and extruded them, like doughnuts. "They were mushy," said Bass. "We decided we'd never do that. Ours would be raw and for the deep-fryer.

"Our breading was special," he said. "It was made by a guy in New York. It was like a big matzoh, 30 feet long, 3 feet wide, and he'd bake it, grind it up, season it with celery salt, and we'd use it for our rings.

The good thing was that it was forgiving. If you gave it a little too much time in the deep-fryer, or had it above the recommended 360 degrees, it would get a high golden color and resist burning."

A big problem was getting onions with a single center, or as Bass put it, onions without a complicated heart. It was these onions that caused the company its thorniest problem. Customers complained that their rings were turning black in the fryer. Finally, one of the women in the lab was able to figure out why. The company had been using a particularly sweet cultivar. When the rings were set aside and allowed to stand for a while between breading and freezing, some of their sugary juices would ooze out. When the onions were placed in the fat, the sugar would caramelize, making the onions black. The company solved the problem by freezing the onions faster.

At first, Bass Brothers Produce cut the onions with commercial bread slicers, but they eventually had to design and build their own equipment. "You couldn't just go to the store and buy it," said Bass. "The company hired a staff welder, who kept the slicers working."

By 1966, the company had two plants, in Akron and Paducah, with 400 employees who prepared and shipped 8 million pounds of onion rings a year. The Paducah plant alone could process 40,000 pounds per day—1,400,000 onion rings that had to be cut, breaded and frozen.

When a frozen-fish processor called Blue Water started making onion rings, Bass decided to merge with that company. One day, however, he found that the Blue Water plant was selling its rings at a lower price than the Bass operation, its subsidiary. So Bass left the company and retired.

"I miss the business and I miss the confusion," said Bass with a chuckle. "And I miss the money. But I don't cry over it. The crying is in the past, when we would be slicing those hundreds of thousands of onions.

"Every day we'd cry for the first 10 or 15 minutes, then we'd get used to it. Everything smelled like onions. My suits smelled like onions. Our Akron plant was near a school. They'd complain about the smell. In Akron, there was always a smell: onions mixed with rubber.

"There was one beautiful young woman who worked for us," said Bass, "and her husband always complained that going to bed with her was like going to bed with a hamburger."

Spicy Fried Onion Rings

THESE CRISP RINGS have a thinner coating than those made with the beer batter. If you are not an aficionado of "hot," add less cayenne and chile powder to the flour. On the other hand, if you like spicy food, you can do as we do, and make a seasoned salt by combining kosher salt with more of the black and white pepper and chile powder and sprinkling the onions as you eat them.

SERVES 4 TO 6

1   jumbo sweet onion, such as Vidalia, Walla Walla or Texas Sweet, cut into ¼-inch slices
3   cups buttermilk
2   cups unbleached flour
2   teaspoons kosher salt
2   teaspoons freshly ground black pepper
2   teaspoons freshly ground white pepper
2   teaspoons cayenne
2   teaspoons medium-hot chile powder or other chili powder
6-8   cups vegetable oil, for deep-frying

Separate onions into rings and place in a deep bowl. Add enough buttermilk to cover and soak for 2 to 3 hours at room temperature.

Pour oil into a deep-fat fryer to a depth of 2 inches and heat to 400 degrees F. Preheat oven to warm (250 degrees).

Combine flour, salt, black and white peppers, cayenne and chile powder in a large bowl; blend well.

Remove onion rings from buttermilk but do not drain well.

When oil is hot, dredge onion rings, a few at a time, in flour mixture and place in the fryer. Fry, without crowding, until golden brown, about 4 minutes. Drain fried rings on paper towels; keep warm in the oven until all rings have been fried. Sprinkle with salt and serve.

Casserole of Creamed Onions & Mushrooms

WE FEEL A THANKSGIVING TABLE is incomplete without these cheesy creamed onions in a casserole. The technique for preparing the mushrooms comes from Jack Czarnecki, the owner of Joe's Restaurant in Reading, Pennsylvania. If you don't have pearl onions, use 3 dozen very small ones, but parboil them for 3 minutes before peeling.

SERVES 8 TO 12

1	pound mushrooms, cleaned and thinly sliced
1	cup water
6	tablespoons (¾ stick) unsalted butter
½	cup unbleached flour
3	cups milk, preferably whole milk, scalded
2	cups grated sharp Cheddar cheese
	Kosher salt and freshly ground white pepper
1	teaspoon dried thyme
⅛	teaspoon cayenne
3	pints pearl onions, peeled (pages 37-38)
½	cup fine dry bread crumbs

Preheat oven to 425 degrees F. Butter a 3-quart baking dish.

In a medium-sized saucepan, combine mushrooms and water. Bring to a boil over high heat. Reduce the heat to low, cover and simmer for 30 minutes.

Meanwhile, in a large, heavy-bottomed saucepan, melt butter over medium-low heat. Whisk in flour and cook, whisking constantly, for 1 minute. Slowly whisk in hot milk and cook, whisking constantly, until mixture is hot and thick, about 7 minutes.

Remove sauce from heat and stir in 1½ cups cheese until completely melted. Stir in salt and white pepper to taste, thyme, cayenne and pearl onions. Drain mushrooms and stir into sauce. Pour mixture into the prepared baking dish; sprinkle with remaining ½ cup cheese. Sprinkle evenly with bread crumbs. Bake onions until top is golden brown, 45 to 55 minutes. Serve spooned into small side dishes.

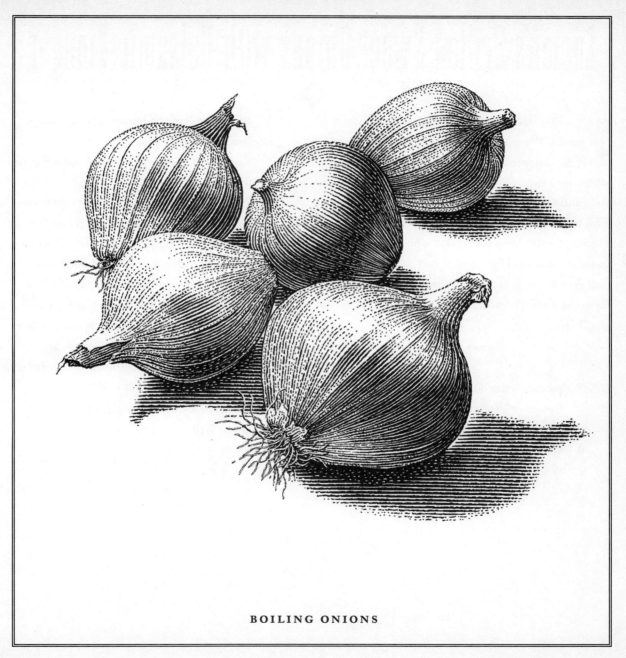

BOILING ONIONS

Lucien's Grilled Sweet Onions with Balsamic Vinegar

THE GRILLING TECHNIQUE for these onions is unusual. We take a whole onion, cut a thin slice off the top, press the flat surface on a hot grill or skillet until lightly browned, then slice that piece off and continue the process until the entire onion is cut. This technique allows for a crisp onion side dish with a subtle, smoky flavor that makes a pleasing accompaniment to grilled fish or poultry. Credit for this dish goes to our dear friend Lucien Vendome, who for many years was executive chef of Stouffer Hotels and Resorts.

SERVES 6

2½-3 pounds sweet onions, such as Vidalia, Texas Sweets or Walla Wallas
About ⅓ cup olive oil
3 tablespoons balsamic vinegar or fruit vinegar

1 tablespoon minced fresh tarragon, basil or lemon verbena leaves
Kosher salt and freshly ground white pepper

Slice off ¼ inch of stem end from each onion and discard. Lightly coat the bottom of a large cast-iron skillet with olive oil and heat until very hot. Place 2 to 3 onions, cut sides down, on the hot skillet and grill until bottoms are browned, 1 to 2 minutes. Quickly remove onions from the skillet and cut off a ¼-inch-thick slice from browned end of onion. Place slices in a large bowl. Continue grilling and cutting, adding oil to the skillet as needed, until all onions are grilled and sliced.

Add vinegar, herbs and salt and pepper to grilled onions and toss well.

Simple Baked Sweet Onions

SCOOP OUT A SMALL PORTION of the center of a whole, sweet onion; fill it with butter and some fresh herbs, and bake it just until tender. What could be better? The towns around Vidalia, Georgia, are rightfully proud of their world-renowned onions. Every cook in the area has a version of this dish. Serve with roasted chicken, grilled fish or alone as a healthful lunchtime snack.

SERVES 4

4   medium-sized Vidalia or other sweet onions
2   teaspoons fresh thyme leaves, preferably
       lemon thyme, or 1 teaspoon dried
2   tablespoons unsalted butter, cut into
       4 equal pieces
       Kosher salt and freshly ground black pepper

Preheat oven to 375 degrees F.

Carefully slice off stem end of each onion. Slice enough of the root off the bottom so each will stand evenly; carefully remove the dry skins. Using an apple corer, bore into the center of each onion, making an opening about ½ inch in diameter. (Do not cut all the way through the bottom.)

Sprinkle some thyme in each cavity; place a piece of butter in each. Arrange onions in a small baking dish and sprinkle generously with salt and pepper; cover dish with foil. Bake until onions are tender when pierced with a knife, about 40 minutes.

Craig Claiborne's Indian Pickled Onions

YEARS AGO, we had a marvelous visit with Craig Claiborne in his Long Island home. That's when we had one of our best dining adventures—an evening's meal of leftovers from his refrigerator. When he heard about this book project, he sent us this appealing recipe. "One of my most memorable dining experiences that I recall from a visit to Delhi," he wrote, "was at an unpretentious and well-known native restaurant called the Moti Mahal. This is a version of a pickle that is much admired." The pickles are piquant and subtly garlicky, and they will remain crunchy for months. We save the marinade, and when the onions are gone, add another pound to the jar. They make a refreshing accompaniment to fiery-hot dishes, but they are equally pleasing with grilled foods.

MAKES I QUART

1 pound large pearl onions, blanched and peeled (pages 37-38)

2 cups red-wine vinegar

2 garlic cloves, sliced lengthwise

2 whole dried red chile peppers

1 tablespoon kosher salt

Wash and sterilize a 1-quart wide-mouthed glass jar with a tight-fitting lid. To prepare onions, use a very sharp paring knife to cut as if to quarter them, but cut only ¾ of the way down so that they stay whole, leaving the 4 sections attached at the bottom. Place the cut onions in the jar.

In a large pitcher, combine vinegar, garlic, chiles and salt, stirring to dissolve salt. Pour mixture over onions. Cover tightly and let stand for 24 hours. Refrigerate and serve as desired.

Paul's Confit of Vidalia Onions

WEDGES OF SWEET ONIONS are slowly stewed in a fragrant mixture of spices until they are richly browned and tender. Cleveland chef Paul Minnillo served this delicious dish to us in his home. As a side dish, these onions are good hot with roasted chicken or a grilled veal chop, and they also make a fine warm appetizer, accompanied by slices of French bread. You can prepare the confit and reheat just before serving. By the way, the spice mixture is terrific rubbed over chicken or duck before roasting.

SERVES 8

2   tablespoons ground cinnamon
1   teaspoon ground coriander
1   teaspoon ground cumin
½   teaspoon ground allspice
¼   teaspoon ground cloves
¼   teaspoon ground cardamom
¼   teaspoon ground ginger
¼   teaspoon freshly grated nutmeg
½   bay leaf, finely crumbled
¼   teaspoon dried thyme
6   medium-sized Vidalia or other sweet onions
½   cup (1 stick) unsalted butter, cut into small pieces
1   cup dry white wine
    Kosher salt and freshly ground black pepper

Preheat oven to 275 degrees F.

In a small bowl, combine all spices and set aside.

Peel onions without removing root end. Cut each onion into quarters, retaining some of the root at the bottom of each piece so wedge will stay intact.

Lightly butter a shallow baking dish large enough to hold onions in a single layer. Arrange onions in the buttered dish. Scatter pieces of butter over onions; sprinkle evenly with wine. Sprinkle with spice mixture; season with salt and pepper to taste. Cover casserole with foil. Bake until onions are very soft, about 3 hours. Store in the refrigerator in a tightly covered container.

Roasted Sweet Onions

BASTING WEDGES OF CARAMELIZED ONIONS with balsamic vinegar and olive oil gives them a sweet-and-tart glaze. This is derived from one of the best onion recipes we have ever made—found in Johanne Killeen and George Germon's *Cucina Simpatica*. Serve at room temperature as an accompaniment to chicken or beef. The leftovers are splendid tossed with pasta, stirred into Stuffed Baked Potatoes Soubise (page 353) or combined with good cheese on a pizza (page 195). If you substitute dried tarragon for fresh, sprinkle it over the onions before cooking.

SERVES 10

4   large Vidalia or other sweet onions
½   cup sherry vinegar
½   cup olive oil
1   teaspoon kosher salt
1   teaspoon freshly ground white pepper
2   tablespoons minced fresh tarragon leaves or
     1 tablespoon dried
1   tablespoon drained capers

Preheat oven to 450 degrees F.

Carefully peel onions without removing root. Cut onions in half, cutting directly through center of root. Cut each half into 8 long wedges, keeping a bit of the root, so that the wedge stays together. Arrange wedges, slightly overlapping, in a single layer in a large, shallow pan. (We use a 14-inch paella pan.) Drizzle vinegar over onions, and drizzle on olive oil. Sprinkle with salt and white pepper.

Cover the dish with foil. Roast for 40 minutes.

Uncover, baste onions with pan juices and roast for 10 minutes.

Remove the dish from the oven and allow to cool for at least 15 minutes before serving. Sprinkle with fresh tarragon, capers and a few more grindings of white pepper before serving.

Janet's Sweet Onion & Rice Casserole

THIS UNUSUAL BROWN RICE CASSEROLE is baked with generous amounts of diced sweet onions, creamy Gruyère, Calvados (or applejack or hard cider) and golden raisins. Janet Podolak, a travel and food writer who lives in our area, was kind enough to share this delicious recipe. "This casserole," she wrote, "was adapted from a dish I had last year in France. It's great as a side dish with chicken or meat and works just as well as a luncheon main course. With a cup of leftover diced ham mixed in, it becomes supper." To make the dish even better, use organic brown jasmine rice from Lowell Farms (see Special Products, page 374).

SERVES 6 TO 8

6   tablespoons (¾ stick) unsalted butter

7   cups finely diced Vidalia or other sweet onions (about 6 onions)

2   cups water

⅔   cup long-grain brown rice

1   cup grated Gruyère cheese

¾   cup half-and-half

⅓   cup chicken stock

2   tablespoons dry white vermouth

2   tablespoons Calvados or applejack

½   cup golden raisins

Preheat oven to 325 degrees F. Butter a 3-quart casserole 8 x 10 x 2¾ inches.

Melt butter in a large skillet over medium heat. Add onions and cook, stirring often, until translucent, about 20 minutes.

Meanwhile, in a small saucepan, bring water to a boil. Add rice and cook for 10 minutes.

Drain rice and add to cooked onions. Mix in cheese, half-and-half, chicken stock, vermouth, Calvados or applejack and raisins.

Pour mixture into the prepared casserole and cover with a lid or foil. Bake for 30 minutes.

Uncover casserole and bake until top is brown and rice is tender, about 40 minutes. Spoon onto heated plates and serve.

Quick Glazed Onions with Thyme

AFTER THESE SMALL ONIONS are tender, we toss them in balsamic vinegar with a touch of sugar and thyme. This dish can easily be increased for a crowd.

SERVES 6

12	creaming or boiling onions (small yellow onions), unpeeled
	Several stalks lovage or 2 celery ribs, halved
3	tablespoons butter
1	tablespoon sugar
¼	cup balsamic vinegar
2	teaspoons fresh thyme leaves, preferably lemon thyme, or 1 teaspoon dried
	Kosher salt and freshly ground white pepper

Combine onions and lovage or celery in a medium saucepan. Add salted water to cover and bring to a boil. Simmer briskly over medium-low heat until onions are tender when pierced with a knife, about 10 minutes. Drain; chill in ice water until cool. Discard lovage or celery and peel onions; set aside.

Shortly before serving, melt butter in a medium-sized nonaluminum skillet over medium heat. Add onions and stir for a few minutes. Sprinkle with sugar, increase heat to high, and stir until sugar melts. Add vinegar and cook, stirring over high heat until onions are nicely glazed, 3 to 5 minutes. Stir in thyme and salt and white pepper to taste. Serve.

Ratatouille

THERE ARE ALMOST as many recipes for this delicious Provençal vegetable stew as there are people in France. Some people think that each ingredient should be cooked separately, others believe that the ingredients should be cooked together. Some like the dish hot, others prefer it cold. Mostly we like it simple, so that we can have it often. A really good ratatouille can be made only during the summer, with luscious, right-from-the-garden ingredients.

SERVES 8 TO 10

1   pound eggplant, peeled, quartered lengthwise and cut crosswise into ½-inch-thick slices

1   tablespoon plus 1 teaspoon kosher salt

⅓   cup olive oil

2   red bell peppers, cut into ½-inch-wide strips

1   green bell pepper, cut into ½-inch-wide strips

1   pound white onions, thinly sliced

1   pound zucchini, trimmed and cut into ½-inch-thick slices

4   garlic cloves, coarsely chopped

1   tablespoon tomato paste

4-6   ripe tomatoes, peeled, seeded and diced

1   teaspoon freshly ground black pepper

1   tablespoon minced fresh thyme leaves or 1½ teaspoons dried

1   tablespoon minced fresh oregano leaves or 1½ teaspoons dried

1   tablespoon minced fresh basil leaves or 1½ teaspoons dried

Sprinkle eggplant slices with 1 tablespoon salt and let stand in a colander for 30 minutes. Rinse and pat dry.

Heat olive oil in a large nonaluminum Dutch oven or casserole over medium-high heat. Add eggplant and stir until golden, about 5 minutes. Reduce heat to medium, add red and green bell peppers, onions, zucchini and garlic and cook, stirring frequently, for 5 minutes. Add tomato paste and stir well. Add tomatoes, 1 teaspoon salt, pepper and all herbs. Add a few tablespoons more oil, if mixture is too dry.

Cover, reduce heat to very low and cook for 40 minutes.

If there is too much liquid, drain some off at this point or cook, uncovered, for about 10 minutes to boil away any remaining liquid, depending upon how "stewy" you like your ratatouille. Serve in a heated bowl or spoon onto heated plates. Store any extra ratatouille tightly covered in the refrigerator.

Steamed Asparagus with Lemon-Shallot Sauce

WE LIKE TO SERVE spears of steamed asparagus with a variety of sauces. Our favorite is sabayon, a foamy cooked sauce of egg yolks, lemon juice and wine. When we add cilantro, it makes a great accompaniment for smoked fowl or grilled fish.

SERVES 6 TO 8

2   pounds asparagus, trimmed and peeled
4   large egg yolks
¼   cup fresh lemon juice
½   teaspoon sugar
    Kosher salt and freshly ground white pepper
¾   cup dry white wine
3   tablespoons Dijon mustard
1   shallot, finely minced
1   tablespoon minced fresh parsley
1   tablespoon minced fresh chives

Steam asparagus according to your preference. Drain and refresh in cold water.

In the top of a double boiler over simmering water, whisk together egg yolks, lemon juice, sugar and salt and pepper to taste. Continue whisking until yolks begin to lighten in color, about 3 minutes. Whisking vigorously, add wine and beat until the volume more than doubles, about 5 minutes. (You need a strong arm and patience, but suddenly this mixture will lighten and swell considerably.)

Whisk in mustard, shallot and herbs; remove from the heat. Spoon sauce over asparagus and serve.

Summer Squash & Onion Sauté

WITH SOUR CREAM & FENNEL

As SOON AS YELLOW SQUASH appear at a nearby farm, we make this dish and serve it as long as the squash are available. It's a good accompaniment to grilled fish or chicken.

SERVES 4

2   tablespoons vegetable oil

3   small yellow squashes, trimmed and cut into ¼-inch slices

1   small onion, sliced

2   tablespoons minced fennel fronds

¼   cup low-fat sour cream

Kosher salt and freshly ground black pepper

1   tablespoon minced fresh chives

Heat oil in a nonstick skillet over medium heat. Add squash and onions and toss until vegetables are coated with oil. Reduce heat to low, cover and cook, stirring from time to time, until vegetables are just tender, about 6 minutes.

Stir in fennel and sour cream; season with salt and pepper to taste. Cook, uncovered, just until heated through, 1 to 2 minutes. Sprinkle with chives and serve.

Timbales of Broccoli & Scallions with Hazelnuts

THESE SMALL broccoli and scallion custards can also be made with baby Vidalias as a late-winter treat. The toasted hazelnuts on the bottom provide delicious crunch. Serve with meats from the grill, roasted leg of lamb or almost any smoked food.

SERVES 8

2	tablespoons unsalted butter, softened
¾	cup hazelnuts
1½	cups coarsely chopped broccoli
½	cup minced scallions, trimmed to include tender green part
1	tablespoon unbleached flour
3	large whole eggs
2	large egg yolks
2	cups half-and-half
1	tablespoon unsalted butter, melted
2	teaspoons minced fresh thyme leaves
2	teaspoons minced fresh chives
	Pinch freshly grated nutmeg
	Kosher salt and freshly ground white pepper

Preheat oven to 425 degrees F. Thoroughly coat 8 four-ounce timbale molds or small custard cups with softened butter.

Place nuts in a single layer on a baking sheet. Roast until skins are very dark, about 10 minutes. Place nuts in a dish towel and wrap tightly until cooled, about 10 minutes. Reduce oven temperature to 350 degrees.

Rub nuts with the towel to loosen the skins. Finely chop nuts medium-fine in a food processor fitted with the metal blade or by hand and set aside.

In a mixing bowl, combine broccoli, scallions and flour; toss well.

In a larger bowl, combine eggs and egg yolks and whisk thoroughly. Gradually whisk in half-and-half, melted butter, thyme, chives and nutmeg. Add vegetable mixture and blend thoroughly. Season with salt and pepper to taste. Pour into prepared molds; sprinkle evenly with hazelnuts.

Arrange timbales in a baking pan just large enough to hold them without touching one another. Pour in hot water to reach halfway up the sides of the molds. Bake timbales until set, about 35 minutes. Remove timbales from the water bath and let stand at room temperature for 5 minutes.

Invert onto a heated plate and serve.

Leeks Vinaigrette

JUST ABOUT EVERY SHOP in France that sells pre-pared food has a version of these poached leeks dressed in a vinaigrette.

SERVES 4

8   slender leeks, trimmed to include tender green part
1   teaspoon kosher salt
1   tablespoon fresh lemon juice
2   tablespoons Champagne vinegar or white-wine vinegar
1   teaspoon Dijon mustard
⅓   cup extra-virgin olive oil
2   tablespoons minced fresh flat-leaf parsley
1   tablespoon minced shallots
1   tablespoon minced fresh tarragon leaves or 1 teaspoon dried
1   teaspoon minced lemon verbena or lemon balm leaves or ½ teaspoon minced lemon zest
    Freshly ground black pepper

Slice leeks lengthwise; carefully rinse to remove any sand. Fill a large saucepan with water, add salt, and bring to a boil over high heat. Add leeks and cook over low heat until just tender, 8 to 10 minutes. Carefully drain; refresh in ice water.

In a small bowl, combine lemon juice, vinegar and mustard. Whisk well to blend, and slowly whisk in olive oil. Add parsley, shallots, tarragon and verbena, balm or lemon zest; blend well. Season with salt and pepper to taste.

Drain leeks and place in a shallow serving dish. Add vinaigrette and toss gently to combine. Cover and chill at least 1 hour before serving, then let stand at room temperature.

Baked Stuffed Potatoes with Roasted Sweet Onions

THIS IS A SIMPLE VARIATION on the old favorite, twice-baked potatoes.

SERVES 4

⅔   cup packed leftover Roasted Sweet Onions (page 340)

4   large russet potatoes, scrubbed and baked

¼   cup (½ stick) unsalted butter, softened

¼   cup low-fat sour cream

¼   cup freshly grated Parmesan cheese, plus more for topping

1   tablespoon minced fresh chives
    Kosher salt and freshly ground black pepper

Preheat oven to 450 degrees F. With a sharp knife, carefully cut roots off roasted onions. Place trimmed onions in the bowl of a food processor fitted with the metal blade and pulse until pureed; set aside.

Cut potatoes lengthwise in half and scoop baked flesh into a mixing bowl, leaving a shell of pulp in potato skin. Add butter and mash thoroughly. Blend in onion puree, sour cream, cheese and chives. Mix well; season with salt and pepper to taste.

Fill potato shells with potato mixture; sprinkle tops with additional cheese. Bake until tops are browned, about 20 minutes.

Chive & Shallot Mashed Potatoes

Thanks to Johanne Killeen and George Germon, authors of *Cucina Simpatica*, we discovered that potatoes mashed with their skins still on them are delicious.

SERVES 4

1¼	pounds small Ruby Red or Yukon Gold potatoes, scrubbed
¼	cup olive oil
1	shallot, minced
¼	cup minced chives
	Kosher salt and freshly ground black pepper

Place potatoes in a saucepan, cover with water and bring to a boil over high heat. Cover the saucepan, reduce heat to medium and cook until potatoes are tender, about 20 minutes.

While potatoes are cooking, combine oil and shallot in a small saucepan and heat until oil is hot, about 1 minute.

Drain cooked potatoes, return them to the pot and thoroughly mash with a potato masher. Mix in warm shallot oil and blend well. Stir in chives and season with salt and pepper to taste.

On his farm in Walla Walla, Washington, Jim Robison grows mainly wheat. But his heart is in his onions and shallots. As we ordered some baby Walla Wallas, he told us about one of his favorite uses for the great sweets. "Cut a really thick slice of a big Walla Walla, at least an inch thick. Then slice a fresh lemon into very thin slices, about an eighth of an inch, including the peel. Put half a dozen of these slices on the onion, sprinkle generously with sugar and enjoy." He swears it's better than candy.

Potatoes Lyonnaise

THIS IS OUR VERSION of a traditional French potato and onion dish that is delicious with meat, fish and poultry. Fred loves to fry any leftovers with some smoked Virginia ham and eggs for a hearty breakfast.

SERVES 6

3   **pounds large white potatoes**
8   **tablespoons (1 stick) unsalted butter**
1   **pound yellow onions, thinly sliced**
2   **teaspoons fresh thyme leaves or**
    1 teaspoon dried
    Kosher salt and freshly ground white pepper

Early in the day, bake potatoes until just tender; they should still be a bit firm. Let cool; chill.

Shortly before cooking, peel potatoes and cut into ¼-inch slices.

In a large cast-iron skillet, melt 4 tablespoons butter over medium heat. Add potato slices and sauté until browned, 7 to 10 minutes per side.

Meanwhile, in a smaller cast-iron skillet, melt 3 tablespoons butter over medium heat. Add onions and sauté until caramelized, 10 to 20 minutes.

When potatoes are browned on both sides, add remaining 1 tablespoon butter to the skillet. Add onions, thyme, salt and pepper to taste. Cook for just a few minutes, turning carefully with a large spatula, so that potatoes and onions are well combined and absorb the flavors of the seasonings, and serve.

Potatoes & Onions, Alsatian-Style

THIS RICH AND CREAMY CASSEROLE is not for the faint of heart. It gets its inspiration from a traditional potato and Muenster cheese combination that we first encountered in the dining room of a tiny inn high in the Vosges Mountains in Alsace. Pont l'Évêque or Port Salut can be substituted for Alsatian Muenster. Not as tasty, though also possible, is Monterey Jack.

SERVES 6

2½-3   pounds Yukon Gold or medium-sized white or red-skinned potatoes, peeled and thinly sliced
1   large sweet onion, thinly sliced
½   pound Alsatian Muenster cheese, shredded (2 cups)
1   garlic clove, minced

Kosher salt and freshly ground black pepper
2   cups half-and-half
1   cup heavy cream
2   tablespoons butter, cut into pieces

Preheat oven to 425 degrees F.

Thoroughly butter a shallow 8-x-10-inch baking dish. Divide potatoes, onion, cheese and garlic into thirds. Layer ⅓ of potatoes in the dish and sprinkle with ⅓ of garlic, onion and cheese. Season with salt and pepper to taste. Repeat layering 2 more times, ending with a cheese layer.

Pour half-and-half and cream over top. Scatter butter on top.

Bake in the middle of the oven for 30 minutes.

Reduce oven temperature to 375 degrees. Bake until potatoes are golden and tender, about 1 hour.

Skillet Potato Cake with Shallots & Chives

WE BAKE THIS CAKE of grated potatoes and shallots in a hot cast-iron skillet in the oven and frequently serve it with chicken dishes.

SERVES 8 TO 10

8   large russet potatoes
½   cup minced shallots
3   tablespoons minced fresh chives
1   tablespoon chopped fresh rosemary leaves
     or 1½ teaspoons dried
1   tablespoon minced fresh parsley
2   teaspoons kosher salt
1   tablespoon freshly ground black pepper
½   cup (1 stick) unsalted butter
     Chopped chives and chive blossoms, for
     garnish (optional)

Early in the day, bake potatoes until just tender but still a bit firm. Cool thoroughly.

Preheat oven to 450 degrees F.

Peel potatoes and coarsely grate into a large mixing bowl. Add shallots, chives, rosemary, parsley, salt and pepper and mix well.

Melt butter in a 9-inch cast-iron skillet. Pour ¾ of it (6 tablespoons) into potato mixture. Thoroughly coat the skillet with remaining 2 tablespoons butter. Place the skillet in the oven and preheat until hot, about 5 minutes.

When the skillet is hot, carefully remove from the oven, fill with potato mixture, and press firmly to make a compact cake. Bake until the edges are browned, about 45 minutes.

Remove the skillet from the oven and let stand for a few minutes. Invert over a platter and cut potato cake into wedges. Sprinkle with more chives and chive blossoms, if using, and serve.

Stuffed Baked Potatoes Soubise

SOUBISE, a French onion sauce, is made by slowly cooking blanched white onions in a covered skillet and adding cream to them. The soubise is then combined with the flesh of baked potatoes and the potatoes are baked a second time. Serve with Grilled Butterflied Leg of Lamb in Onion-Herb Marinade (page 292) or a thick, juicy grilled steak.

SERVES 8

2   pounds white onions, thinly sliced
1   teaspoon kosher salt
    Pinch sugar
6   tablespoons (¾ stick) unsalted butter
½   cup heavy cream
8   large russet potatoes, baked
    Freshly ground white pepper
3   tablespoons chopped fresh chives
1   cup grated sharp Cheddar or Dry Jack
    cheese (¼ pound)

Place onions in a large saucepan and cover with water. Add salt and sugar, and bring to a boil over medium heat. Boil for 1 minute; drain well.

In a large nonstick skillet, melt butter over very low heat. Add onions, cover and cook until onions are very tender, but not browned, about 40 minutes. Keep heat low and stir occasionally.

Add cream to onions and stir well. Cover and cook over very low heat for 30 minutes.

Meanwhile, cut each baked potato lengthwise in half. Scoop out pulp into a mixing bowl, leaving a shell of pulp in potato skin. Thoroughly mash pulp with a potato masher.

Preheat oven to 450 degrees F.

When onions are done, transfer to a food processor fitted with the metal blade. Puree thoroughly. Add onion puree to mashed potatoes and blend well. Season with salt and pepper to taste; add chives and blend well. Spoon filling into potato skins.

Arrange potato skins on a baking sheet.

Sprinkle potatoes with grated cheese. Bake until filling is heated through and tops are browned, 20 to 30 minutes.

Potatoes & Onions Boulangère

BOULANGÈRE MEANS "baker style" in French. When we plan to serve this with chicken, we use stock instead of water to cook the potatoes.

SERVES 6

1   tablespoon butter
5   large russet potatoes, peeled and thinly
    sliced
1   large white onion, thinly sliced
    Kosher salt and freshly ground black pepper
5-6 tablespoons olive oil
    About 1 cup boiling water or chicken stock

Preheat oven to 325 degrees F. Butter a 10-inch round baking dish. Arrange ⅓ of the potatoes in an even layer, scatter with ⅓ of the onions, sprinkle with salt and pepper and drizzle with about 1½ tablespoons olive oil. Repeat 2 more times.

Add enough boiling water or stock to reach about ¾ of the way up the sides of the dish. Drizzle top with remaining 1½ tablespoons olive oil; sprinkle with more salt and pepper.

Place the baking dish in the oven and bake for 1¼ hours, adding more hot water or stock at the edges if potatoes look too dry, until potatoes are very tender and top is browned.

Souffléed Sweet Potatoes with Deep-Fried Leeks

ALTHOUGH THIS DISH calls for some last-minute finishing, it's a good addition to the Thanksgiving table. We like it with turkey, roast goose and venison roast.

SERVES 6 TO 8

4	pounds sweet potatoes or yams, baked and peeled
½	cup (1 stick) unsalted butter, softened
½	cup half-and-half
⅓	cup minced shallots
¼	cup firmly packed dark brown sugar
4	large egg yolks
1	teaspoon ground ginger
¾	teaspoon freshly ground white pepper
½	teaspoon kosher salt
½	teaspoon ground cinnamon
¼	teaspoon ground cloves
¼	teaspoon freshly grated nutmeg
2	tablespoons orange-flavored liqueur
5	large egg whites
¼	cup finely chopped pecans
2	plump leeks, cleaned, trimmed and julienned
2-3	cups vegetable oil for deep-frying

Butter a 2-quart soufflé dish and set aside.

In a large bowl, combine sweet potatoes and butter. Mash with a potato masher until very smooth. Using a mixer or masher, beat in half-and-half, shallots, brown sugar, egg yolks, salt, pepper, spices and liqueur. Set aside.

Shortly before baking, preheat oven to 375 degrees F.

In a mixing bowl, beat egg whites until they form stiff, but not dry, peaks. Spoon ¼ of the whites into sweet potato mixture and stir well. Fold in remaining whites.

Pour mixture into the prepared soufflé dish; sprinkle with pecans. Bake in the middle of the oven for 1 hour, or until puffed and brown on top.

Meanwhile, while soufflé is baking, put julienned leeks in a large bowl of cold water and let stand for 45 minutes. Drain and pat dry with paper towels.

Shortly before soufflé is done, pour oil into a deep-fryer or wok to a depth of 1½ inches. Heat until hot enough to brown a cube of bread that is dropped into it. Toss in ½ of the leeks and deep-fry until golden, 2 to 3 minutes. Remove and drain on paper towels; fry remaining leeks. Scatter fried leeks over top of soufflé and serve.

Sweet Potato & Red Onion Hash

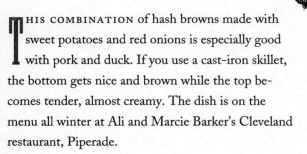

THIS COMBINATION of hash browns made with sweet potatoes and red onions is especially good with pork and duck. If you use a cast-iron skillet, the bottom gets nice and brown while the top becomes tender, almost creamy. The dish is on the menu all winter at Ali and Marcie Barker's Cleveland restaurant, Piperade.

SERVES 4 TO 6

6   cups grated sweet potatoes (2-3 large)

1   large red onion, grated

6   tablespoons (¾ stick) unsalted butter, softened

2   tablespoons minced shallots

¼   cup plus 2 tablespoons heavy cream
     Kosher salt and freshly ground black pepper

¼   cup minced scallions

In a large bowl, combine sweet potatoes and red onion; blend thoroughly and set aside.

In a small bowl, thoroughly blend butter and shallots.

Heat a large cast-iron skillet over high heat for 30 seconds. Add ½ of the shallot butter and swirl until melted and hot. Add potato mixture and press firmly and evenly over the bottom of the pan. Cook over high heat for 4 minutes.

Reduce heat to medium, add remaining butter, and stir potatoes with a wooden spoon until evenly blended. Continue to cook hash, stirring until potatoes begin to brown, about 5 minutes.

Add cream and salt and pepper to taste. When cream boils, reduce heat to low and cook until bottom begins to brown and potatoes are cooked through, about 4 minutes.

Use a spatula to serve, flipping browned portions, top side up. Sprinkle each portion with scallions.

Oniony Curried Potatoes, Cauliflower & Green Beans

WHEN THE WEATHER gets cold, we like to make this Indian-style vegetable stew inspired by Ismail Merchant's *Indian Cuisine*. Feel free to create your own vegetable combinations. For example, you could add chunks of winter squash for color, or broccoli for more texture. Sometimes this is our whole meal; at other times, we'll serve it with Roasted Chicken Dijon with Shallots & Onions (page 302) or Ground Lamb & Onion Kabobs with Minted Yogurt (page 281).

SERVES 4 TO 6

3 tablespoons vegetable oil

1 tablespoon curry powder

2 teaspoons black mustard seeds

2 whole cloves

½ teaspoon cayenne

2 dried red chile peppers, crushed

1 plump garlic clove, thinly sliced

8 small red-skinned or yellow potatoes, scrubbed and left whole

3 small white onions, quartered, with some root remaining

½ small cauliflower, broken into florets

¼ pound green beans, trimmed

¼ cup chicken stock

Juice of ½ lemon

Kosher salt and freshly ground white pepper

½ cup plain yogurt

In a heavy nonaluminum saucepan over medium-low heat, heat oil with curry powder, mustard seeds, cloves, cayenne, chile peppers and garlic. Stir often and cook for 3 minutes.

Add potatoes, onions, cauliflower, beans, chicken stock, lemon juice and salt and white pepper to taste. Cover and cook over low heat, stirring occasionally, until vegetables are tender, about 30 minutes.

Carefully stir in yogurt and serve.

Baked Beans with Onions, Flanken & Pork

THESE SLOWLY BAKED BEANS have a thick, somewhat sweet sauce, pungent from the addition of whisky, dry mustard and ginger.

SERVES 12 TO 16 PEOPLE

2	pounds navy beans
1	tablespoon butter, softened
2	cups medium-diced white onions
1	pound boneless flanken (beef short ribs cut from the plate), cut into 1-inch chunks, or other boneless short ribs
⅔	pound salt pork, finely diced
4	whole cloves
½	cup firmly packed dark brown sugar
1	tablespoon ground ginger
2	teaspoons dry mustard
2	teaspoons coarsely ground black pepper
1	tablespoon kosher salt
⅔	cup Canadian Club whisky
½	cup black molasses, unsulfured preferred
½	cup maple syrup
1	12-ounce bottle Bennett's chili sauce or another spicy chili sauce
1	bay leaf

Early in the morning, place beans in a large saucepan and cover with several inches of water. Bring to a boil. Remove from heat and let stand for 1½ hours.

Return the saucepan to high heat and bring to a boil. Reduce heat and simmer, adding water, if needed, to keep beans covered, until beans are tender, 1 to 1½ hours. Drain cooked beans, reserving cooking liquid.

Preheat oven to 275 degrees F.

Thoroughly coat a 5-quart bean pot or cast-iron Dutch oven with butter. Place ¼ of the beans in the pot, and scatter with ¼ of the onions, ¼ of the flanken and ¼ of the salt pork. Place 1 clove in the layer. Repeat layers, ending with a layer of salt pork and a clove.

In a large bowl, blend together brown sugar, ginger, mustard, pepper and salt. Whisk in whisky. Stir in molasses, maple syrup, chili sauce and 3 cups reserved bean liquid. Pour mixture over beans. Place bay leaf on top.

Cover pot and bake for 6½ hours, adding hot water if beans look too dry.

Remove bay leaf and cooking beans, uncovered, until a thin crust forms on top, about 45 minutes.

Winter Squash, Red Onion & Corn Cakes

RED KURI SQUASH has a marvelous flavor and a heavy, coarse texture that suits these mashed squash-corn cakes, but other varieties can be used. This dish is a good accompaniment to poultry.

To bake a winter squash: Split squash in half and remove the seeds. Place the halves, cut side down, in a roasting pan with just enough water to cover the bottom. Bake at 425 degrees until tender, about 45 minutes. Scoop out the cooked flesh and mash it.

MAKES 8 TO 10 CAKES

2 cups cooked, mashed flesh from a Red Kuri or other winter squash, such as butternut, Hubbard or acorn

1 cup fresh or frozen corn kernels

1 cup finely diced red onions

2 scallions, finely minced

1 teaspoon fresh thyme leaves or ½ teaspoon dried

2 large eggs, beaten

⅔ cup unbleached flour

½ cup cornmeal

2 teaspoons baking powder

½ teaspoon salt

½ teaspoon freshly ground black pepper

3 tablespoons low-fat sour cream

½ cup vegetable oil

Minced fresh chives for garnish

In a large bowl, combine squash, corn, onions, scallions and thyme; blend thoroughly. Stir in eggs, flour, cornmeal, baking powder, salt and pepper. Fold in sour cream. If using a moister winter squash, add more flour, 1 tablespoon at a time, until mixture is the texture of mashed potatoes.

Generously coat the bottom of a large cast-iron skillet with oil and preheat until hot. Spoon about ½ cup squash mixture into the skillet to make cakes about 4 inches in diameter and ½ inch thick. Reduce heat to medium-low and fry about 3 cakes at a time until bottoms are nicely browned, about 3 minutes. Turn and fry until undersides are browned. Remove and keep warm. Add oil as needed and fry remaining cakes until all are made.

Sprinkle with minced chives.

Northern Sweets

THERE IT WAS. In the *New England Farmer*, a monthly newspaper, Jim Cunning of Stokes Seeds in Buffalo, New York, was proudly showing off a new contender, the "Kelsey Sweet Giant." It is, said the *Farmer*, "the Northeast's answer to Texas Grano and Vidalia onions."

We had heard the name before. Someone had told us it was a variety that had become popular in England and that some specimens had weighed as much as five pounds.

In the laboratory at the Stokes company, we got the real story from Terry McIntee, a botanist-researcher who has been involved with the development of the Kelsey Sweet for a decade.

"It's a wonderful onion, very sweet," he said. "And yes, it can be huge. We've seen them at six pounds."

The Stokes company sells the Kelsey Sweet mainly to home gardeners who live in the North. McIntee recommends planting them as early as January in flats under grow lights. They should be transplanted to the garden as soon as they are well established and the soil is soft enough to be worked. They will produce leaves until the longest day, and then on that day, the first day of summer, bulbs will be triggered.

We wondered why farmers in the North don't try to grow the Kelsey Sweet and go into competition with the folks in Vidalia. McIntee says there is already overproduction of sweet onions, and it wouldn't make good business sense to get into that highly competitive field. Besides, buyers of northern onions expect them to be "keepers"; they don't like onions that say, "Eat me or lose me."

Squash & Onion Pie with Virginia Ham & Cheese

A CRUSTLESS QUICHE-LIKE vegetable pie, this can be served as a side dish with pork or poultry, or it can shine as the main course for brunch or lunch.

SERVES 8

1 tablespoon butter, softened

2 tablespoons fine dry bread crumbs

4 large eggs, beaten

1 cup low-fat sour cream, plus more for serving

2 cups milk

¼ pound shredded sharp Cheddar cheese (1 cup)

½ pound shredded Fontina or Monterey Jack cheese (2 cups)

¼ cup unbleached flour

1 teaspoon baking powder

2 teaspoons fresh thyme leaves or 1 teaspoon dried

½ teaspoon kosher salt

½ teaspoon freshly ground white pepper

2½ pounds winter squash, such as Hokaido, Red Kuri or butternut

½ pound white onions, thinly sliced

5 ounces smoked Virginia ham or prosciutto, thinly sliced

Fresh thyme leaves or parsley for garnish

Preheat oven to 375 degrees F.

Coat an 11-inch round ceramic baking dish with butter. Coat the dish with bread crumbs. Invert dish to dislodge excess crumbs.

In a large mixing bowl, whisk together eggs and sour cream. Whisk in milk, both cheeses, flour, baking powder, thyme, salt and white pepper; set aside.

Cut squash in half and discard seeds. Cut into quarters, then into thin slices. Remove and discard skin. Arrange alternating layers of the squash, onions and ham or prosciutto in the prepared baking dish. Cover with egg mixture, making certain that liquids soak under vegetables along sides.

Bake pie until mixture is set, about 1 hour. Let rest on a rack for 5 minutes before slicing.

Serve, garnished with a dollop of sour cream and a sprig of thyme or parsley.

Braised Green Beans & Onions

WITH SMOKED HAM HOCKS

TRADITIONALLY, Southern country-style beans are cooked until they fall apart, but we prefer them to retain some texture. This recipe has all of the traditional flavors, but leaves the beans with some crunch. The onions for this dish can be chopped in a food processor.

SERVES 6

6	tablespoons (¾ stick) unsalted butter
1½	cups finely chopped yellow onions
5	cups water
1½	pounds smoked ham hocks
1½	tablespoons freshly ground black pepper
2	pounds fresh green beans, trimmed and cut into 1-inch pieces
	Kosher salt

Melt 4 tablespoons butter in a large, heavy-bottomed saucepan. Add onions and cook over very low heat until wilted, about 5 minutes. Add water, ham hocks and pepper. Partially cover and bring to a boil over high heat. Reduce heat to low, cover completely and simmer for 10 minutes

Add beans and cook for 10 minutes. Pour bean mixture into a colander and drain.

Return beans and onions to the pan. Skin ham hocks, slice meat into small pieces and stir into beans and onions. Stir in remaining 2 tablespoons butter and salt to taste and let stand until butter melts. Serve in a heated bowl or spooned onto warm plates.

Caramelized Red Onions & Beet Leaves

LARGE BEET LEAVES are delicious like this, sautéed with sweet, browned red onions and finished with a splash of balsamic vinegar and white pepper.

SERVES 4

3 tablespoons unsalted butter
1 medium-sized red onion, diced
1 teaspoon sugar
½ pound beet leaves, stems removed
1 tablespoon balsamic vinegar
½ teaspoon kosher salt
½ teaspoon freshly ground white pepper

In a large nonaluminum skillet, melt butter over medium heat. Add onion, increase heat, and sauté, stirring frequently, until it begins to brown, about 3 minutes.

Add sugar and increase heat to high. Sauté, stirring, until onions begin to caramelize, about 2 minutes.

Add beet leaves and stir over high heat until leaves wilt, 1 to 2 minutes. Add balsamic vinegar, salt and white pepper; cook for 1 minute to reduce sauce. Serve on heated plates.

L'Étoile's Braised Cremini Mushrooms

WITH LEEKS, HERBS & CHEESE

THESE STUFFED MUSHROOM CAPS can accompany a roasted chicken or grilled fish, or they can be served as an appetizer. We thank Odessa Piper, owner of L'Étoile restaurant, for sharing her recipe.

SERVES 4

4   cups chicken stock
2   teaspoons olive oil
2   large shallots, finely diced
½   cup Madeira wine
3   fresh thyme sprigs, plus 1 tablespoon
     chopped thyme leaves or
     1¼ teaspoons dried
1   fresh rosemary sprig, plus 1 teaspoon
     chopped rosemary leaves or ¾ teaspoon
     dried
     Salt and freshly ground black pepper
12   large cremini mushrooms (about ½ pound),
     stems discarded
2   leeks, white parts only, cleaned and
     chopped
2   tablespoons chopped fresh parsley

¼   cup finely shredded aged goat cheese or
     other aged hard cheese, such as aged Asiago

In a medium saucepan, bring chicken stock to a boil over high heat. Boil until reduced to 1 cup.

Preheat oven to 350 degrees F.

In a large nonstick sauté pan, heat 1 teaspoon oil over medium heat. Add shallots and sauté until lightly browned, 5 to 7 minutes. Remove from heat, add Madeira and carefully return to high heat. Boil until reduced to a syrup. Add reduced chicken stock, thyme and rosemary sprigs (or ¼ teaspoon each dried) and a pinch of salt and pepper. Cook over high heat until mixture is slightly reduced, 3 to 5 minutes.

Pour into a shallow casserole, add mushroom caps, stem sides up. Cover and braise in the oven for 30 minutes.

Take casserole from oven, remove mushroom caps and set aside. Strain braising liquid and set it aside.

Heat remaining 1 teaspoon oil in a nonstick sauté pan over medium-high heat. Add leeks and stir until translucent. Add braising sauce and cook until sauce is thick and thoroughly coats leeks, 5 to 8 minutes. Cool sauce slightly; stir in chopped fresh thyme and rosemary (or 1 teaspoon dried thyme and ½ teaspoon dried rosemary) and parsley. Stuff mushroom caps with leek filling; arrange caps on a small baking sheet.

Preheat broiler.

Just before serving, sprinkle stuffed mushrooms with cheese. Broil until heated through and cheese melts, about 1 minute.

**Wine: Selene Sauvignon Blanc "Hyde Vineyard"
(California: Napa Valley, Carneros)**

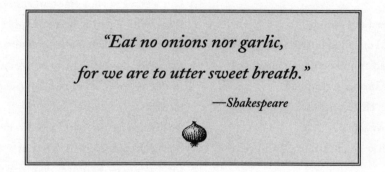

*"Eat no onions nor garlic,
for we are to utter sweet breath."*

—*Shakespeare*

Baked Red Onions

STUFFED WITH WILD RICE, SPINACH & MUSHROOMS

RED ONIONS MAKE a handsome and delicious casing for a stuffing made of sautéed mushrooms, spinach, wild rice and Fontina cheese. This dish is good with grilled chicken or fish.

SERVES 8

8	medium-sized red onions
¼	cup (½ stick) unsalted butter or margarine
4-6	ounces mixed shiitake and portobello or cremini mushrooms, chopped
2	plump garlic cloves, minced
2	teaspoons soy sauce
6	ounces fresh spinach, trimmed and coarsely chopped
1	tablespoon minced fresh tarragon leaves or 1½ teaspoons dried
1	cup cooked wild rice (about ½ cup raw)
⅓	cup sour cream
⅓	cup (1½ ounces) shredded Fontina or Monterey Jack cheese
2	tablespoons minced fresh parsley

	Kosher salt and freshly ground white pepper
1½	cups dry red wine

Preheat oven to 400 degrees F. Cut a slice from root end of each onion so that it will stand upright. Cut a straight slice off stem end; peel off and discard skin. With a paring knife or apple corer, bore into the center of each onion, creating an onion shell that can hold the stuffing (do not cut all the way through to the bottom). Reserve all of the onion flesh you remove.

Fill a large pot with salted water and bring to a boil. Add onion shells, a few at a time, and blanch for 4 minutes. Remove onions and drain upside down on paper towels.

Chop enough reserved onion flesh to yield ⅓ cup. In a large nonaluminum skillet, melt butter over medium heat. Stir in chopped onion, mushrooms, garlic and soy sauce. Reduce heat to low, cover and cook, stirring from time to time, for 5 minutes. Uncover and add chopped spinach and tarragon. Stir over low heat until spinach wilts, about 4 minutes.

Remove skillet from heat. Stir in rice, sour cream, cheese, parsley and salt and white pepper to taste. Stuff onion shells, mounding filling over tops. Arrange onions in a well-oiled baking dish large enough to hold onions snugly. Pour wine into the bottom of the pan; cover pan loosely with foil. Bake for 25 minutes.

Uncover and bake until onions are tender, about 20 minutes more.

Tofu & Scallions Braised in White Wine

W E FIRST LEARNED how good braised tofu could be in 1981 when we visited the Chinese city of Hangzhou and ate lunch in a Buddhist temple near the beautiful West Lake. Slices of tofu are coated in a light batter of flour and egg, quickly browned, then punctured to absorb the braising mixture of white wine, scallions and ginger. This simple dish is a wonderful addition to any Chinese meal. Even people who disdain tofu will rave about it. While we've always prepared it in an electric frying pan, you can fry it in any large skillet.

SERVES 6 TO 8

1	square firm tofu (bean curd)
⅔	cup unbleached flour
2	large eggs, lightly beaten
4	scallions, minced
1	tablespoon minced peeled fresh ginger
⅓	cup chicken stock
¼	cup dry white wine
2	teaspoons Oriental sesame oil
½	teaspoon kosher salt
½	cup peanut oil, for frying tofu

Cut tofu into ½-inch-thick slices. Quarter each slice crosswise. Dredge pieces first in flour and then in egg; set aside on wax paper.

Combine scallions and ginger and set aside. Combine chicken stock, wine, sesame oil and salt in another bowl and reserve.

Lightly cover the bottom of the frying pan with oil and preheat over medium-high heat until hot. Arrange tofu pieces in a single layer over the bottom of the pan and fry until golden, 2 to 3 minutes. Turn, add more oil if needed, and fry until underside is golden, 2 to 3 minutes. Reduce the heat to low, and quickly pierce each piece of tofu with a fork. Sprinkle evenly with scallion mixture; sprinkle with chicken stock mixture. Cook, uncovered, until liquids are absorbed, 3 to 5 minutes.

Hungarian Sautéed Cabbage, Onions & Noodles

GRATE CABBAGE AND ONIONS, sauté them slowly in oil until tender, add good paprika, mix with cooked noodles, and bake until done." That's *kapotszatsz,* according to Margaret Wine, a friend who grew up outside of Budapest in the town of Nagy-Varad. We doubt if there is a better Hungarian cook. "Always keep your paprika in the refrigerator," she admonishes. "And for this dish, use bow ties instead of plain noodles. Bow ties hold the cabbage and onions better."

SERVES 8 TO 10

1	12-ounce package bow tie egg noodles
2½	pounds cabbage, quartered
2	large yellow onions, coarsely grated
¾	cup canola or other vegetable oil
1½	teaspoons sweet Hungarian paprika
1	teaspoon kosher salt
½	rounded teaspoon freshly ground black pepper

In a large pot of boiling salted water, cook bow ties until just tender, about 10 minutes. Drain well and rinse in cool water; set aside.

Grate each cabbage quarter on the large holes of a hand grater into a large nonaluminum sauté pan. Discard core and finely chop any whole leaves. Add onions and mix well with cabbage. Pour oil over the mixture. Cook over medium heat, stirring often, until cabbage is tender but not mushy, about 20 minutes.

Stir in paprika, salt and pepper. Increase heat to high and stir-fry to release the flavor of paprika, about 2 minutes.

Spoon ⅓ of the bow ties evenly over the bottom of a shallow 3-quart casserole. Evenly distribute ⅓ of the cabbage mixture over bow ties. Repeat layering, ending with a layer of cabbage. Loosely cover casserole with foil; set aside at room temperature until just before cooking.

Preheat oven to 350 degrees F. Loosen foil cover. Bake casserole until piping hot and top layer of cabbage steams, 20 to 40 minutes.

Maui Corn Cakes

THESE CORN CAKES with sweet onions have a wonderful fragrance as they cook. For an added touch, garnish them with some Confit of Red Onions & Cherries (page 81) or a bit of Red Onion-Corn Relish (page 224). Or serve them with maple syrup and grilled ham for a yummy brunch.

SERVES 8

1	cup unbleached flour
¾	cup yellow cornmeal
1	scant tablespoon baking powder
½	teaspoon baking soda
1	tablespoon sugar
¼	teaspoon cayenne
½	teaspoon freshly ground black pepper
½	teaspoon kosher salt
2	large eggs, separated
6	tablespoons (¾ stick) butter, melted
1½	cups buttermilk
1	cup finely diced Maui or other sweet onion
1	cup fresh or frozen corn kernels
¼	cup minced scallions
2	tablespoons finely diced red bell pepper
1	tablespoon minced fresh cilantro leaves
1	tablespoon minced fresh chives
	About ½ cup vegetable oil for frying

Combine flour, cornmeal, baking powder, baking soda, sugar, cayenne, pepper and salt in a large mixing bowl. Beat egg yolks lightly and stir into dry ingredients, along with melted butter and buttermilk. Blend well. Add onions, corn, scallions, bell pepper, cilantro and chives. Fold lightly to blend; mixture should be thick enough to make a good pancake. If too thick, stir in a bit more buttermilk. If too thin, add more cornmeal, 1 tablespoon at a time, and blend carefully.

Beat egg whites just until they hold firm peaks. Mix some into the batter; lightly fold in the rest of whites.

Pour 3 tablespoons oil into a large cast-iron skillet and set over medium-high heat. When oil begins to sizzle, drop about ⅓ cup batter into the pan to make 3-inch round cakes; do not crowd cakes. Cook until bubbles begin to appear on the surface, about 2 minutes. Turn and brown on other side, about 2 minutes. Remove finished cakes and keep warm on a baking sheet in a low (250-degree) oven, and cook remaining cakes, adding more oil as needed. Serve hot.

Roasted Gray Shallots

COMMONLY GROWN in France, gray shallots have a thick gray-beige exterior skin. When roasted in oil and splashed with balsamic vinegar and a sprig of rosemary, the flesh inside becomes opulently creamy and flavorful. The recipe is from Odessa Piper's Wisconsin restaurant, L'Étoile. Serve these shallots hot or at room temperature, with any simple chicken dish. To eat, pick them up, one at a time, with your fingers, and squeeze the soft insides into your mouth. If you cannot get gray shallots, you can certainly use the more commonly available red shallots, peeled, and eat them with a fork.

SERVES 4

1   pound gray shallots, root and stem ends removed

1   cup olive oil
1   fresh rosemary branch (about 4 inches long)
1   long fresh thyme sprig
¼   cup balsamic vinegar
1   teaspoon kosher salt
    Freshly ground black pepper
¼   cup water

Preheat oven to 380 degrees F. (If you cannot set your oven to this temperature, set it to 375 degrees and roast for 55 to 65 minutes.)

Place all ingredients in a small, heavy ceramic casserole. Cover and roast for 45 to 55 minutes, until shallots are very tender when pierced with the tip of a knife.

Serve warm or at room temperature.

Grow Your Own

WE UNDERSTAND FROM Shepherd Ogden, the guru of the organic vegetable garden, that onions are difficult to grow. But when you walk through one of the giant farms that grows bulb onions, you get the feeling that onions are tough, hardy and resilient.

They are—provided that the grower has planted a variety specifically developed for the particular soil, latitude, altitude and average temperature of the region, as well as one with built-in resistance to pests and diseases and that won't go to seed.

If you are thinking about growing onions, first do your research. Get a good book. Read the seed catalogs. Order the right cultivar, or variety—usually the one that has done best for most people in your area.

Plant at the right time in the right soil. Watch out for weeds. Understand the onion's water needs. And then, unless there is a weather disaster, you will have onions.

In the northern regions, seeds can be started inside under light and taken outside when the temperatures are right. In the South, you can plant the seeds outside and transplant them.

Sets—immature, diminutive bulbs that have been dried and held in storage—are the easiest to deal with.

Most seed companies ship onion, garlic and shallot plants separately at the correct time for planting in your area.

Selected Sources for Seeds, Sets and Seedlings

The following companies carry bulb onions, leeks, shallots and garlic:

THE COOK'S GARDEN
Box 535
Londonderry, Vermont 05148

JOHNNY'S SELECTED SEEDS
Foss Hill Road
Albion, Maine 04910

NATIVE SEEDS SEARCH
2509 North Campbell Avenue
Box 325
Tucson, Arizona 85719

SEED SAVERS EXCHANGE
Rural Route 3, Box 339
Decorah, Iowa 52101

SHEPHERD'S GARDEN SEEDS
6116 Highway 9
Felton, California 95018

SOUTHERN EXPOSURE
SEED EXCHANGE
Box 158
North Garden, Virginia 22959

Alliums by Mail

Vidalias

Vidalia onions are usually found in the stores from mid-April through June. You can order them by mail for the October-December release. Baby Vidalias are available by mail through the winter.

BLAND FARMS
P.O. Box 506
Highway 169
Glenville, Georgia 30427
(800) 843-2542

G & R FARMS
Route 3, Box 35A
Glennville, Georgia 30427
(912) 654-1534

Walla Wallas

Walla Wallas are available in July. Baby Walla Wallas are available in the spring.
ROBISON RANCH
P.O. Box 1018
Walla Walla, Washington 99362
(509) 525-8807
Jim Robison

Shallots & Leeks

THE ALLIUM CONNECTION
1339 Swainwood Drive
Glenview, Illinois 60025
(708) 729-4823
John F. Swenson
Brittany shallots (imported), red shallots and garlic.

KINGSFIELD GARDENS
Blue Mounds, Wisconsin 53517
(608) 924-9341
Richard Abernethy and Erika Koenigsaecker
Gray and red shallots, leeks and bottle onions (Red Torpedo).

ROBISON RANCH
P.O. Box 1018
Walla Walla, Washington 99362
(509) 525-8807
Jim Robison
Shallots, French demi-long leeks, Robison Ranch varietal (jumbo and colossal).

Herbs

ART FORM NURSERIES
15656 Chillicothe Road
Chagrin Falls, Ohio 44022
(216) 338-8102
Patty and Michael Artino
Chives and other herbs.

WOODLAND HERB FARM
7741 N. Manitou Trail
Northport, Michigan 49670
(616) 386-5081
Pat Bourdo
Chives, curly chives, garlic chives, caraway thyme and a wide variety of other herbs; fruit and herb vinegars.

Special Products by Mail

Cheeses

APPEL FARMS
6605 Northwest Road
Ferndale, Washington 98248
(206) 384-4996
Quark.

HAWTHORNE VALLEY FARM
R.D. 2, Box 225A Harlemville
Ghent, New York 12075
(518) 672-7500
Quark.

LOOMIS CHEESE
220 Felch Street
Ann Arbor, Michigan 48103
(313) 741-8512
Janet, Bill and John Loomis
Cheshire cheese.

PELUSO CHEESE INC.
429 H Street
Los Banos, California 93635
(209) 826-3744
Teleme cheese.

QUILLISASCUT CHEESE
2409 Pleasant Valley Road
Rice, Washington 99167
(509) 738-2011
Lora Lea and Rick Misterly
Fresh chèvre (goat cheese).

SMITH COUNTRY CHEESE
20 Otter River Road
Winchendon, Massachusetts 01475
(508) 939-5738
Dave Smith
Farmstead gouda.

VELLA CHEESE COMPANY
315 Second Street East
Sonoma, California 95476
(707) 938-3232
Ignazio Vella
Vella Dry jack cheese.

WESTFIELD FARM GOAT CHEESE
Hubbardston, Massachusetts 01452
(508) 928-5110
Letty and Bob Killmoyer
Fresh chèvre (goat cheese).

Dried Products

AMERICAN SPOON FOODS
1668 Clarion Avenue
Petoskey, Michigan 49770
(800) 222-5886
Dried cherries and other berries.

THE FOWLER'S MILLING COMPANY
12500 Fowler's Mill Road
Chardon, Ohio 44022
(216) 286-2024
Rick Erickson
Stone-ground cornmeal and grits.

LOWELL FARMS
311 Avenue A
El Campo, Texas 77437
(409) 543-4950
Lowell and Linda Raun
White jasmine and brown jasmine rice.

MANITOK WILD RICE
Box 97
Callaway, Minnesota 56521
(800) 726-1863
Dave Reinke, Manager
Lake-grown certified organic wild rice.

ORLANDO CASADOS
P.O. Box 1149
San Juan Pueblo, New Mexico 87566
(505) 852-4482
Orlando Casados
Dried chiles, pozole (dried) and New Mexico chile powders.

Meats

S. WALLACE EDWARDS & SONS, INC.
P.O. Box 25
Surry, Virginia 23883
(800) 222-4267
Virginia ham, Wigwam ham, smoked bacon and smoked sausage.

Bibliography

Bacheller, Barbara. *Lilies of the Kitchen*, New York: St. Martin's Press, 1986.

Ball, Frank and Feltman, Arlene. *Trucs of the Trade*. New York: HarperPerennial, 1992.

Bayless, Rick and Bayless, Deann Groen. *Authentic Mexican*. New York: William Morrow, 1987.

Beard, James. *Delights and Prejudices*. New York: Simon & Schuster, 1964.

Bianchini, F. and Corbetta, F. *Fruits of the Earth*. London: Bloomsbury Books, 1975.

Child, Julia, et al. *Mastering the Art of French Cooking*. New York: Alfred A. Knopf, 1963.

Claiborne, Craig. *The New York Times Cookbook*. New York: Harper & Row, 1990.

Comin, Donald. *Onion Production*. New York: Orange Judd, 1946.

Comstock, Jim. *Best of Hillbilly*. Richwood, West Virginia: Droke House, 1968.

Damrosch, Barbara. *The Garden Primer*. New York: Workman Publishing, 1988.

Darby, William J., Ghalioungui, Paul, and Grivetti, Louis. *Food: The Gift of Osiris*. Vol. 2. London: Academic Press, 1976.

Derecskey, Susan. *The Hungarian Cookbook*. New York: Perennial Library, 1972.

Edwards, John. *The Roman Cookery of Apicius*. Point Roberts, Washington: Hartley & Marks, 1984.

Fernald, Merritt Lyndon. *Gray's Manual of Botany*. New York: D. Van Nostrand, 1970.

Folkard, Richard. *Plant Lore, Legends and Lyrics*. London: Emerson Low, 1884.

Guinness Book of World Records. New York: Bantam Books, 1994.

Hausman, Patricia. *The Healing Foods*. New York: Dell, 1989.

Hazan, Marcella. *Essentials of Classic Italian Cooking*. New York: Alfred A. Knopf, 1992.

Hein, Peg. *Tales and Tastes from Texas*. Austin, Texas: Peg Hein, 1984.

Helck, Wolfgang, Westendorf, Wolfhart, and Otto, Eberhard. *Lexikon der Ägyptologie*. Wiesbaden: Otto Harrassowitz, 1985.

Hess, John and Hess, Karen. *The Taste of America*. Columbia, South Carolina: South Carolina Press, 1989.

Jashemski, Wilhelmina F. *The Gardens of Pompeii*. New Rochelle, New York: Caratzas Brothers, 1979.

Jones, Henry A. *Hybrid Onions*. El Centro, California: The Dessert Seed Co., n.d.

Jones, Henry A. and Mann, Louis K. *Onions and Their Allies*. New York: Interscience Publishers, Inc., 1963.

Killeen, J. and Germon, G. *Cucina Simpatica*. New York: HarperCollins, 1991.

Kovi, Paul. *Paul Kovi's Transylvanian Cuisine*. New York: Crown, 1985.

Manniche, Lise. *An Ancient Egyptian Herbal*. Austin, Texas: University of Texas Press, 1989.

Marshall, Lydie Pinoy. *Cooking with Lydie Marshall*. New York: Alfred A. Knopf, 1982.

The Maui Onion Book. Kula, Hawaii: Maui County Farm Bureau, 1988.

McCallum, Barbara Beury. *Mom and Ramps Forever*. Charleston, West Virginia: Mountain State Press, 1983.

McGee, Harold. *On Food and Cooking*. New York: Scribner's, 1984.

Mendelsohn, Oscar A. *A Salute to Onions*. New York: Hawthorne Books, 1965.

Merchant, I. *Ismail Merchant's Indian Cuisine*. New York: St. Martin's Press, 1986.

Morash, Marian. *The Victory Garden Cookbook*. New York: Alfred A. Knopf, 1982.

New York Botanical Garden Illustrated Encyclopedia of Horticulture. Ed. by Thomas H. Everett. New York: Garland Publishing, 1981.

Ody, Penelope. *The Complete Medicinal Herbal*. New York: Dorling Kindersley, 1993.

Ogden, Shepherd. *Step by Step Organic Vegetable Gardening*. New York: HarperCollins, 1992.

Onion Lovers' Dishes and Delectable Desserts. Greeley, Colorado: National Onion Association, n.d.

Passmore, Jacki. *The Encyclopedia of Asian Food and Cooking*. New York: Hearst Books, 1991.

Root, Waverley. *Food*. New York: Simon & Schuster, 1980.

Simmons, Amelia. *American Cookery*. Hartford, Connecticut: n.p., 1796.

Singer, Marilyn. *The Fanatic's Ecstatic Aromatic Guide to Onions, Garlic, Shallots and Leeks*. New York: Prentice-Hall, 1981.

Tannahill, Reay. *Food In History*. New York: Stein & Day, 1973.

Tropp, Barbara. *The Modern Art of Chinese Cooking*. New York: William Morrow, 1982.

Waldron, Maggie. *Cold Spaghetti at Midnight*. New York: William Morrow, 1992.

Index